Ecclesiastical Authority
God's Sabbath and Biblical Calendar

James Malm

ISBN: 978-1-7753510-4-7
Copyright 2018
All Rights Reserved

Dedication

This work is dedicated to the Great God whose house is eternity; the Father and Sovereign of all that exists and the sum of all Truth, Wisdom, Love, Justice and Mercy.
May God's house be filled with children whose chief joy is to be like Him!

For in depth studies on these subjects visit our website
theshininglight.info

Table of Contents

The Priesthood 5

    Introduction 6

    In the Beginning 8

    The Priesthood 11

    The Ezra Restoration 27

    The New Covenant Ministry 36

    Qualifications for the Priesthood/Ministry 47

    Ordination 53

    Godly and Ungodly Religious Leaders 60

    The Primacy of Peter 69

    Binding and Loosing 80

    The Keys and Door of Eternal Life 88

    The Mark of the Beast 104

    Legitimate Ministerial Authority 111

God's Sabbath Day 125

    God's Holy Sabbath 126

    Sabbath Activities 133

    What does God want us to do on His Sabbaths? 139

    Nehemiah on the Sabbath 147

    Common Excuses for Sinning Against God's Sabbath 153

    The Biblical Sabbath to Sunday Change 157

    Catholics and Protestants on Sunday and the Sabbath 162

The Biblical Calendar 181

    The Biblical Calendar Explained 182

    God Chooses Jerusalem 185

    A History of Today's Rabbinic Calendar 188

    New Moons in Ancient Israel 194

    Establishing the New Moon and New Year 202

    Calendar References and Sources 214

The Priesthood

Introduction

The whole of scripture was written and preserved for our instruction and for our example, not just the New Testament.

2 Timothy 3:16 All scripture is given by inspiration of God, and is profitable for doctrine, for reproof, for correction, for instruction in righteousness: **3:17** That the man of God may be perfect, thoroughly furnished unto all good works.

1 Corinthians 10:11 Now all these things happened unto them for examples: and they are written for our admonition, upon whom the ends of the world are come.

Romans 15:4 For whatsoever things were written aforetime were written for our learning, that we through patience and comfort of the scriptures might have hope.

All aspects of the Mosaic Covenant are an instructional allegory of a New Covenant (Jer 31:31), so that by learning the Mosaic things we can have a much better understanding of the spiritual things of the New Covenant.

Jesus [Hebrew: Yeshua] taught that men are to live by every Word of God

Matthew 4:3 And when the tempter [Satan] came to him, he said, If thou be the Son of God, command that these stones be made bread.

4:4 But he answered and said, It is written, **Man shall not live by bread alone, but by every word that proceedeth out of the mouth of God.**

Which God did Jesus know and refer to? The very King of the universe, God the Father in heaven!

4:5 Then the devil taketh him up into the holy city, and setteth him on a pinnacle of the temple, **4:6** And saith unto him, If thou be the Son of God, cast thyself down: for it is written, He shall give his angels charge concerning thee: and in their hands they shall bear thee up, lest at any time thou dash thy foot against a stone.

4:7 Jesus said unto him, It is written again, **Thou shalt not tempt the Lord thy God.**

4:8 Again, the devil taketh him up into an exceeding high mountain, and sheweth him all the kingdoms of the world, and the glory of them; **4:9** And saith unto him, All these things will I give thee, if thou wilt fall down and worship me.

4:10 Then saith Jesus unto him, **Get thee hence, Satan: for it is written, Thou shalt worship the Lord thy God, and him only shalt thou serve.**

Most religious people would agree that we should follow and obey God our Father in heaven, but this belief is complicated by the questions of the Covenants and the concept that men have the authority to bind and loose the Word of God.

This claimed binding and loosing authority of men over God's Word, is further complicated by the claim that what a "man of God" binds or looses has been inspired by the Holy Spirit of God and therefore must be accepted and obeyed.

This book will study into these questions directly from the scriptures themselves; with the intent to demonstrate from the Word of God the answer to Peter's question:

Acts 4:19 But Peter and John answered and said unto them, **Whether it be right in the sight of God to hearken unto you more than unto God, judge ye.**

In the Beginning

The Implementing Creator: The First High Priest

Genesis 1:26 And God (Elohim, plural: Mighty Ones) said, Let us make man in **our** image, after **our** likeness:..

From the very beginning, creation is represented as a collaborative effort of two Mighty Beings.

Genesis 3:22 reflects the same plurality of Beings in the same Family of Beings, And the LORD God said, Behold, the man is become as **one of us**, to know good and evil: and now, lest he put forth his hand, and take also of the tree of life, and eat, and live for ever:..

Genesis 1:1 In the beginning God [Elohim; Mighty Ones] created . . . The term translated as "God" here means "Mighty Ones;" the singular of Elohim being El meaning a Lord or Mighty One, a judge or ruler.

Later, because men had made many gods [mighty ones] it was no longer adequate to simply call the true God, Elohim [Mighty Ones]; since any particular Elohim would only be one of multitudes of gods. The Creator Mighty One therefore identified himself to Moses as YHVH to separate YHVH from all the other mighty ones or gods of the nations, and to separate himself from the mighty ones [gods] of Egypt.

This introduced a specific name for the True God Family to differentiate the Creator from other mighty ones [Elohim].

The term Elohim originally meant - until men perverted it - a family of at least two Creator beings; one the Executive Creating Authority who later became God the Father, and one the Implementing Creating Authority who later gave up his God-hood to become the Son.

The term Elohim meant at least two creating Beings and the word YHVH also refers to the same two Creator Beings as eternally existing and as separate from all other mighty ones.

The name YHVH means simply "I AM" or "I Am eternally self-existent;" and this description fits and is applicable to BOTH God the Father and the one who became the Son.

In the beginning there were two eternal God Beings called Elohim who characterized themselves as being the YHVH FAMILY of self-existing eternal ones.

The Being who was later called God the Father was and is the Executive Authority over the entire universe; and the One who was the actual Implementing Creator and gave up his Godhood to be made flesh and dying for the sins of mankind, was then resurrected and ascended back to the Father.

Once mankind was created, God the Father left the One who later gave up his Godhood to become flesh as the Son, to care for the man and his wife.

God the Father left because mankind sinned, separating humanity from God the Father by their sin and rebellion against the Word of God to do as they decided for themselves instead of living by every Word of God

The moment that the woman and the man sinned by acting contrary to the Word of God [the tree in the garden was a test of obedience for them, which they failed] that sin separated them from God the Father.

Sin Separates Humanity From God, Requiring an Intercessor (Is 59:1)

Once mankind was separated from God the Father by their sin; humanity needed a High Priest [a Mediator between humanity and God the Father] to reconcile humanity back to God the Father!

From the very beginning, God knowing that man could sin and would therefore need reconciliation, the two Beings who became the Father and the Son, together established the means that such a reconciliation could be effected.

That plan of reconciliation between man and God required the sincere repentance of the sinner, an effective sacrifice for sin, and a commitment by the repentant to stop sinning and to sin no more. The plan also called for a Mediator or High Priest to reconcile the repentant sinner to God the Father.

When man sinned, humanity was cut off and separated from God the Father by that sin (Is 59:1-2); yet the Being who became the Son remained with humanity working to reconcile mankind to God the Father, thereby fulfilling the role of a spiritual High Priest [at that time a High Priest made of spirit].

In that role the Implementing Creator was still spirit, yet he appeared in human form from time to time and spoke with many people over many centuries.

The One who became flesh as Jesus Christ was the Implementing Creator and after man sinned, this Implementing Creator became the High Priest of God the Father, a Mediator [which mediation between God and man is the job of a High Priest] between God the Father and humanity.

This spiritual High Priest or Intercessor between God the Father and humanity, appeared to Adam and Eve in the form of a man and spoke with Cain, Noah, Abraham and doubtless others.

The last time we hear of him in the scriptures before he became flesh, was by the name of Melchizedek, when he spoke to Abraham and later he was seen by Ezekiel and certain prophets.

The Priesthood

The Levites

After the Creator called Israel out of Egypt, he called Levi out of the twelve tribes of Israel to become the tribe of God. At that time - in order to maintain the tribes of Israel at twelve - the tribe of Joseph was split into two portions, Joseph being given a double portion through his two sons Ephraim and Manasseh.

Then after Levi was called out of Israel to be the tribe of God, Aaron and his sons were called out of the tribe of Levi to be the priests of God. All priests were Levites, but all Levites were not priests.

From that time the Levitical Priests were to offer the Daily and Festival Sacrifices on behalf of the whole nation and to officiate in offering the sacrifices brought by individuals, they were also to judge all Israel in matters of the law of God; while the remainder of Levi were to help and support the Priests by fulfilling all other necessary functions.

Those Levites who were not descendants of Aaron, served as aides to the priests, doing things like helping to prepare the sacrifices.

The Levites carried the Tabernacle and its vessels during the wanderings in the desert. Later Levites served as the honor guard, gatekeepers, singers and musicians of the Temple. They also assisted the Priests [*Kohanim*] in preparing the offerings and in other aspects of the Temple's functioning.

The non-priest Levites made repairs when needed, and served as musicians, singers and doorkeepers, including security and crowd management (Numbers 1:50-53; 3:6-9; 4:1-33; I Chronicles 23). They would also have made the priestly garments and such utensils as were needed in the Tabernacle - Temple service.

The Levites also pastured the tithed animals in their suburbs, from which the animals for the Daily and Festival Sacrifices were taken, as well as animals for their own sustenance.

The Levites and Priests together were also tasked to be the teachers of Israel

Deuteronomy 33:8 And **of Levi** he said, Let thy Thummim and thy Urim be with thy holy one, whom thou didst prove at Massah, and with whom thou didst strive at the waters of Meribah; **33:9** Who said unto his father and to his mother, I have not seen him; neither did he acknowledge his brethren, nor knew his own children: for they have observed thy word, and kept thy covenant. **33:10 They shall teach Jacob thy judgments, and Israel thy law:** they [and those Levites called out to be Priests] shall put incense before thee, and whole burnt sacrifice upon thine altar.

Josiah tell us that the Levites were the teachers of Israel

II Chronicles 35:3 And said unto **the Levites that taught all Israel**, which were holy unto the Lord, Put the holy ark in the house which Solomon the son of David king of Israel did build; it shall not be a burden upon your shoulders: serve now the Lord your God, and his people Israel,

The Ezra revival began with the Priests and Levites teaching the Word of God to the people

Nehemiah 8:5 And Ezra opened the book in the sight of all the people; (for he was above all the people;) and when he opened it, all the people stood up: **8:6** And Ezra blessed the Lord, the great God. And all the people answered, Amen, Amen, with lifting up their hands: and they bowed their heads, and worshipped the Lord with their faces to the ground. **8:7** Also Jeshua, and Bani, and Sherebiah, Jamin, Akkub, Shabbethai, Hodijah, Maaseiah, Kelita, Azariah, Jozabad, Hanan, Pelaiah, **and the Levites, caused the people to understand the law**: and the people stood in their place.

The Levites and Priests together set up Synagogues [David writes of such meeting places or schools in Psalm 74] throughout the land, teaching the people the Word of God from their 48 Levitical cities and also served as God's scribes, copying and preserving the Holy Scriptures (II Chronicles 34:13).

Part of the inheritance of the Levites including the Levitical Priests; consisted of forty-eight cities spread throughout the land (Numbers 35:6-7).

Of these forty-eight cities, six were designated as cities of refuge. The cities were Kedesh, Shechem, Hebron, Bezer, Romath, and Golan (Joshua 20:7-8). These six cities served as Judicial Centres to which persons accused of murder could seek justice from the Priests. These six cities would have been primarily occupied by the Levitical Priests because the Priests were to be the nation's judges.

Israel also had a civil administration of seventy elders to judge the people; and if issues, particularly involving God's law, were too difficult for the Civil Administration they were to be referred to the Priesthood.

Deuteronomy 17:8 If there arise a matter too hard for thee [a matter that the civil administration cannot handle] in judgment, between blood and blood, between plea and plea, and between stroke and stroke, being matters of controversy within thy gates: then shalt thou arise, and get thee up into the place which the Lord thy God shall choose; **17:9** And thou shalt come unto **the priests the Levites**, and unto the judge that shall be in those days, and enquire; and they shall shew thee the sentence of judgment:

The Levitical Priests were teachers and judges in Israel concerning the Word of God

Deuteronomy 21:5 And **the priests the sons of Levi** shall come near; for them the Lord thy God hath chosen to minister unto him, and to bless in the name of the Lord; and **by their word shall every controversy and every stroke be tried**:

I Chronicles 23:4 So when David was old and full of days, he made Solomon his son king over Israel. **23:2** And he gathered together all the princes of Israel, **with the priests and the Levites**. **23:3** Now the Levites were numbered from the age of thirty years and upward: and their number by their polls, man by man, was thirty and eight thousand. **23:4** Of which, twenty and four thousand [Levites and Priests] were to set forward the work of the house of the Lord; and **six thousand** [Levites and priests] **were officers and judges**:

The priests were also responsible for the accuracy of weights and measures used in Israel (I Chronicles 23:29; Leviticus 19:35-36).

Whereas the other tribes worked the land, the Levites [including the priests] were dependent on small suburbs around their cities to pasture the livestock tithed to them and depended for much of their income on the tithes and gifts of others.

Service for the Levites began at the age of 25 (though later changed to 20 under King David) and continued until they reached the age of 50 (Numbers 8:24; I Chronicles 23:3,24-32).

Levites were made to be economically dependent on God and received their wages from the people for their service to them on behalf of God. In exchange for his life's service, the Levites [including the priests] received God's ordained sustenance through the required tithing of the nation.

The Levites [along with the Levitical Priests] had periods of faithfulness and of apostasy through history and often fell away from God; and their failure to teach the nation to live by every Word of God was a root cause - along with apostate rulers - of the nations repeated drift into apostasy. This repeated apostasy finally resulted in the Babylonian captivity.

This repeated apostasy of the Levites and Levitical Priests and the correction of those who followed them away from God, is a lesson for us today that even the ministry can often go astray, and we are not to make idols of any ministry or man; we are to remain faithful to live by every Word of God even if a priest or minister falls into error.

The Male Priesthood and Ministry

After Levi was called out of Israel to be the tribe of God, Aaron and his sons were called out of the tribe of Levi to be the Priests of God.

Exodus 28:1 And take thou unto thee **Aaron thy brother, and his sons with him**, from among the children of Israel, that he may minister unto me in the priest's office.

This command of God signifies that only males may serve as the priests or ministry of God. Women may serve as teachers and may even be called to become prophetesses, or even Judges [Deborah being an example] and rulers of the people in the Civil Administration, but they may not serve as priests.

This is because the priests or ministry, serve as types of the spiritual High Priest Melchizedek [the very Creator God who gave up his Godhood to become flesh and give himself as a perfect sacrifice as Jesus Christ]; who as the Husband of Israel must be represented as a male.

The law says that the man is the head of his wife (Gen 3:16, 1 Cor 11:3) and our spiritual High Priest is our Husband and our Head, it is therefore only proper that those acting on behalf of his headship and priesthood also be male.

Melchizedek was always presented as a male and Jesus Christ was a man, therefore those that are types of our spiritual High Priest must be male.

Melchisedec

Melchisedec [from the Greek] is also spelled Melchizedek [from the Hebrew].

Genesis 14:18 And Melchizedek king of Salem brought forth bread and wine: and he was the priest of the most high God [God the Father].

Melchizedek blesses Abram by God the Father; showing that Melchizedek was not the Father in heaven and was the High Priest and Intercessor between man and God the Father in heaven.

Genesis 14:19 And he blessed him, and said, Blessed be Abram of the most high God, possessor of heaven and earth: **14:20** And blessed be the most high God [he blessed God the Father showing that he was not God the Father but the Intermediary between humanity and God the Father], which hath delivered thine enemies into thy hand. And he [Abram] **gave him tithes of all** [everything including the spoils of the battle].

Notice that Abram recognizes this Being and immediately acknowledges his authority over Abram by giving him a tithe of all. There is no: "Who are you?" or "Why should I give anything to you that came at the risk of life?"! No, there was only an immediate recognition of authority and an immediate submission to that authority. From this it is clear that Adam had experience with and KNEW this Being from previous encounters.

We know that the Creator walked with and taught Adam, Abel and Cain; and was likely seen by Noah and many others. We shall also see that the Creator High Priest Melchisedec did visit Abram several times and that Abram had no surprise at seeing him. That was because the Implementing

Creator appeared to Abram as Melchizedek on multiple occasions and was well known to Abram.

This is the first place that tithes are mentioned in the Bible, and here Abram gives this Melchizedek tithes of the spoil of battle; showing that while Israel was later specifically commanded to tithe on agriculture [because they were an agricultural people]; God the Father is entitled to a tithe of ALL: because he is ultimately the sustainer of ALL things.

Who made you and the earth you stand upon? Who made the air you breath? Who gave you the wisdom and skill to make clothes or cars? Who provided the metals and minerals you utilize?

To claim that God requires tithes in payment for land used agriculturally only; and then ignore that God is the maker, and overseer, and owner of ALL things; is myopic and self-delusional. Shall we say then, that the potter, the tailor, or the inn keeper need not go up to the Feasts of God because they have no tithe on their labours? Shall we say that God is not equitable; taking from one endeavor and not from others?

Israel was at that time an agrarian society so God commanded them in agrarian terms; but the principle that we are to acknowledge the gifts of God to us is not limited to agricultural things at all!

Abram gave a tenth of the spoil to acknowledge that God had given him victory with safety, and had delivered his nephew will al the captives! There was nothing agricultural in the motives and the giving at all. The law plainly says that the labourer is worthy of his wages, no matter what his job; and that those who serve in the gospel should have a reasonable living from their work.

Tithing on all our net increase, acknowledges God the Father [and the other God Being who gave up his Godhood to be made flesh as the Son] as ALL in all; the fountain of all knowledge and wisdom, and all of creation!

Notice that the tithe was given to the spirit High Priest who was later made flesh as Jesus Christ in the form of Melchizedek, revealing that this Melchizedek had a right to receive our tithes being the ultimate Implementing Creator of humanity!

This makes it clear that the priesthood of the Implementing Creator who became Jesus Christ has the overriding right to receive tithes [by virtue of having made and owning all things] even above the Aaronic priesthood.

Genesis 14:18 And Melchizedek king of Salem brought forth bread and wine: and he was the priest of the most high God [The Most High God; that is God the Father].

The name Melchizedek means: "king of righteousness" consisting of two words, Melek-King, Zedek-Righteousness; which is the interpretation of his name. This person was also known as the King of Salem meaning king of peace.

This Being was the King of Righteousness, meaning that he was the ultimate example of righteousness which is something exclusive to God, therefore this Being was a member of the God Family!

The whole Word of God is the righteousness of God defined in print; and that Word, being the righteousness of God, brings peace; first between man and God and then between like-minded people.

Therefore this Melchizedek as king of peace and the king of righteousness was the ultimate Mediator between mankind and God the Father, the ultimate spirit High Priest of all humanity.

Melchizedek is spelled with a "Z" from the Hebrew; and with an "S" when translated from the Greek.

Hebrews 7:1 For this Melchisedec, king of Salem [peace], priest of the most high God, who met Abraham returning from the slaughter of the kings, and blessed him; **7:2** To whom also Abraham gave a tenth part of all; first **being by interpretation King of righteousness, and after that also King of Salem, which is, King of peace**; **7:3** Without father, without mother, without descent, having neither beginning of days, nor end of life; but made [was] **like unto the Son of God;** abideth a priest continually.

The word Melchisedec means ruler or king or high priest by divine right; having an absolute authority and an absolute right to that office, because he was righteousness personified and was the Implementing Creator of all things.

Melchisedec is here referred to as the king of Salem, the word Salem meaning peace; referring to him as our High Priest bringing reconciliation and peace between man and God the Father.

Melchisedec was King of Righteousness and King of Peace. And both of those titles fit and apply to Jesus Christ.

7:4 Now consider how great this man was, unto whom even **the patriarch Abraham gave the tenth of the spoils. 7:5** And verily they that are of **the**

sons of Levi, who receive the office of the priesthood, have a commandment to take tithes of the people according to the [Mosaic] **law**, that is, [to take tithes] of their brethren, though they come out of the loins of Abraham: **7:6** But he whose descent is not counted from [he who existed BEFORE and was not descended from Levi, FIRST took tithes] them received tithes of Abraham, and blessed him [Melchisedec (who later became Jesus Christ) blessed Abraham and through Abraham also blessed Levi] that had the promises. **7:7** And without all contradiction the less is blessed of the better.

That is, although he was not a descendant of Levi, Melchisedec existed before Levi and being the very Creator was greater than Levi.

Levi payed tithes to Christ [the Melchisedec priesthood] through his ancestor Abraham; later Levi was called to be God's tribe, yet he was still only taking tithes on behalf of Christ, as the representative of the Husband of Israel; Melchisedec who later became flesh as Jesus Christ! This means that we are to tithe to the New Covenant priesthood of Melchisedec today just as Abraham did!

7:8 And here men that die receive tithes; but there he receiveth them, of whom it is witnessed that he liveth. **7:9** And as I may so say, **Levi also, who receiveth tithes, payed tithes in Abraham. 7:10 For he was yet in the loins of his father** [Abraham], **when Melchisedec met him** [received tithes of Abraham].

7:11 If therefore perfection were by the Levitical priesthood, (for under it the people received the law,) what further need was there that another priest should rise after the order of Melchisedec, and not be called after the order of Aaron?

The Death of the Husband, Ended the Mosaic Covenant and its Aaronic Priesthood

The law concerning the priesthood of Aaron was annulled by the end of the Mosaic Covenant with the death of the Husband of that Covenant, God made flesh,; and the pre-existing priesthood of Melchisedec has been restored through the resurrection of Jesus Christ back to his former glory.

7:12 For the priesthood being changed, there is made of necessity a change also of the law.

The Implementing Creator and spiritual High Priest Intercessor between man and God the Father - called Melchizedek, was the Being who married Israel at Sinai. He was not only the Husband of Israel but also the spiritual High Priest of Israel, above the physical Aaronic priesthood; which physical priesthood was only an allegory of the spiritual priesthood

Isaiah 54:5 For **thy Maker is thine husband**; the Lord of hosts is his name; and thy Redeemer the Holy One of Israel; The God of the whole earth shall he be called.

The Mosaic Covenant placed a son of Levi as a physical High Priest; and when the Mosaic Covenant ended by the death of the Husband, the Creator of all things was Husband of Mosaic Israel and spiritual High Priest who later gave up his Godhood to be made flesh; a new spiritual Covenant (Ez 11:19, 36:26, Jer 31:31) was offered to the called out of all nations to become a spiritual Israel with a restored High Priest; not of Aaron, but a restoration of the direct Priesthood of Melchisedec [the resurrected Jesus Christ].

Jesus Christ [Melchisedec] was God; who gave up his God-hood to be made flesh and placed in the womb of Mary to be born into Judah.

7:13 For he of whom these things are spoken pertaineth to another tribe [Judah], of which no man gave attendance at the altar. 7:14 For it is evident that our Lord sprang out of Juda; of which tribe Moses spake nothing concerning priesthood.

7:15 And it is yet **far more evident: for that after the similitude of Melchisedec there ariseth another priest, 7:6 Who is made, not after the law of a carnal commandment, but after the power of an endless life. 7:17** For he testifieth, **Thou art a priest for ever after the order of Melchisedec.**

The physical priesthood of Aaron could only mediate the physical Mosaic Covenant which had no spiritual promises and no promise of eternal life. Therefore there was need of a better spiritual High Priest to mediate a true spiritual reconciliation with God the Father and bring in a spiritual New Covenant with better promises.

7:18 For **there is verily a disannulling of the commandment going before** [the Mosaic Marriage Covenant ended with the death of the Husband] **for the weakness and unprofitableness thereof**.

The New Covenant has an Eternal Spirit High Priest

The spiritual New Covenant gives humanity a better hope [of eternal life as spirit] and therefore a better [a spiritual] High Priest to reconcile us to God the Father, bringing the gift of the Holy Spirit and eternal life to all who would live by every Word of God.

A better New Covenant, with a better sacrifice than animals, with better promises, and with the empowerment of the Holy Spirit to enable us to KEEP that New Covenant; is now overseen directly by an eternal spirit High Priest.

Indeed the Melchizedek priesthood had always existed and was even mediating between God the Father and a few spiritually called out, during the Mosaic Aaronic dispensation. We know this because Moses, Joshua and others were given the Holy Spirit via that spiritual mediation.

The Mosaic Covenant and the priesthood of Aaron was limited to mediating the physical Mosaic Covenant, as an instructional allegory of the spiritual priesthood of Melchisedec [Jesus Christ], which reconciles the sincerely repentant with God the Father on the spiritual level of the New Covenant.

7:19 For the law made nothing perfect, but **the bringing in of a better hope did; by the which we draw nigh** [are reconciled to God the Father] **unto God.**

The New Covenant makes one perfect through sincere repentance, the atoning sacrifice of the Lamb of God and the indwelling of God's Holy Spirit, married to a dedicated zeal to become like God our Father in heaven.

The Mosaic law made nothing perfect, being unable to atone for repented PAST sin.

The physical sacrifices of the Mosaic Covenant were an allegorical type of the spiritual New Covenant, but could not reconcile anyone spiritually to God the Father.

Only the sacrifice of the Creator himself could reconcile the sincerely repentant to God the Father; for the wages of sin [which is death] must be paid.

7:20 And inasmuch as not without an oath he [Christ] was made [High] priest: **7:21** (For those priests [of Levi] were made without an oath; but this with an oath by him that said unto him, The Lord sware and will not repent, Thou art a priest for ever after the order of Melchisedec:) **7:22** By so much was Jesus made a surety of a better testament [the High Priest of the New Covenant].

Because the men of Levi died in their generations there was a continual change of high priests; but the High Priesthood of Jesus Christ is eternal; existing from Adam as Melchisedec, right to the present; and the priesthood of Levi actually served the spiritual High Priest, the Husband of Israel, Jesus Christ [Melchisedec].

The Mosaic high priest and priesthood served Mosaic Israel under the spiritual High Priesthood of Melchisedec, therefore the passing of the Mosaic priesthood left the priesthood of Melchisedec as the only remaining priesthood of God!

Melchisedec [Jesus Christ] was the spiritual Husband of Israel that Levi served! After he gave up his Godhood to become flesh and die for humanity, the Mosaic Marriage Covenant and with it the Aaronic priesthood ended; but with the resurrection of Melchisedec, Jesus Christ [Hebrew: Yeshua Mashiach], the High Priesthood of Melchisedec between mankind and God the Father was established as an eternal spiritual High Priesthood, Mediating and reconciling all humanity to God the Father on the spiritual level of the New Covenant!

The New Covenant is only offered to Israel, yet it will save all humanity; because all humanity will be grafted into a new spiritual Israel composed of all nations and peoples!

7:23 And they truly were many priests, because they were not suffered to continue by reason of death: **7:24** But this man, because he continueth ever, hath an unchangeable priesthood. **7:25** Wherefore he is able also to save them to the uttermost that come unto God by him, seeing he ever liveth to make intercession for them.

7:26 For such an [spiritual] high priest [was suitable to be an eternal High Priest] became us, **who is holy, harmless, undefiled, separate from sinners** [without sin and set apart from all sinners], **and made higher than the heavens;**

Jesus Christ the eternal High Priest offered up himself as the Creator of Humanity made flesh, who being worth more that all humanity and being without any sin; was a perfect sacrifice and need be offered only once to atone for all the sins of all humanity; While the physical sacrifices of animals only served to keep people in the physical Mosaic Covenant and had NO spiritual promises, and animals needed to be killed on a continual basis

7:27 Who needeth not daily, as those high priests, to offer up sacrifice, first for his own sins, and then for the people's: for this he did once [being a perfect sinless sacrifice of the Creator himself], when he offered up himself.

7:28 For the law maketh men high priests which have infirmity; but the word of the oath, which was since the law, maketh the Son, who is consecrated [an eternal spirit High Priest] for evermore.

The Perfect Sacrifice and Spirit High Priest

Our High Priest, Jesus Christ will now live forever and will be able to make continual intercession for us, for all eternity. And His sacrifice being perfect, no longer has to be made again and again. He doesn't have to be killed day after day, year after year. No!

However, every time someone repents, that perfect sacrifice needs to be REAPPLIED to the repentant sinner.

The difference is in the actual dying as opposed to the actual applying of the sacrifice. They are two different things.

Christ died, regardless of whether any man ever repents or not. He was dead and He was resurrected. That has nothing to do with whether men repent, or turn from sin or not. However, when men do sincerely repent, the sacrifice is now there and available to be applied to them.

The priesthood of Aaron has been superseded by the High Priesthood of Jesus Christ, who is our spiritual Intercessor High Priest forever after the order of Melchisedec.

He is our High Priest of the New Covenant for all eternity. And He has superseded the priesthood of Aaron; and in doing this, He has fulfilled the promises that God made to the patriarchs and the prophets of old days (Jeremiah 31:31-37).

When we see the words "forever" and "without beginning or end" and we begin to take a deep prayerful think on Hebrews 7 we end up with some remarkable understanding.

Jesus Christ was the Creator and he began conversing with man as soon as man was created, for on the seventh day the Creator and Adam and Eve spent the day together.

We then have the record of some of the various conversations of the Creator with Adam and Eve, Cain, Abel, the ancients including Noah, right up to Abraham, Isaac, Jacob and beyond.

In all these things Jesus Christ was speaking with human beings in place of [as a High Priest of] God the Father.

In the time of Abraham the Creator Jesus Christ was known by the name of Melchisedec, and when he presented himself to Moses he revealed himself as the Great "I Am" which means the same thing as Melchisedec: "the forever existing one." Without beginning or end, without father or mother!

We can see that Melchisedec [the Creator who became Jesus Christ] was the spiritual High Priest [appearing in human form] between God the Father and all humanity from Adam, appearing in the form of a man.

It was when he revealed himself in a part of his glory on Mt Sinai that the people demanded a human high priest or mediator; and the priesthood of Aaron was given to Israel, to be an allegory of the High Priesthood of the Creator Melchisedec, who gave up his God-hood to become fully flesh as Jesus Christ.

The lesson in this is that the Creator Melchisedec who became flesh as Jesus Christ was a spiritual High Priest interceding between humanity and God the Father: from the very beginning of Creation!

The physical priesthood of Aaron was only a temporary expedient for the Mosaic Covenant; **and even in the Mosaic Covenant: the priesthood of Aaron was really serving the spiritual High Priest, the Creator Melchisedec, who was the spiritual Husband of Israel and later became flesh as Jesus Christ.**

Both the Mosaic Covenant and the Aaronic priesthood were instructional allegories of the spiritual New Covenant and its spiritual High Priest; who was/is the Creator; and in the Mosaic Covenant and the priesthood of Aaron, they actually served [whenever they were faithful] Jesus Christ as their Husband who came between them and God the Father [which is the role of a High Priest].

The physical high priest acted out the function of a physical mediator between man and God which is the role of Jesus Christ as the ONLY spiritual Mediator and Intercessor between man and God on the spiritual level.

1 Timothy 2:5 For there is one God [the Father], and one mediator between God [the Father] and men, the man Christ Jesus;

The one who became Jesus Christ gave up his Godhood and as a physical man came and gave his life for us, after which he was resurrected back to spirit and returned to God-hood as the ONLY Intercessor between God the Father and humanity.

2:6 Who gave himself a ransom for all, to be testified in due time.

The Function of a Priesthood

The function of a priesthood is to:

- Mediate between men and God and to
- Offer sacrifices on behalf of men to God, and to
- Teach people to live by every Word of God, and to
- Judge and rebuke all sin and

So reconcile the sincerely repentant to God the Father.

The Priests were to be God's teachers of godliness to bring people to the righteousness of God, and also to judge the people (Deuteronomy 17:8-9; 21:5; I Chronicles 23:4; II Chronicles 19:8; Ezekiel 44:15, 24).

The Mosaic Aaronic priesthood offered the sacrifices of various physical animals, which atoned for the nation and for individuals in a physical sense, to keep them in good standing within the physical Mosaic Covenant.

Melchisedec on the other hand, offered the perfect sacrifice of the very Implementing Creator of all things [the true Passover Lamb of God], to atone for the sins of humanity and to redeem us from the penalty of death for our sins; thereby reconciling the sincerely repentant with God the Father and setting before us the gift of a change to spirit and eternal life at peace with God.

The Aaronic Priesthood offered sacrifices on behalf of the whole nation and officiated over the offering of personal sacrifices, which duties they faithfully carried out at the Tabernacle during the post Sinai life of Moses and Joshua. Then through the period of the Judges and king Saul their ministrations seem to have been intermittent at best with many periods of laxity.

It was the job of the Aaronic priesthood to offer physical sacrifices as an instructional allegory of the offering of a perfect sacrifice of and by our spiritual High Priest Jesus Christ. Once the reality had happened, there was no longer a need for the physical allegory of that reality.

Since 31 A.D. our High Priest Jesus Christ has been resurrected back to spirit and to the glory which he had given up to be made flesh; and now sits at the right hand of God the Father in heaven and daily intervenes on our behalf interceding for us with God the Father.

Psalm 110:1 The Lord said unto my Lord, Sit thou at my right hand, until I make thine enemies thy footstool.

A History of Repeated Apostasy

The physical ministrations of the Aaronic priesthood would have been largely restored by the zeal of king David and the young king Solomon.

Later in the reign of Solomon the king fell astray and led the nation away from God and from that time there were a few good kings and many wicked ones.

The priesthood also fell away from God with regularity.

After the reign of Solomon, God rent the ten tribes from Benjamin / Judah and gave them to Jeroboam who immediately abandoned God and set up pagan altars.

In spite of the work of various prophets including Elijah and Elisha the ten tribes of Israel remained adamant in sin and were finally removed from the land by God through the hand of the Assyrians. Israel fell in a series of wars and without doubt many of Israel that were trying to be faithful to God fled south and were assimilated into Judah / Benjamin.

Years later, after a few good kings restored the service of the priests and many bad rulers restored paganism in Judah [some of whom went as far as to set up pagan altars in God's Temple], Judah / Benjamin was sent into corrective captivity to Babylon.

The follow up studies for this lesson on The Priesthood, is a study through the book of Hebrews.

The Ezra Restoration

Moses was called to be the Judge or leader of Israel under God, and under Moses were the elders and the Seventy ruling over the various tribes of Israel, and under them were the officers of thousands and hundreds etc. which ruled all Israel. This was the Mosaic Civil Administration.

The Religious Administration consisted of the tribe of Levi and from Levi the sons [male descendants] of Aaron were called to be the priests; the priests officiating over the sacrificial system and the Levites assisting the priests in all matters except the actual offering of the sacrifices.

Throughout the history of the Judges and Kings the priests of Aaron, the Levites and the Administrative System officials repeatedly fell far away from God.

Israel

Solomon departed from God and God rent the ten tribes of Israel away from Judah/Benjamin and gave them to Jeroboam. Jeroboam immediately led Israel into idolatry and great wickedness so that not one of the kings of Israel was righteous and God finally removed them from the land by the hand of the Assyrians who replaced them.

2 Kings 17:22 For the children of Israel walked in all the sins of Jeroboam which he did; they departed not from them; **17:23** Until the Lord removed

Israel out of his sight, as he had said by all his servants the prophets. So was Israel carried away out of their own land to Assyria unto this day. **17:24** And the king of Assyria brought men **from Babylon**, and from Cuthah, and from Ava [cities of Babylon], and from Hamath [modern Homs Syria, at that time the Hamathites were a Hamitic race, and are included among the descendants of Canaan. (Genesis 10:18)] , and from Sepharvaim [Sippara on the east bank of the Euphrates is now called Abu-Habba], and placed them in the cities of Samaria instead of the children of Israel: and they possessed Samaria, and dwelt in the cities thereof.

Without doubt there were some faithful to God through the years in Israel as God had told Elijah that he had 7,000 still in Israel during the days of Elijah (1 Kings 19:18).

Some of the faithful would have fled south to Judah at the warnings of the prophets and the approaching armies, after which they were assimilated into Judah.

Judah

Because of the Temple at Jerusalem and several good kings, Judah had periods of revival among the periods of apostasy and Judah remained until Jerusalem was destroyed in c 586 B.C. Judah then fully entered the Babylonian Captivity and was largely removed from the land to Babylon by Nebuchadnezzar.

They remained in captivity in Babylon until 536 B.C. during which time the Mosaic Administration of the Seventy and the officers over the people gained almost complete ascendancy over the tribe of Judah; the Priests and Levites fading because there was no longer a tabernacle or a temple or even an Ark.

The Scribes who were from the Levites with some from the Priests [who were also descendants of Levi], prospered because they preserved the scriptures and were the only remaining Levites and Priests relevant to the situation.

Rebuilding the Temple

Cyrus assumed the title of "king of Babylon" in 536, claiming to be the descendant of the ancient kings, and made rich offerings to all the temples and religions, to maintain the peace of the population by gaining the support of the religions leaders; in a continuation of the "church state" system of Babylon.

In celebration he decreed that the foreign populations who had been deported to Babylon could return to their old homes, carrying with them the images of their gods; and restore their national religions. Among these populations were certain Jews, who, as they had no images, took with them the sacred vessels of the temple and some 50,000 went back to Judea to rebuild the Temple.

At that time leaders of the Jewish people throughout Babylonia urged them to return to the Judah and to begin working on rebuilding the Temple.

This included Zerubavel ben She'altiel, a descendant of King David; Yohoshua [Joshua] ben Yehotzadak [Jehozadok], the High Priest; Nechemiah [Nehemiah]; Mordechai; and the Prophets; Chaggai [Haggai], Zechariah and Malachi. Yehoshua and Zerubavel appointed the Levites to supervise the work, while the questions of halachah [law] which arose in the course of construction were decide by the Sages of the Sanhedrin [the Seventy elders], among who were many prophets. [HOJP I, 25].

Ezra

Ezra the Scribe came to Jerusalem only after the Temple was built. The Persian king appointed Ezra as the chief judge over the Jews, and authorized him to enforce his decisions. When Ezra arrived in Jerusalem he quickly discovered the truth of the many reports concerning the disappointing spiritual level of the local Jews.

The physical construction of the Temple was completed but the spiritual condition of the people was not. Ezra summoned all the men of Yehudah [Judah] and Benjamin [Benjamin] to Jerusalem.

So great was Ezra's impact on the people that they all promised to divorce their foreign wives. All that winter, until the first of Nissan, the Seventy now called the Sanhedrin in Jerusalem and the various local courts [the administrative officials remember the Mosaic Administration] occupied themselves with establishing the family purity of the returnees.

The society's need for national spiritual leadership was met by the creation of a special body called the Knesses HaGedolah, or Great Assembly which assisted Ezra in restoring true religion to Judah, this body of the Seventy was eventually called the Sanhedrin.

The Great Assembly later called the Great Sanhedrin, under Ezra took steps to revive the religion.

Seeing that the lack of biblical scholars and teachers was the cause of Judah's downfall, Ezra sent scholars to the different communities restoring the synagogue school system with a synagogue [meeting place] in every town.

Era being a deeply converted and an appointed Judge [ruler] Levite, Priest, prophet and Scribe, restored the Synagogue system and sent Biblical Scholars to teach the nation.

They translated the Bible into the Aramaic [common speach of the people] vernacular and canonized the scriptures into a single authoritative version. Ezra also ordained that all sacred texts be again written in Ashuri script, a sacred square-letter script.

Ezra and the Great Assembly also restored the method of determining the new month by a special committee of the Sanhedrin examining witnesses to the first visible light of the new moon, precise sacrificial ritual with its various prayers, the temple period Passover service [which is not the same as today's Rabbinic Seder service], the water pouring ceremony, the ceremony of light and the method of rejoicing with branches at the Feast of Tabernacles.

After Ezra, from the time of Alexander into the first century there was a continual struggle for dominance between the Saducee's, Scribes and the Pharisees, especially between the Mosaic loyalists and those who had been Hellenized.

The Pharisees

Alexander the Great 356-323 B.C.

By introducing Hellenic culture into Syria, Babylon and Egypt, he had probably more influence on the development of today's Judaism than any one individual not a Jew by race. After the siege of Tyre, 332 B.C., he marched through Palestine unopposed and visited Jerusalem.

By the first century, the Seventy came to be called the Sanhedrin, while the scholarly officials came to be called Pharisees. The priests were called Saducee's and those who copied the scriptures were called Scribes. The Pharisees came to be deeply influenced by Hellenic culture and reasoning which was spread by Alexander, who had been taught by Aristotle, who was taught by Plato, who was taught by Socrates.

Those Pharisees who remained faithful to God lived mostly in Judea, while those willing to apply the reasoning of the Greeks to their religion, had many in Judea and dominated the Jews who remained in Babylon or lived in Alexandria.

The Mosaic or faithful Pharisees became very proud and eventually made God's Word of no effect through their many added traditions. They rejected Christ, who stripped away their false traditions and taught the pure and true Word of God. These folks were largely destroyed along with the Jerusalem Temple Sadducee's and Scribes by the Romans in the first century.

The demise of the Mosaic Pharisees meant the end of Mosaic Judaism and a long struggle between the Scribes [Karaites] and the Hellenized Pharisees, resulting in the rise of modern Rabbinic Judaism.

Jesus said: **Matthew 23:2** "Saying The scribes and the Pharisees sit in Moses' seat:"

He was speaking of the Mosaic Pharisees and Scribes who were faithful to Moses and taught the Word of God in Judea at that time.

Those Mosaic Pharisees were not the Sadducee's [priests] they came from the Seventy and from the Mosaic System of Officials over thousands and hundreds, who were scholars of the scriptures!

Let's look at the Mosaic Administration again; what kind of people were to be chosen to help rule the people? **Exodus 18:21** Moreover thou shalt provide out of all the people **able men, such as fear God, men of truth, hating covetousness**; and place such over them, to be rulers of thousands, and rulers of hundreds, rulers of fifties, and rulers of tens:

Jesus said that it was these scholars of God's Word who sat in Moses seat, because they were the heirs of the Mosaic Administrative System!

Then he said **Matthew 23:3** All therefore whatsoever they bid you observe, that observe and do; but **do not ye after their works: for they say, and do not.**

The chief problem with the Mosaic Pharisees is that they added their own traditions to the Word of God and were just as zealous for their traditions as they were for the Word of God, thereby making the Word of God of no effect through their zeal for the traditions of men; which is exactly the problem in today's Ekklesia!

He was not speaking of the Hellenized Pharisees who interpreted the scriptures using Greek logic, twisting the scriptures to appear to mean things quite different from what they actually said, and falsely claiming a secret tradition from Moses to deceive people into accepting their apostate teachings.

How do we know that there is no secret tradition from Moses? Because God commanded that all that he had told Moses was to be taught to the people!

Leviticus 10:11 And that ye may **teach the children of Israel all the statutes which the Lord hath spoken unto them by the hand of Moses**

Deuteronomy 5:31 But as for thee, stand thou here by me, and **I will speak unto thee all the commandments, and the statutes, and the judgments, which thou shalt teach them**, that they may do them in the land which I give them to possess it.

Any person who teaches anything different from the Holy Scriptures is a false teacher and a false prophet, for we are to live by every Word of God in the Holy Scriptures.

Deuteronomy 5:31 But as for thee, stand thou here by me, and **I will speak unto thee all the commandments, and the statutes, and the judgments, which thou shalt teach them**, that they may do them in the land which I give them to possess it. **5:32** Ye shall observe to do therefore as the Lord your God hath commanded you: **ye shall not turn aside to the right hand or to the left.**

Deuteronomy 8:3 And he humbled thee, and suffered thee to hunger, and fed thee with manna, which thou knewest not, neither did thy fathers know; **that he might make thee know that man doth not live by bread only, but by every word that proceedeth out of the mouth of the Lord doth man live.**

Deuteronomy 13:1 If there arise among you a prophet, or a dreamer of dreams, and giveth thee a sign or a wonder,

13:2 And the sign or the wonder come to pass, whereof he spake unto thee, saying, Let us go after other gods, which thou hast not known, and let us serve them;

13:3 Thou shalt not hearken unto the words of that prophet, or that dreamer of dreams: for the Lord your God proveth [tests] you, to know whether ye love the Lord your God with all your heart and with all your soul.

13:4 Ye shall walk after the Lord your God, and fear him, and keep his commandments, and obey his voice, and ye shall serve him, and cleave unto him.

There is NO secret instruction or traditions from Moses, we are to live by every Word of God contained in the Holy Scriptures and any teaching which is different from the Holy Scriptures is false.

Ezra's Synagogue Education System
Bet Sefer

Children around six years old would have gone to a local synagogue school called a Bet Sefer. It means house of the book. In the days of Moses and Joshua a synagogue or school system of education was set up to be run by the Levites. The godliness of these schools often fluctuated into paganism as David prophesied in **Psalm 74:8** They said in their hearts, Let us destroy them [Judah in the Babylonian captivity] together: they [because Judah had forsaken God] have burned up all **the synagogues of God** in the land.

Then after the punishment and captivity in Babylon some of the Jews returned to Judea and the godly synagogue education system was restored by Ezra.

This system continued until the Roman wars when the Temple and the religion of the Judean Pharisees and Sadducee's was destroyed; to be succeeded by the followers of Yeshua [Jesus; true faithful Christians]; and by the Babylonian Hellenized Pharisees who developed into the modern rabbinate of today.

From the days of Ezra, a child usually attended a Bet Sefer from age 6 to age 10.

This school would be attended five or six days a week . There would be a local synagogue teacher who would begin teaching the Books of Moses; Genesis, Exodus, Leviticus, Numbers and Deuteronomy; along with reading, writing and other subjects of a general basic education.

It is said that on the first day of class a rabbi would give each child some honey. He would then say, "Now class, There is nothing sweeter, than honey, taste the honey". And as the students tasted, the teacher would say, "May the words of God be sweet to your taste, sweeter than honey to your mouth" (Psalm 119:103). May the words of God be the most pleasurable, the most enjoyable thing you could ever comprehend.

As a child you were introduced to the Scriptures and taught that there was nothing more enjoyable in the entire universe than; tasting, receiving and fully learning and internalizing the Words of God and making them a part of your life.

This is how boys were introduced to the Scriptures. From ages 6-10 they would be taught the entire five Books of Moses as well as the "ABCs" of reading writing and arithmetic and complete the Bet Sefer schooling.

Bet Talmud

Bet Talmud means house of learning and does not refer to the Talmud compiled hundreds of years later. Roughly from ages 10-14 in Bet Talmud you would learn the rest of the Hebrew Scriptures all the way to Malachi.

Bet Midrash [Discipleship]

At the end of your study at Bet Talmud, when you were around 14-15 years old, you would proceed to learn a trade; or if you were interested in advanced religious studies you would go and seek out a respected and knowledgeable Rabbi to study with.

The rabbi would ask you lots of questions, to find out if you were a suitable candidate for a discipleship. This was because each rabbi wanted to teach very advanced studies designed to make the novice into a rabbi himself. This was akin to a modern Bible School to train people for the ministry, although much more personal, like having a personal tutor, and was called the yoke of learning. This rabbi wanted to know, when he was questioning the applicant, his potential disciple: "Is this boy able to become a rabbi himself and to teach and spread my yoke?" So the rabbi would ask all kinds of questions.

And if the rabbi believed that you had potential to become a rabbi, He would say, "Lech Acharai – Come, follow me," and you would be accepted to become his disciple student ,and you would spend the next few years to learning from that rabbi. Would Yeshua [Jesus] settle for anyone but the very best and wisest rabbi to apprentice to? Would the teachers not have heard of this prodigy and seek him for their student? There is much reason to believe that Jesus was trained by the leading scholar of his time Gamaliel.; and that he was trained alongside the brightest Jewish students of his day, perhaps Saul himself.

At the age of 30 years the diligent student would "graduate" to become a Rabbi himself.

The New Covenant Ministry

The God who married Israel was made flesh and dwelt among men, dying for the sins of humanity. Marriages last only as long as both parties live and with the death of the Husband of Israel; the Mosaic marriage Covenant ended and Israel became a widow.

Israel was to remain a widow from that moment on, until she entered into a New Covenant of marriage to God (Jer 31:31, Ez 36), and once Israel enters into a permanent New Covenant she shall no longer be called a widow.

Isaiah 54:4 Fear not; for thou shalt not be ashamed: neither be thou confounded; for thou shalt not be put to shame: for thou shalt forget the shame of thy youth, and shalt not remember the reproach of **thy widowhood** any more.

At the moment of Christ's death Israel became a widow and the Mosaic Covenant ended because of the death of the Husband of Israel. Yet as soon as Jesus Christ was resurrected to spirit and accepted for us he became an eternal High Priest of a New and Eternal Covenant.

The plan of God for the salvation of mankind involves the calling out of an early harvest with a resurrection at the end of six thousand years for ll those who have overcome all sin. This resurrection will be followed the removal of Satan from influencing mankind for a thousand years, during which all those living after the resurrection to spirit would also be filled with God's Spirit and would be changed to spirit at the end of their lives throughout the millennial period.

Those called out to be set apart to God in the New Covenant are NOT spiritual priests in this physical life. They are called out to BECOME priests and kings for eternity (Rev 1:6, 5:10). God does not want a priesthood or kings [rulers] who will continually rebel like the priests and rulers of physical Israeli did!

God established the Mosaic rulers and priesthood as an instructional allegory to teach those called out to the New Covenant spiritual priesthood of Jesus Christ - from both good and bad examples; how to become faithful spiritual rulers and priests forever.

I ask, was Abel or Noah or Abraham or even Jesus Christ while in the flesh a priest or king? No, for they all died NOT having inherited the promises (Heb 11).

The priesthood of Aaron has ended with the end of the Mosaic Covenant; which ended with the death of the Husband of Israel.

1. At this time with the end of the priesthood of Aaron, there is no longer any physical priesthood on the earth,

2. All of those called out to become first fruits, are called to persevere and learn godliness, to become spiritual priests and kings [judges and officials] after the resurrection to spirit.

3. At the present time, for the sake of order in the assemblies and the spiritual growth of the brethren, as well as the public preaching of the Gospel of Salvation, there are of necessity certain offices of responsibility within the Ekklesia.

4. These offices are offices of service through setting a godly example and teaching all people to live by every Word of God.

5. All of the called to God are in training to BECOME priests and rulers while in the flesh, but will not achieve that dignity until the resurrection to spirit.

6. All authority - especially moral authority - comes from God; and the only moral authority any man has is the authority of the Word of God. Therefore when a person [no matter what title he claims] departs from any part of the Word of God he has abandoned the source of his moral authority and has forfeited all religious authority being apostate.

7. The brethren MUST NOT OBEY apostates, and must follow and obey only those who live by every Word of God and teach men to do likewise.

Brethren: We are presently In Training to become kings and priests, and we will not become priests and kings [rulers or judges and officials, as well as priests] until we successfully complete the course and are chosen to be resurrected to spirit. It is only after we are chosen and changed to spirit that we will be set apart [consecrated] as full priests and kings [rulers]; inheriting our place in the priesthood of Jesus Christ!

At the resurrection to spirit of the chosen we will be consecrated as priests before the throne of God in heaven.

Today there is NO Physical Priesthood!

The function of a priesthood is to mediate between mankind and God, to teach godliness to the people and to offer sacrifices on behalf of repentant people to God, so as to reconcile men to God the Father.

The Mosaic Aaronic priesthood offered the sacrifices of various physical animals, which atoned for the nation and for individuals in a physical sense, to keep them in good standing within the physical Mosaic Covenant.

That physical priesthood ended with the end of the Mosaic Covenant at the death of the Husband of Israel

Melchisedec offered the perfect sacrifice of the very Implementing Creator of all things [the true Passover Lamb of God], to atone for the sins of humanity and to redeem us from the penalty of death for our sins; thereby reconciling the sincerely repentant with God the Father, and setting before us the gift of a change to spirit and eternal life at peace with God.

The Aaronic Priesthood offered sacrifices on behalf of the whole nation and officiated over the offering of personal sacrifices, which duties they faithfully carried out at the Tabernacle during the post Sinai life of Moses and Joshua; after which their ministrations seem to have been intermittent at best with many periods of falling away.

Since 31 A.D. our resurrected spiritual High Priest sits at the right hand of God the Father in heaven and daily intervenes on our behalf interceding for us with God the Father.

Since the resurrection of Jesus Christ as our spiritual High Priest, the Daily Sacrifice has been spiritual, being the regular daily application of the sacrifice of the Lamb of God before the Father in heaven [even though the physical sacrifices lasted for a few more years]; where he also intervenes on behalf of repentant individuals!

Today's ministry are NOT priests or Levites in either the physical or the spiritual sense, they are brethren and priests In Training, like all of the Called Out; but they have been given certain responsibilities to help their brethren overcome and persevere to the resurrection to spirit.

Today the entirety of God's spiritually called out are in training to BECOME priests forever under the High Priesthood of Jesus Christ, but we are not there yet, we are not yet qualified, and we are not yet chosen and changed to spirit.

1 Peter 2:5 Ye also, as lively stones, are built up a spiritual house, [we are called to become] an holy priesthood, to offer up spiritual sacrifices, acceptable to God by Jesus Christ.

1 Peter 2:9 But ye are a chosen generation, a royal priesthood, an holy nation, a peculiar [special] people; that ye should [we are called to] shew forth the praises of him who hath called you out of darkness into his marvellous light;

Only by continually growing in Faith and the Knowledge of God and by diligently applying that Knowledge so as to live by every Word of God, and by persevering no matter how difficult the conditions; will we be qualified to enter the resurrection into eternal life where our lot will be to be made priests of the High Priesthood of Jesus Christ at that time and not before!

For it is written that it is those who have attained to the first resurrection who will be made priests of God the Father in the High Priesthood of Jesus Christ.

Revelation 20:6 Blessed and holy is **he that hath part in the first resurrection**: on such the second death hath no power, but **they shall be priests of God and of Christ**

Why? Because today the priesthood of Jesus Christ is a spiritual priesthood which flesh cannot enter! Because the physical priesthood of Aaron failed and often went astray from their duty, God will no longer allow a physical priesthood to come between Him and the brethren.

During the New Covenant age the physical priesthood of Aaron has ended, and with it all physical priesthoods have ended.

The New Covenant priesthood is the priesthood of the resurrected High Priest Jesus Christ as the ONLY intercessor between people and God the Father.

The job of the priests is to mediate between God and people and Almighty God has decreed that ONLY the resurrected Jesus Christ may mediate between people and God in this dispensation.

1 Timothy 2:5 For there is one God, and one mediator between God and men, the man [now resurrected back to spirit] Christ Jesus;

God does not want another "failed physical priesthood," therefore God is now TRAINING a spiritual priesthood, which priesthood will be formally consecrated before the Throne of God the Father in heaven, ONLY after the resurrection of the Chosen (Rev 15).

Today, ALL of the called out are called to become a royal [rulers, teachers and judges and officials] priesthood of priest kings of Jesus Christ in the resurrection to spirit.

Yet, of necessity, today God has given various persons different Gifts of His Spirit and ordained different offices of responsibilities in the brotherhood for the express purpose of teaching and encouraging the brethren, and helping them to become the spiritual image [to become like] of Jesus Christ and God the Father.

Ephesians 4:11 And he gave some, apostles; and some, prophets; and some, evangelists; and some, pastors and teachers;

Why? **4:12** For the perfecting [exhortation and instruction] of the saints, for the work of the ministry, for the edifying [teaching and building up in spiritual knowledge] of the body of Christ:

4:13 Till we all come in the unity of the faith [until every person comes into the full knowledge of godliness and lives by every Word of God as Jesus does], and of the knowledge of the Son of God, unto a perfect man, [we must all become fully Christ-like and ready to enter the same priesthood of Jesus Christ] unto the measure of the stature of the fulness of Christ:

These offices have nothing to do with actually being priests at this time, and today's ministry is NOT some kind of spiritual Levites or Priests at all!

These offices of responsibilities are gifts of the Holy Spirit from God, to assist every called out person to grow into the fullness of Jesus Christ [to become LIKE Jesus Christ in every way], so that God will raise us up to spirit to become a part of those chosen to enter THE SAME SPIRITUAL PRIESTHOOD as Jesus Christ.

Today's Christian Dispensation ministry which began in 31 A.D. and will last only until the coming of Christ to rule the nations, when a new priesthood made of resurrected spirits will officiate on the earth [with the physical descendants of Zadok officiating in the physical things of the Ezekiel Temple]; is only a temporary expedient to help, instruct and build up the called out, until we are properly prepared to be resurrected into the spiritual priesthood of Jesus Christ.

All of the called out brethren since righteous Abel have been or are In Training until they die. In training to be chosen and resurrected as a royal spirit priesthood; in training so that we will be a perfect priesthood made o0f spirit which will last forever, instead of a priesthood which regularly falls away like the priesthood of Aaron: However God in his mercy and wisdom has provided offices of responsibility to help each of us to attain to the purpose of our calling!

Discipleship to Jesus Christ

The calling of God the Father is to the school of discipleship to Jesus Christ. All of the called out since righteous Abel have been called out to God the Father through Jesus Christ. They and we, have all been called out to godliness and to living by every Word of God during extremely adverse circumstances, so that we can learn godliness and also learn the weakness of the flesh and the power of God so that we can learn mercy for others through suffering as Jesus did.

Hebrews 2:18 For in that he himself hath suffered being tempted, he is able to succour them that are tempted.

Hebrews 5:8 Though he were a Son, yet learned he obedience by the things which he suffered;

A Disciple of Christ

Jesus said: "If you will enter life: keep the commandments". **John 15:10** If ye keep my commandments, ye shall abide in my love; even as I have kept my Father's commandments, and abide in his love.

Luke 14:26 If anyone comes to Me and does not hate his father and mother, wife and children, brothers and sisters, yes, and his own life also, he cannot be My disciple.

This means that godliness must be our FIRST priority; it does NOT mean that we should literally hate our relatives. This does mean that our love for God and his commandments should be so strong, that we will be ready to give up all things for that "Pearl of Great Price". Should you love your family? Yes! But love God the Father and the Son; many times more!

Matthew 16:24 "Then Jesus said to His disciples, If anyone desires to come after Me, let him deny himself, and take up his cross and follow Me.

To deny oneself means to say 'no' to personal desires and pleasures in order to say 'yes' to God.

This means that we are to put God at the very center of our lives. It means denying and forsaking anything that hinders our walk with God (Luke 14:33). It means "seeking first the kingdom of God and His righteousness" (Matthew 6:33). It means maintaining a passionate Christ-like zeal to live by every Word of God the Father.

A Disciple of Christ, follows Christ everywhere, and lives by every Word of God just as Christ does

Matthew 4:4 But he answered and said, It is written, Man shall not live by bread alone, but by every word that proceedeth out of the mouth of God.

In **John 8:31** "Jesus said … 'If you abide in My word, you are My disciples indeed'.

If we do not eat for several days we will get weak and even ill. The only people who do not eat are either sick or dead. The same is true spiritually. The Word of God is spiritual food. It is like milk, like water, like bread, like honey, like meat …

The people who do not eat [internalize] God's Word will become either spiritually sick or spiritually dead.

That is why we must always be diligent to be faithful to our Beloved Espoused Husband and his Father, reading in God's Word, continually thinking on God's Word, discussing godliness with other faithful persons, discussing the Word with God our Father in prayer; and APPLYING and LIVING what we learn! Following the example and instructions of Jesus Christ and living by every Word of God with enthusiasm!

John 13:35 says, By this all will know that you are My disciples, if you have love for one another.

What kind of love is this? It is more than just the being polite and kind.

1 John 3:16 says, Hereby perceive we the love of God, because He laid down His life for us: and we ought to lay down our lives for the brethren.

By being willing to tell the truth in love and helping to focus others on the way to life eternal, we are showing far more love than those who would give a physical gift.

Love begins with loving God and his Word enough to live by God's Word at all times; and then progresses to love towards man.

The second great commandment does not eclipse the first, because the first is the foundation of the second.

Matthew 22:37 Jesus said unto him, Thou shalt love the Lord thy God with all thy heart, and with all thy soul, and with all thy mind. **22:38** This is the first and great commandment. **22:39** And the second is like unto it, Thou shalt love thy neighbour as thyself. **22:40** On these two commandments hang all the law and the prophets.

Proverbs 27:5 Open rebuke [correction from error] is better than secret love. **27:6** Faithful are the wounds of a friend; but the kisses of an enemy are deceitful.

Very often demonstrations and claims of love and of affection are only a deceitful con job to lead men into following others to their own hurt and to the advantage of the other.

BEWARE the man who says; "I love you, come and follow me, for to follow me is to follow God": TEST him out by the Word of God; because such men are often con artists who will teach their own traditions and will not stand on the Word of God.

It is the man who insists that all men follow God and NOT themselves; that is far more likely to be of God.

Once any man or organization starts pushing love and organizational unity instead of teaching a passionate zeal to live by every Word of God; they have apostatized from God; for the godly man and organization will always push unity with God, and love for God and his Word. Godly men will never teach "go along ot get along" for the sake of organizational loyalty.

Unity with others and love for mankind is secondary to love for God and his Word and Will.

Loving God and all his Word and Will is the foundation upon which love for mankind is based; and NOT the other way around.

Those who are offended by God's Word and the person who teaches it; have no understanding of the love being offered to them that engenders the gift of eternal life to them.

Love is NOT only a matter of saying "have a good day" and then allowing a brother to rush to his destruction; love is telling him the truth and if necessary warning him to turn top godliness.

The shallowest and most superficial kind of love is about physical things; while the deepest and most sublime love is love on a spiritual plane! We should love on BOTH the physical and spiritual levels.

A Disciple produces Good Spiritual Fruits

In John 15 Jesus said, By this My Father is glorified, that you bear much fruit, … and that your fruit should remain; … so you will be My disciples.

God wants each of us to bear "fruit that remains" and to do that we must remain grafted into the true vine of Jesus Christ; whose foundation is every Word of God the Father!

Those who do not bear fruit will be gathered up and thrown into the fire.

A Disciple is called to study and learn; to become a "trained" person.

Becoming a disciple of Jesus comes through being selected and called; by God the Father!

Discipleship itself is a training process. True Christians follow Christ in living by every Word of God:

1 By imitating His life and diligently following his example, that means that we are also to work hard at setting the very same good Christ-like godly example ourselves;

2 By obeying all of our Master's instructions and commandments, which includes living by every Word of God the Father (Mat 4:4) as Jesus does;

3 We are to diligently study as Jesus diligently studied throughout his lifetime.

2 Timothy 2:15 Study to shew thyself approved unto God, a workman that needeth not to be ashamed, rightly dividing the word of truth.

We are to copy the example of and internalize the full nature of God the father and Jesus Christ!

It is by their fruits that we can discern the false from the true man of God:

Matthew 7:15 Beware of false prophets, which come to you in sheep's clothing, but inwardly they are ravening wolves.

7:16 Ye shall know them by their fruits. Do men gather grapes of thorns, or figs of thistles? **7:17** Even so every good tree bringeth forth good fruit; but a corrupt tree bringeth forth evil fruit. **7:18** A good tree cannot bring forth evil fruit, neither can a corrupt tree bring forth good fruit.

7:19 Every tree that bringeth not forth good fruit is hewn down, and cast into the fire. **7:20** Wherefore by their fruits ye shall know them.

7:21 Not every one that saith unto me, Lord, Lord, shall enter into the kingdom of heaven; but **he that doeth the will of my Father which is in heave**n.

I encourage you to make God the Father, Jesus Christ and every Word of God your focus, to get close to them again; to walk as they walk, to live as they live!

God will not walk with you; if you will not live as he lives.

A good Disciple - especially one desiring an office of responsibility - should be fully versed in ALL the Holy Scriptures and must be enthusiastically zealous to live by every Word of God; and his example of love for God's Word should be proven over a very lengthy period of time.

He should be seen as a good example of godliness and fully experienced and mature in the faith and in his personal life.

Brethren, Christ was dedicated to studying the scriptures and did so all of his life. That should be no surprise to anyone. Christ loved his Father and he would have been buried in the scriptures or in prayer throughout his life.

At the tender age of 12 Christ deeply impressed the wise men in Jerusalem at the Temple and as an adult He became thoroughly learned in the Word of God and probably was well respected; until he began to go beyond their teachings of the letter of the law and began to teach the spirit and intent of the law.

With that he passed beyond their understanding and offended the religious leaders of the time.

So it was that they demanded: "Who taught you these things" when he explained new things about the purpose and spirit of the scriptures; for they had never heard of such things before.

John 7:14 Now about the midst of the feast Jesus went up into the temple, and taught. **7:15** And the Jews marvelled, saying, How knoweth this man letters, having never learned? [never been taught by their teachers] **7:16** Jesus answered them, and said, My doctrine is not mine, but his that sent me [God the Father's].

Qualifications for the Priesthood/Ministry

In reality we are ALL called out to become priests and kings and these things are the qualifications which we ALL must meet to be among the resurrected chosen first fruits!

It is required for all "elders" to be mature men, heads of families, capable men of strong moral character, fearing God, men of truth and integrity. The same things are required of all of us in order to be in the resurrection to spirit and enter the resurrection to the priesthood of Jesus Christ for all eternity.

If we are to be good teachers of godliness; then we must KNOW the Word of God.

Exodus 18:20 And thou shalt teach them ordinances and laws, and shalt shew them the way wherein they must walk, and the work that they must do. **18:21** Moreover **thou shalt provide out of all the people able men, such as fear God, men of truth, hating covetousness;** and place such over them, to be rulers of thousands, and rulers of hundreds, rulers of fifties, and rulers of tens:

Elders were men who were full of the Holy Spirit (Numbers 11:16-17); they were supposed to be capable men, full of wisdom, discernment, and experience; impartial and courageous men who would intercede, teach, and judge righteously and fairly.

Deuteronomy 1:13 Take you wise men, and understanding, and known among your tribes, and I will make them rulers over you. **1:14** And ye answered me, and said, The thing which thou hast spoken is good for us to do. **1:15** So I took the chief of your tribes, wise men, and known, and made them heads over you, captains over thousands, and captains over hundreds, and captains over fifties, and captains over tens, and officers among your tribes. **1:16** And I charged your judges at that time, saying, Hear the causes between your brethren, and judge righteously between every man and his brother, and the stranger that is with him. **1:17** Ye shall not respect persons in judgment; but ye shall hear the small as well as the great; ye shall not be afraid of the face of man; for the judgment is God's: and the cause that is too hard for you, bring it unto me, and I will hear it.

All of those characteristics were involved in the Jewish understanding of the term "elder" (*presbuteros*). So the concept and responsibility of being an elder was not new to the early church. The use of the term "elder" to describe church leaders emphasizes that they needed to be mature men of integrity, having years of experience and proven to be strong and consistent in all moral character.

In the New Covenant, the office of elder was regarded as the highest level of LOCAL church leadership. Therefore, the office carried a great amount of sobriety and responsibility. The elders were charged with the care and spiritual guidance of the entire congregation, but it was not to be the kind of authority exercised by unconverted rulers.

The behavior of elders should never be self-aggrandizing or bullying; but the setting of a godly example and tirelessly teaching and exhorting all people to live by every Word of God.

In 1 Timothy 3, and Titus 1, Paul gives a clear-cut list of the qualifications necessary for the office of pastor/bishop/elder and describes the kind of mature character and reputation that is required of a pastor in order to fill and continue to fill this office.

1 Timothy 3:1 This is a true saying, if a man desire the office of a bishop, he desireth a good work. **3:2** A bishop then must be blameless [without sin], the husband of one wife, vigilant, sober, of good behaviour, given to hospitality, apt to teach; **3:3** Not given to wine, no striker, not greedy of filthy lucre; but patient, not a brawler, not covetous;

3:4 One that ruleth well his own house, having his children in subjection with all gravity; **3:5** (For if a man know not how to rule his own house, how shall he take care of the church of God?) **3:6** Not a novice, lest being lifted up with pride he fall into the condemnation of the devil. **3:7** Moreover he must have a good report of them which are without; lest he fall into reproach and the snare of the devil.

The Bible is very clear about how elders and pastors and all godly people, are to conduct themselves. We all need to be familiar with these Scriptures to help us to discern that those we are following are truly exemplifying the qualifications that God requires for those who claim any ecclesiastical office.

They are to be godly men of the highest moral integrity; those who have crucified any carnal lusts for control, power, money and pleasure; men that are not easily angered or frustrated.

In other words all candidates for ordination [and that includes all candidates for the resurrection to spirit] must be people that have proved that they can rightly rule themselves and master their human nature and inordinate emotions and are patient teachers of others. They must know how to manage alcohol and not given over to overindulgence of wine or strong drink. They are men who hold fast to the faithful Word of God and teach only sound doctrine and are able (skilled) to firmly oppose those who try to subvert them or their congregations to follow after false doctrines and heresies. They are not to be tainted by any of the Works of the Flesh.

They are to be above reproach in all things, also being excellent examples in their own family lives and in how they treat their women and children. An elder is to be a good husband having only one wife and having wisely taught their children.

The qualifications of an elder, then, go far beyond good moral characteristics. An elder must be demonstrably skilled as a teacher and manager of his own life before he can teach and manage a congregation. His life must reflect these qualities, and, if he does not meet these qualifications, he is not to be ordained.

To be ordained to an office of responsibility one must not be a new convert to the faith, for it takes time for a man to grow and become spiritually grounded in sound doctrine and to mature and gain wisdom through the experiences of life.

In addition, elevating someone who is new to the faith to a position of leadership in the assembly could possibly make that person conceited and think of himself as more important than others.

This list of qualifications informs us that an elder, in addition to being of the highest moral character, must also have a spotless reputation with those inside and outside the congregation. His business and social activities in the community, the assemblies and within his family, in fact his whole life, must also be above reproach in order to qualify him for ordination.

Brethren, such qualifications for an office in the flesh reveal that at least the same high qualifications will be required to receive the gift of eternal life and an eternal spiritual priesthood [eldership]! We must all be striving to live by every Word of God and to gain a Christ-like mastery over ourselves!

Titus 1:5 For this cause left I thee in Crete, that thou shouldest set in order the things that are wanting, and ordain elders in every city, as I had appointed thee: **1:6** If any be blameless, the husband of one wife, having faithful children not accused of riot or unruly. **1:7** For a bishop must be blameless, as the steward of God; not selfwilled, not soon angry, not given to wine, no striker, not given to filthy lucre; **1:8** But a lover of hospitality, a lover of good men, sober, just, holy, temperate; **1:9** Holding fast the faithful word as he hath been taught, that he may be able by sound doctrine both to exhort and to convince the gainsayers.

Another qualification for eldership at any level is that a person must love God and God's flock [people], being willing to die to live by every Word of God and for each individual.

We can look at John 10 to see that a true shepherd of the sheep loves the sheep and is not like one that thinks of being a shepherd as just a job to earn a paycheck and retirement benefits. A true shepherd is willing to give up his own life for the benefit of the flock. This can mean to die for them, but more typically it can mean that he is willing to give up his own hopes, dreams, and desires and the kind of life that others have, in order to devote his life to the care of the sheep.

John 10:12 But he that is an hireling, and not the shepherd, whose own the sheep are not, seeth the wolf coming, and leaveth the sheep, and fleeth: and the wolf catcheth them, and scattereth the sheep.

10:13 The hireling fleeth, because he is an hireling, and careth not for the sheep. **10:14** I am the good shepherd, and know my sheep, and am known of mine. 15 As the Father knoweth me, even so know I the Father: and I lay down my life for the sheep.

From Old Testament times there were stringent instructions and guidelines beginning with Moses as to the qualifications for elders, and they were carried over into the New Covenant Ekklesia and those qualifications apply right up to today and beyond.

Those who are called to offices in the assemblies are placed in a position to give aid and assistance to the body of Christ; they are to lead the sheep just as Christ would lead them and they are to lead the sheep to God the Father and not to try to lead them to follow themselves, as we have seen happen so often.

Peter also exhorted the elders in his congregations to be sure that they were living up to the very highest standards of what it meant to be a shepherd over the flock.

1 Peter 5:1 The elders which are among you I exhort, who am also an elder, and a witness of the sufferings of Christ, and also a partaker of the glory that shall be revealed: **5:2** Feed the flock of God which is among you, taking the oversight thereof, not by constraint, but willingly; not for filthy lucre, but of a ready mind. **5:3** Neither as being lords over God's heritage, **but being examples to the flock**.

It is a great disservice and even dangerous when men who call themselves elders and leaders fail to do as Peter charges them, and act as hirelings in the pursuit of enriching themselves at the expense of the people who look to them as their spiritual shepherds.

In verse 3, Peter warns elders not to act as control freaks (lords over God's heritage) and it is a great sin when ordained leaders do not provide godly righteous examples for those who look to them as leaders. The most important way a person can be a leader is to be an example of what he teaches to others and to be a mentor to them.

If we do not practice what we teach we are hypocrites which behavior is strongly condemned by Jesus Christ.

Paul is also very adamant in spelling out the kind of conduct that God requires in one who is called to be a guide to others; he condemns those that set themselves up to be leaders, but are hypocrites when it comes to teaching others what they themselves are unwilling to do.

Romans 2:19 And art confident that thou thyself art a guide of the blind, a light of them which are in darkness, **2:20** An instructor of the foolish, a teacher of babes, which hast the form of knowledge and of the truth in the law. **2:21** Thou therefore which teachest another, teachest thou not thyself? thou that preachest a man should not steal, dost thou steal? **2:22** Thou that sayest a man should not commit adultery, dost thou commit adultery? thou that abhorrest idols, dost thou commit sacrilege? **2:23** Thou that makest thy boast of the law, through breaking the law dishonourest thou God?

How can one be an effective leader if we ourselves do not live the kind of life that we preach to others?

It is very important for the sheep to be alert to the kind of men who would pastor and teach us. If we come to see that an elder, pastor of teacher is not acting like a true shepherd or that he lacks the qualifications that are required by Scripture, then it is in our best interest to move on and not support those that mislead or set bad examples for us and our families.

Ordination

Public ordination by men while desirable is not always the case. Who ordained Moses, or Paul, or John Baptist, or Jesus Christ? In fact the only "Judge" of Israel to be ordained by a man was Joshua. Who ordained Elijah, or Noah, or Abraham, or most of the prophets?

The scriptures indicate that people who demonstrate by their fruits that God has already called them to an office, are to be publicly appointed to their office. The Greek word for "appoint" is KATHISTÉMI (Strong's # 2525) and means: to set in order, appoint, "to ordain".

Ordination is meant to publicly recognize those whom God has already selected, with a public announcement setting men aside for special responsibilities. An example is when Timothy was ordained to his office and had hands laid on him.

Here, Paul is encouraging Timothy to give full devotion to his calling and not neglect it.

1 Timothy 4:14 Neglect not the gift that is in thee, which was given thee by prophecy, with the laying on of the hands of the presbytery.

The laying on of hands is an acknowledgment of what God has already revealed through the person's fruits (Mat 7): acknowledging that God has already set this person apart to the work for which God has called him.

Those laying on hands, are acknowledging and affirming that God has already officially placed the person in that office and are requesting God's aid to help the person to fulfill the responsibilities of the office.

Paul also warned Timothy, that in choosing and ordaining other men to an office, he needed to be very careful about whom he ordained. It is imperative that the leaders doing the ordaining seek God's will and approval of each person that is ordained.

Ordination must only come after a person has proved (over time, not by a quick snap decision) that he does have the calling and the qualifications to be ordained into the office.

1 Timothy 5:22 Lay hands suddenly on no man, neither be partaker of other men's sins: keep thyself pure.

A believer must demonstrate godliness over time and also show that he would be capable of handling the office; that he does have the qualifications, all the while demonstrating that he is totally loyal to the whole Word of God and to living by it.

Then after a period of time and when it becomes clear that God is choosing him, he can be publicly acknowledged as one who is to be trusted in the service of shepherding others.

The gift of a responsibility from God is a serious calling; the person must be willing to serve in this way, not because he is being compelled or pressured into it by friends and family; or because he seeks the adulation of the people, or seeks to earn money. He must want to do it because God has placed that desire in his heart.

1 Peter 5:2 Feed the flock of God which is among you, taking the oversight thereof, **not by constraint, but willingly; not for filthy lucre**, but of a ready mind.

Those who would be elders must desire and be willing to do whatever the calling requires them to do, to serve in this capacity because of their devotion to their LORD. That is one of the indications that God is calling them and gifting them for the position.

1 Timothy 3:1 This is a true saying, if a man desire the office of a bishop, he desireth a good work."

A man of God who is being called will desire the office, will sanctify [separate] himself from the ways of the world, and he will devote himself to prayer and to living by every Word of God. No one will have to talk him into the office; because serving God is his heart's passion.

In truth, a godly man who loves and is passionate to serve God in ANY office and would be glad to be in any position high or low just to please God; is the person who is fit for ordination to whatever office God calls him to.

Furthermore, he serves "voluntarily, according to the will of God" because he knows that God has spoken to him and he knows that he must obey the call of God upon his life no matter what anyone else wants for him.

Acts 13:1 Now there were in the church that was at Antioch certain prophets and teachers; as Barnabas, and Simeon that was called Niger, and Lucius of Cyrene, and Manaen, which had been brought up with Herod the tetrarch, and Saul.

13:2 As they ministered to the Lord, and fasted, the Holy Ghost said, Separate me Barnabas and Saul for the work whereunto I have called them.

13:3 And when they had fasted and prayed, and laid their hands on them, they sent them away. **13:4** So they, being sent forth by the Holy Ghost, departed unto Seleucia; and from thence they sailed to Cyprus.

In Acts 13:2 the writer says that as these leaders were worshiping and fasting, the Holy Spirit distinctly instructed them to set apart Paul and Barnabas for a certain work that God had called them to perform. It was God's choice, not the choice of the men that were present, and He made it known to them. A call from God to do something or to fulfill a calling is very serious and is not to be taken lightly or ignored.

Unfortunately, in today's Ekklesia there have been many who were chosen and ordained to be elders without the leaders seeking God's will, nor did they consider all the qualifications as listed by Paul in his letters.

Many were chosen for their loyalty to a man or group and not for their loyalty to God; and many who were not scripturally qualified were ordained. Many men were ordained for the wrong reasons and some were ordained before they spiritually matured and had gained enough experience in the art of living godly lives. They just did not have the experience and wisdom yet to handle the responsibilities of being a shepherd over others and the whole Ekklesia has suffered as a consequence of this.

The will of God - and the candidate's loyalty to God and zeal to live by every Word of God - must always be considered when choosing any person for positions in the Body. Ordination should be a public acknowledgment and confirmation of what God has already decided, and the ones doing the choosing and ordaining must take all things in consideration and wholeheartedly seek God first, before laying hands on anyone to ordain him to a certain office.

The ones doing the ordaining, too, must be devoted men of God who are very close to God and who can discern what God's will is. When the leaders are corrupt or are lacking in godly leadership skills and lack the qualifications of an elder, it is very unlikely that they will be able to discern godly qualifications in others. They generally choose others who are more like themselves.

When the ministry goes astray it is God himself who choses and sends his choice to warn and correct the ministry and brethren; in that case the ones God sends are called prophets.

The biblical way of ordaining elders is clearly spelled out in the scriptures and ideally it will work if we all do things God's way. Elders are to be a group of specially called and ordained men who have a passionate love and zeal to serve and please God.

It will be evident by the fruits in their character and in the testimony of their lives, that they are being called to an office by God. Only then are they to be appointed and ordained, and then only if they show-forth evidence of being qualified through their consistent, genuine, pure and godly life in the eyes of God.

Paul and the other apostles sought God's choice concerning who was to be appointed as elders in the assemblies, with prayer and fasting.

It is of utmost importance to only choose deeply converted, godly, faithful men of high moral character whom God would approve.

Only those who have given themselves completely over to God to live by every Word of God will be capable of teaching sound doctrine; only these whop are zealous to live by every Word of God can make good helpers of the Ekklesia.

Acts 14:23 And when they had ordained them elders in every church, [in every assembly] and had prayed with fasting, they commended them to the Lord, on whom they believed.

Paul's Own Example and His Instruction for Elders

When Paul was about to depart from Miletus, he sent for the elders of the assemblies and delivered a farewell message delivering a somber mandate that they follow the kind of example he had set for the brethren; he wanted them to realize that they had been called to feed, protect and cherish God's beloved sheep.

He warned them that there would be wolves that would come in amongst the flock and would do much spiritual damage to the sheep, so they would need to be vigilant in watching out for them.

These wolves would attempt to draw away the members of the Ekklesia to follow after themselves, teaching them perverse things and to following false traditions, men and their organizations rather than putting God and His Word above all things.

This kind of infiltration and apostasy from sound doctrine is rampant in our own day as well.

He charged them to be on guard for such people and to protect the brethren from them. This was a warning for the elders of his day, but is also a warning for those in today's modern day Ekklesia.

He gave them his own example of laboring tirelessly to care for the flock and instructed them that they, too, should follow his example of doing so from a heart devoted to a godly love for them and not for what they could gain materially.

These people loved Paul and he loved them; we can pick up on this as we see the kind of apostle/pastor that he was from the following passages.

Paul had the kind of love that wanted the best for the brethren and he never backed down from telling his followers when they were wrong and he could be quite harsh with them at times, he allowed no compromising; because he wanted all of the brethren to be a part of the first fruits resurrection and was not willing that any should fall away and perish (2 Corinthians 11:2).

This section in Acts is very instructional to all those who would be called to care and shepherd God's people.

Acts 20:17 And from Miletus he sent to Ephesus, and called the elders of the church. **20:18** And when they were come to him, he said unto them, Ye know, from the first day that I came into Asia, after what manner I have been with you at all seasons,

20:19 Serving the Lord with all humility of mind, and with many tears, and temptations, which befell me by the lying in wait of the Jews:

20:20 And how I kept back nothing that was profitable unto you, but have shewed you, and have taught you publickly, and from house to house, **20:21** Testifying both to the Jews, and also to the Greeks, repentance toward God, and faith toward our Lord Jesus Christ.

20:22 And now, behold, I go bound in the spirit unto Jerusalem, not knowing the things that shall befall me there: **20:23** Save that the Holy Ghost witnesseth in every city, saying that bonds and afflictions abide me.

20:24 But none of these things move me, neither count I my life dear unto myself, so that I might finish my course with joy, and the ministry, which I have received of the Lord Jesus, to testify the gospel of the grace of God.

20:25 And now, behold, I know that ye all, among whom I have gone preaching the kingdom of God, shall see my face no more. **20:26** Wherefore I take you to record this day, that I am pure from the blood of all men. **20:27** For I have not shunned to declare unto you all the counsel of God.

Further preparing these elders for the work ahead, Paul addressed these elders and said that the Holy Spirit had made them overseers. He also said that their duty was to feed the church [flock] of God. Paul further gave them a charge and a warning about wolves who would try to divert the people from godliness to follow themselves.

20:28 Take heed therefore unto yourselves, and to all the flock, over the which the Holy Ghost hath made you overseers, to feed the church of God, which he hath purchased with his own blood. **20:29** For I know this, that after my departing shall grievous wolves enter in among you, not sparing the flock.

23:30 Also of your own selves shall men arise, speaking perverse things, to draw away disciples after them. **20:31** Therefore watch, and remember, that by the space of three years I ceased not to warn every one night and day with tears. **20:32** And now, brethren, I commend you to God, and to the word of his grace, which is able to build you up, and to give you an inheritance among all them which are sanctified.

20:33 I have coveted no man's silver, or gold, or apparel. **20:34** Yea, ye yourselves know, that these hands have ministered unto my necessities, and to them that were with me.

20:35 I have shewed you all things, how that so labouring ye ought to support the weak, and to remember the words of the Lord Jesus, how he said, It is more blessed to give than to receive.

20:36 And when he had thus spoken, he kneeled down, and prayed with them all. **20:37** And they all wept sore, and fell on Paul's neck, and kissed him, **20:38** Sorrowing most of all for the words which he spake, that they should see his face no more.

Scripture makes it clear that there are those appointed to be leaders on order to fulfill various responsibilities as helpers of the brethren. Whether it is an office of teacher, pastor, elder, prophet or apostle their primary function is to be the spiritual caregivers of God's flock and to preach the true Gospel of Salvation through Jesus Christ to all flesh.

The supreme model of pastoral/shepherding ministry is seen in the work of Jesus himself. Descriptive titles of Jesus include: a Teacher from God, the Good Shepherd and the Great Shepherd.

The analogy of the shepherd who cares and provides for the flock is a key analogy that defines the work of the local pastor.

The End of the Christian Dispensation

Just before the first coming of Christ in the flesh, the Mosaic Pharisees became proud, self-satisfied and full of themselves, exalting their own traditions and making the Word of God of no effect by following the false traditions of men.

Matthew 15:9 But in vain they do worship me, teaching for doctrines the commandments of men.

Just before the second coming of Christ the very same situation exists today; As in the first century it is those who are humble and seeking God who will recognize the signs of the times and will be ready for the coming of their Master.

Godly and Ungodly Religious Leaders

The Laodicean (Rev 3) attitude is an exact replica of the primary attitude of the Mosaic Pharisees during the physical ministry of Christ.

Contrary to popular belief the Mosaic Pharisees were NOT zealous for the law; rather they made the law of God of no effect by their own false traditions, just as today's modern Ekklesia does!

In Matthew 15:9 Jesus said of the Mosaic Pharisees; and this is a very precise description of today's Ekklesia:

Matthew 15:7 Ye hypocrites, well did Esaias prophesy of you, saying, **15:8 This people draweth nigh unto me with their mouth, and honoureth me with their lips; but their heart is far from me. 15:9 But in vain they do worship me, teaching for doctrines the commandments of men.**

Matthew 23 describes the Pharisaic attitude during the physical ministry of Jesus Christ; and it also accurately describes today's church of God groups right before Christ comes to rule: today!

Matthew 23:1 Then spake Jesus to the multitude, and to his disciples,

At that time the scribes and Pharisees sat in Moses seat; that changed with the end of the Mosaic Covenant at the death of the Husband of Israel made flesh as Jesus Christ, who when resurrected became God's eternal High Priest.

We are to obey men when they speak the truth of God, and we are NOT to obey them when they depart from the Word of God!

23:2 Saying The scribes and the Pharisees sit in Moses' seat: **23:3** All therefore whatsoever they bid you observe, that observe and do; but do not ye after their works: for they say, and do not. **23:4** For they bind heavy burdens and grievous to be borne, and lay them on men's shoulders; but they themselves will not move them with one of their fingers.

With the death of the Husband of Israel; the Mosaic Covenant marriage between physical Mosaic Israel and Christ ended, and so did the authority of the Mosaic Priesthood and the Pharisees!

When Jesus Christ ascended into heaven and was accepted by God the Father as a sacrifice for us; He became our High Priest, and the Mosaic priesthood was superseded by the restoration of the High Priesthood of Melchizedek.

From that time on; neither Levi, nor the Rabbins; have any lawful spiritual authority. The only lawful spiritual authority in existence at this time and forever more is the authority of God the Father and our eternal spirit High Priest, Jesus Christ.

The true and only existing Priesthood of God today is that of our High Priest Jesus Christ.

All of those who have been called out to God through Christ; have the potential to become spirit priests under the spirit High Priest, Jesus Christ, at the resurrection of the chosen. All of those who have been called to God over the past six thousand years were/are in training to become priests forever in that spiritual priesthood of Jesus Christ [Melchizedek].

We are not to rely on a Covenant which has ended and been replaced by a New Covenant! We are to rely on the New Covenant of Jeremiah 31 and the whole body of scriptures!

God's governmental system is Family, with God the Father as the HEAD, and the firstborn son Jesus Christ as the second Head under God the Father, and then the Husbands over their own families.

Offices of ecclesiastical authority exist as helps to keep us focused on God the Father, Jesus Christ and the Word of God.

Their authority comes from the Word of God and the truth that they teach, and once they depart from the Word of God they lose all moral authority!

1 Timothy 2:5 For **there is one God, and one mediator between God and men, the man Christ Jesus; 2:6** Who gave himself a ransom for all, to be testified in due time.

The Nicolaitane idea of a pyramidal structure of layers of human authority between men and God is an abomination to God (Rev 2:6, 2:15). It is the job of ALL religious leaders to focus all people on the Father and Christ.

They are NEVER to COME BETWEEN the people and God; but must always act as facilitators in helping men to focus DIRECTLY on God the Father through our ONLY High Priest, Intercessor and Mediator; Jesus Christ!

1 Corinthians 11:3 But **I would have you know, that the head of every man is Christ; and the head of the woman is the man; and the head of Christ is God.**

We are to prove the words of ALL men, by the Word of Almighty God! We are NOT to interpret God's Word by the words of men; but to prove the words of men by the Word of Almighty God!

Matthew 23:11 But he that is greatest among you shall be your servant.

We are all to desire to humbly and passionately serve our God and not to exalt ourselves. God will exalt or abase anyone as HE sees fit.

23:12 And whosoever shall exalt himself shall be abased; and he that shall humble himself shall be exalted.

23:13 But woe unto you, scribes and Pharisees, hypocrites! for ye shut up the kingdom of heaven against men: for ye neither go in yourselves, neither suffer ye them that are entering to go in.

How? By paying lip-service to the law while making it of no effect by the traditions of men; and through compromise in its practical application; By making corporate idols and idols of men instead of faithfully putting God and His Word above all men, no matter what titles they claim.

23:14 Woe unto you, scribes and Pharisees, hypocrites! for ye devour widows' houses, and for a pretence make long prayer: therefore ye shall receive the greater damnation.

Demanding money of poor widows, and then making a show of flowery prayer

23:15 Woe unto you, scribes and Pharisees, hypocrites! for ye compass sea and land to make one proselyte, and when he is made, ye make him twofold more the child of hell than yourselves.

How? By teaching them to obey men, organizations and false traditions, instead of focusing them on repentance and a diligent passionate obedience to every Word of God.

23:16 Woe unto you, ye blind guides, which say, Whosoever shall swear by the temple, it is nothing; but whosoever shall swear by the gold of the temple, he is a debtor! **23:17** Ye fools and blind: for whether is greater, the gold, or the temple that sanctifieth the gold? **23:18** And, Whosoever shall swear by the altar, it is nothing; but whosoever sweareth by the gift that is upon it, he is guilty. **23:19** Ye fools and blind: for whether is greater, the gift, or the altar that sanctifieth the gift? **23:20** Whoso therefore shall swear by the altar, sweareth by it, and by all things thereon.

Today's corporate Ekklesia exalts mammon and numbers above repentance, faith and obedience to every Word of God.

23:21 And whoso shall swear by the temple, sweareth by it, and by him that dwelleth therein. **23:22** And he that shall swear by heaven, sweareth by the throne of God, and by him that sitteth thereon.

The important thing is NOT the numbers of responses, but the quality of the message!

The important thing is not some building or organization, but serving and obeying the Eternal God and serving the God who shall most certainly judge us by our works; whether of faithful uncompromising obedience; or of compromising with HIS Word!

23:23 Woe unto you, scribes and Pharisees, hypocrites! for ye pay tithe of mint and anise and cummin, and have omitted the weightier matters of the law, judgment, mercy, and faith: these ought ye to have done, and not to leave the other undone.

Demanding every last cent that can be demanded or extorted, while ignoring and not rebuking sin, nor teaching repentance from evil doing, and expounding and exhorting faith, mercy and sound judgment founded on the basics of God's word and commandments.

We are to be merciful to the poor in their needs; we are to be merciful to the repentant instead of condemning them for being over righteous!

We are to preach a message of warning and repentance and the mercy of God [the Father] or the sincerely repentant; who gave his only begotten son that sinners might be reconciled to Him [the Father].

23:24 Ye blind guides, which strain at a gnat, and swallow a camel.

This is a figure of speech that simply means that we strain at the little unimportant things like money and numbers; and neglect the really important things like zeal for our God.

23:25 Woe unto you, scribes and Pharisees, hypocrites! for ye make clean the outside of the cup and of the platter, but within they are full of extortion and excess. **23:26** Thou blind Pharisee, cleanse first that which is within the cup and platter, that the outside of them may be clean also. **23:27** Woe unto you, scribes and Pharisees, hypocrites! for ye are like unto whited sepulchres, which indeed appear beautiful outward, but are within full of dead men's bones, and of all uncleanness. **23:28** Even so ye also outwardly appear righteous unto men, but within ye are full of hypocrisy and iniquity.

We have no business reaching out to the world with tainted messages, while we are full of sin inside ourselves and our organizations.

We need to clean up our own spiritual lives and get right with God. We need to rekindle our passionate zeal for God and his commandments; we need to get rid of those traditions not consistent with scripture; we need to start practicing what we preach, and to start setting a godly example instead of acting so shamefully.

We need to stop exalting men and organizations above God; we need to STOP equating loyalty to men, as being equal to loyalty to God. We need to repent and turn to our God with passionate enthusiastic consummate zeal; and then we need to begin to preach the Gospel of warning and repentance that Christ has commanded us to preach.

23:29 Woe unto you, scribes and Pharisees, hypocrites! because ye build the tombs of the prophets, and garnish the sepulchres of the righteous, **23:30** And say, If we had been in the days of our fathers, we would not have been partakers with them in the blood of the prophets.

We honour the prophets and ancient men of God, while persecuting those who today are filled with a similar zeal: Showing ourselves that we are no better than those who persecuted the saints of old.

23:31 Wherefore ye be witnesses unto yourselves, that ye are the children of them which killed the prophets. **23:32** Fill ye up then the measure of your fathers.

Today the Ekklesia persecutes the zealous for God just as the ancients persecuted the prophets and holy men, and the Pharisees persecuted Christ and his true faithful disciples.

23:33 Ye serpents, ye generation of vipers, how can ye escape the damnation of hell? **23:34** Wherefore, behold, I send unto you prophets, and wise men, and scribes: and some of them ye shall kill and crucify; and some of them shall ye scourge in your synagogues, and persecute them from city to city: **23:35** That upon you may come all the righteous blood shed upon the earth, from the blood of righteous Abel unto the blood of Zacharias son of Barachias, whom ye slew between the temple and the altar.

Those who do such things are likened to vipers who hide along the path waiting to strike the unwary. When a person goes to them with questions, they reason with them that they should not be zealous like the Mighty Men of God, but should be lukewarm like themselves, then they make a note to persecute such zeal by calling the zealous Pharisaic, when it is they themselves who are Pharisaic; filled with zeal for their own groups and traditions, while being lukewarm and compromising with the Word of God.

Since Cain slew Abel, it has ever been thus; that the faithless and compromised; have always persecuted the faithful and zealous. Those who exalt the Lord their God; will face resistance from outside and from inside these organizations,

The faithful should REJOICE at the persecution from their wayward brethren, because they have been given an opportunity to set an example, that their persecutors will later remember and be convicted by.

The persecuted faithful should REJOICE, for they are being tempered and tested to become pillars in the Family of The Great God for all eternity.

They that stand unshakable on the foundation of the Word of Almighty God; without turning, no matter what the stress; will be made fit by God to stand on that sure foundation of the Word of God as pillars, helping to hold up the entire family of God for all eternity!

23:36 Verily I say unto you, All these things shall come upon this generation.

These persecutions did come upon the saints by the religious establishment of that day, and have continued to this day.

23:37 O Jerusalem, Jerusalem, thou that killest the prophets, and stonest them which are sent unto thee, how often would I have gathered thy children together, even as a hen gathereth her chickens under her wings, and ye would not! **23:38** Behold, your house is left unto you desolate.

This is about the city, Jerusalem whose people persecuted the godly through history, and is figuratively about the faithless who persecute the faithful today. Jesus Christ would have saved them, if only they would accept his deliverance and turn to him abandoning sin and compromise with the Father's Word.

Both Jerusalem and today's faithless Ekklesia, will be made desolate in the tribulation; it is then that they will sincerely repent and turn to God in sincere repentance!

23:39 For I say unto you, Ye shall not see me henceforth, till ye shall say, Blessed is he that cometh in the name of the Lord.

When they see Christ come, Jerusalem, and all those who persecuted the saints will be in a humbled and repentant attitude, and will no longer reject Christ and the teachings of the whole Word of God; instead they shall Shout for Joy at his appearance; crying out "Blessed is he that cometh in the name of the Lord"!

The Holy and the Profane

Jesus illustrated the difference between a holy attitude and a profane and unacceptable attitude in this parable.

These prayers are not just words; they reveal the attitude of the person praying, for out of the abundance of the heart the mouth speaks.

Luke 18:9 And he spake this parable unto certain which trusted in themselves that they were righteous, and despised others:

18:10 Two men went up into the temple to pray; the one a Pharisee [an unrepentant proud self-willed person], and the other a publican [someone who acknowledged they sin and repented].

18:11 The Pharisee stood and prayed thus with himself, God, I thank thee, that I am not as other men are, extortioners, unjust, adulterers, or even as this publican.

18:12 I fast twice in the week, I give tithes of all that I possess.

18:13 And the publican [a sincerely repentant sinner], standing afar off, would not lift up so much as his eyes unto heaven, but smote upon his breast, saying, God be merciful to me a sinner.

18:14 I tell you, this man went down to his house justified rather than the other: for every one that exalteth himself shall be abased; and he that humbleth himself shall be exalted.

Today the true faithful pillars are scattered throughout the Ekklesia, which are overwhelmingly Pharisaic.

Today we exalt ourselves to live by our own false traditions and reject any true humble passion for the Mighty One who could deliver us! Proud and thinking ourselves rich in spiritual things and thinking we know it all: We have become spiritually dead, apostate from our Master.

Conclusion

The various church attitudes of Revelation two and three may have dominated at various historical tines, but the seven churches also existed together at the same time in the first century and each one is an instructional example for us, that all of these problems and strengths will also exist together at the same time in these last days.

Today like Ephesus, we have lost the passionate zeal of our first love for truth and godliness and the whole Word of God.

Today like Smyrna, there are some who are faithful to God and God's Word and suffer much persecution.

Today like Pergamos, there are some who have not denied the authority of God and the scriptures and yet tolerate Nicolaitane bullying.

Today like Thyatira, there are those who are full of good works, but in our zeal to do good to our neighbor we have lost sight of our obligations to God. Do NOT mistake love of man; for love of God!

As a bride is to be faithful to her husband, our first duty is to our spiritual Husband and all good works to others are secondary. Many unconverted people are also full of good works towards humanity and do not obey God;

how are we different from them if we are also full of good works for humanity and forget our LORD?

We should be filled with good works towards men; while not forgetting to put our LORD first in our lives!

What say you? If a bride put her personal charitable works ahead of her love and obedience to her husband, will the husband think that she loves her own works more than she loves him? It is a very good thing to do good works for people, but such good works should not overtake our zeal for our LORD!

Today, like Smyrna the Ekklesia is largely spiritually dead, having no fire of zeal to live by every Word of our LORD.

Today, like Philadelphia there are some faithful standing on the foundation of the whole Word of God; who are scattered like pillars throughout the various assemblies and standing alone.

Today like Laodicea in Revelation 3, the Ekklesia is overwhelmingly proud, arrogant and unteachable by God. They reject large parts of God's Word and very much truth, to follow their idols of men and false traditions. They will not respond positively to God's warnings and the only way to save them from certain eternal death is to afflict the flesh to humble them so that the spirit might be saved.

Those who do sincerely repent and overcome in the end will be chosen and resurrected to spirit and will then be consecrated before the very throne of God the Father in heaven as priests of the Most high God after the order of Melchizedek the eternal order of Jesus Christ

The Primacy of Peter

Since the most ancient of times great empires and even the smallest of kingdoms have had the problem of controlling their people, at the same time every kind of people followed their own gods.

Rulers quickly learned that it was a big help to have oneself also declared a god; which idea would be accepted by most people because, after all you would still be only one god among many gods.

When the people thought that you were a mere man they might risk physical death to rise up, but if they thought you were a god who had power over eternity, most would not dare to rise up against a god.

If a ruler were only a physical man, some would risk the death of the flesh for the hope of success; but if the ruler were a god who had the power to give eternal life and eternal blessings, or to consign to eternal death or worse eternal torment: That was real power which very few would dare to resist.

Then along came a man named Paul who turned the whole Roman world upside down by declaring that there was only one God and that the Roman emperor was not God.

As this new religion began to spread and the idea that the emperor was not God took hold even among unbelievers, the Roman emperors fought as hard as they could to destroy this upstart sect.

The reason for the persecution of Christians had nothing to do with their God or doctrines because after all they were only one religion among many; the reason they were persecuted was the fact that they rejected the Emperor as a God and also rejected all the other gods of the people.

The Roman emperor's felt trapped in the position of persecuting the Christians who were good citizens, or facing the possibility of widespread revolt if they admitted that they were not gods.

The tragic situation is made clear in Pliney's letter to Emperor Trajan and his response.

Letters of Pliny the Younger and the Emperor Trajan

Translated by William Whiston

These letters concern an episode which marks the first time the Roman government recognized Christianity as a religion separate from Judaism, and sets a precedent for the massive persecution of Christians that takes place in the second and third centuries.

In the year 112 A.D., Pliny the Younger was faced with a dilemma. He was the governor in the Roman province of Bithynia (modern day Turkey) when a number of Christians were brought into his court. It is unclear what the initial charges are, but he ultimately decided, despite the fact that the Christians seemed generally harmless to him, that he should execute them if they refused to recant their faith. Because he is unsure as to whether he can kill them legally for no other crime than their faith, he writes to his friend the Emperor for advice. The Emperor replies that he did the right thing in executing them, but advises him not to seek out Christians for prosecution.

PLINY'S EPISTLE TO TRAJAN ABOUT 112 CE

Sir,

It is my constant method to apply myself to you for the resolution of all my doubts; for who can better govern my dilatory way of proceeding or instruct my ignorance? I have never been present at the examination of the Christians [by others], on which account I am unacquainted with what uses to be inquired into, and what, and how far they used to be punished; nor are my doubts small, whether there be not a distinction to be made between the ages [of the accused]? and whether tender youth ought to have the same punishment with strong men? Whether there be not room for pardon upon repentance?" or whether it may not be an advantage to one that had been a Christian, that he has forsaken Christianity? Whether the bare name, without any crimes besides, or the crimes adhering to that name, be to be punished?

In the meantime, I have taken this course about those who have been brought before me as Christians. I asked them whether they were Christians or not? If they confessed that they were Christians, I asked them again, and a third time, intermixing threatenings with the questions. If they persevered in their confession, I ordered them to be executed; for I did not doubt but, let their confession be of any sort whatsoever, this positiveness and inflexible obstinacy deserved to be punished.

There have been some of this mad sect whom I took notice of in particular as Roman citizens, that they might be sent to that city. After some time, as is usual in such examinations, the crime spread itself and many more cases came before me. A libel was sent to me, though without an author, containing many names [of persons accused].

These denied that they were Christians now, or ever had been. **They called upon the gods, and supplicated to your image, which I caused to be brought to me for that purpose, with frankincense and wine; they also cursed Christ; none of which things, it is said, can any of those that are ready Christians be compelled to do;** so I thought fit to let them go.

Others of them that were named in the libel, said they were Christians, but presently denied it again; that indeed they had been Christians, but had ceased to be so, some three years, some many more; and one there was that said he had not been so these twenty years.

All these **worshipped your image, and the images of our gods;** these also cursed Christ. However, they assured me that the main of their fault, or of their mistake was this:-That they were wont, on a stated day, to meet together before it was light, and to sing a hymn to Christ, as to a god, alternately; and to oblige themselves by a sacrament [or oath], not to do anything that was ill: but that they would commit no theft, or pilfering, or adultery; that they would not break their promises, or deny what was deposited with them, when it was required back again; after which it was their custom to depart, and to meet again at a common but innocent meal, which they had left off upon that edict which I published at your command, and wherein I had forbidden any such conventicles.

These examinations made me think it necessary to inquire by torments what the truth was; which I did of two servant maids, who were called **Deaconesses:** but still I discovered no more than that they were addicted to a bad and to an extravagant superstition.

Hereupon I have put off any further examinations, and have recourse to you, for the affair seems to be well worth consultation, especially on account of the number of those that are in danger; for there are many of every age, of every rank, and of both sexes, who are now and hereafter likely to be called to account, and to be in danger; for this superstition is spread like a contagion, not only into cities and towns, but into country villages also, which yet there is reason to hope may be stopped and corrected.

To be sure, **the temples** [of the gods], **which were almost forsaken,** begin already to be frequented; and the holy solemnities [of the pagan gods like the Saturnalia and Astarte's Day], which were long intermitted not kept], begin to be revived. The sacrifices begin to sell well everywhere, of which very few purchasers had of late appeared; whereby it is easy to suppose how great a multitude of men may be amended, if place for repentance be admitted.

TRAJAN'S EPISTLE TO PLINY IN RESPONSE

My Pliny,

You have taken the method which you ought in examining the causes of those that had been accused as Christians, for indeed no certain and general form of judging can be ordained in this case. These people are not to be sought for; but if they be accused and convicted, they are to be punished; but with this caution, that he who denies himself to be a Christian, and makes it plain that he is not so by supplicating to our gods [anyone who accepts that the Emperor is a god and who acknowledges the gods of the people as being Gods will be pardoned], although he had been so formerly, may be allowed pardon, upon his repentance. As for libels sent without an author, they ought to have no place in any accusation whatsoever, for that would be a thing of very ill example, and not agreeable to my reign.

From

The Works of Josephus,
translated by William Whiston
Hendrickson Publishers, 1987

All of the persecutions of Rome could not avail against this new revelation that the emperor was not a god, and a new method of controlling the people needed to be found.

The problem was finally resolved with the emperors backing up the popes and the popes declaring that the Emperor was CHOSEN by God; reviving and transferring the Holy Roman Empire System of ancient Babylon to Rome.

This was the system used by Nebuchadnezzar in Babylon as the head of the statue of Daniel 2 - the Babylonian Mystery Religion church state empire system - and adopted by all the empires which followed Babylon; Media-Persia, Greece and finally the Holy Roman Empire.

Constantine established the bishop of Rome as preeminent in the Catholic world and in exchange the bishop of Rome consecrated the emperors of Rome. From the time of Constantine forward, the Roman Emperor was no longer a god, but he was considered to be God's choice having been sanctified by the papacy; and to rebel against him was the same as rebelling against God.

The question discussed in this chapter is: does the priesthood or ministry really come between the people and God?

In modern times many religious leaders including in today's Ekklesia have adopted this same deception that they are God's chosen and therefore must be obeyed no matter what they do.

In proving any issue always watch that premise! Today's Ekklesia claims to be God's chosen and to constitute a layer of authority between God and the people; that is their premise! Is this true?

The truth is that if anyone is the servant of God, he would never make any decision contrary to God's Word, he would be faithfully living by - and teaching - every Word of God

Romans 6:16 Know ye not, that to whom ye yield yourselves servants to obey, his servants ye are to whom ye obey; whether of sin unto death, or of obedience unto righteousness?

Jesus said this in a slightly different way, saying:

John 8:34 Jesus answered them, Verily, verily, I say unto you, Whosoever committeth sin [sin is living contrary to any part of the Word of God (1 Jh 3:4)] is the servant of sin.

If we are the servants of God: we would be doing whatever God's Word says and we would NEVER do what we want instead! If we are not living and teaching every Word of God: we are NOT God's servants!

It's just that simple! The premise that men are the servants of God is false if they teach or live contrary to the Word of God!

The ultimate power that any man can have over his fellow man, is for people to allow him to come between them and God as their Ultimate Moral Authority in place of the Word of God.

The usual means of religious deception today is to proclaim that some person or persons are God's ministers or priests and must be obeyed as if they were God in the absence of God.

Of course this is not true since God is not absent at all. God is present in his people through God's Holy Spirit and through the Word of God.

Deceivers will falsely claim that since they are God's choice; and to disagree with them - even when they teach contrary to God's Word - is to disagree with God; and finally they will claim that Jesus Christ gave them the moral authority to Bind and Loose the Word of God as they see fit.

Those who believe these things have fallen victim to the ultimate deception that a man or priesthood holds a position between them and God. the priesthood or ministry being a kind of gatekeeper that can provide access to God or prevent such access according to whether we obey such men or not.

Everyone who believe this feels obligated to obey them and exalt them above the Word of God; and if we bow to this deception we have made them our gods indeed, by exalting them as our idols above the Word of the Eternal.

Claiming the power to deny or facilitate access to God and therefore the power to keep people out of or allow people access into an eternal life of blessings; these deceivers hold the ultimate power over those who believe them.

If some man were to proclaim "follow me for I am greater than God and I know better than God does," he would have very few followers; very few people would think that he was a sane and intelligent man. Yet, large numbers of people believe this very thing because the issue is presented in a much more subtle way.

The primary scriptures used to support the claim that some man has the authority to bind or loose [to change] any part of the Word of God, are found in Matthew 16 and 18.

Matthew 16:18 And I say also unto thee, That thou art Peter [a pebble], and upon this rock [a huge bolder; Jesus Christ the Rock of our salvation] **I will build my church** [Ekklesia, the faithful]**; and the gates of hell** [the grave, death] **shall not prevail against** [A prophecy of the resurrection; the grave will not prevail against Christ and the faithful to God] **it**.

The Rock Revealed

When you study the Greek text you will find that the word "Peter" and the word "Rock" on which Christ was to build His church; are two separate and distinct words, each having a different meaning.

The word Peter in in Greek is petros, which means "a piece of rock; a stone; a single stone; movable, insecure, shifting, or rolling, a pebble."

The word "rock" in Greek is petra, which means "a rock; a cliff; a projecting rock; a huge mother rock; huge mass; solid formation; fixed; immovable; figurative of enduring; a MOUNTAIN of strength."

Petros in the Greek [Peter] is in the masculine gender; and the word Petra for the ROCK is in the feminine gender.

Petros [pebble] and Petra [mountain] are therefore two distinct words in the Greek. Petros [Peter] is a shifting, rolling, or insecure stone, a pebble; while Petra is a solid, immovable, huge rock.

In the English language the gender is not specified by the article. We say the fork, the spoon, and the knife. The three words have the same article, but in the Greek, as in many languages, each noun and corresponding article; is in the masculine, feminine, or neuter gender. In many cases it is an arbitrary arrangement, regardless of sex.

The article in Greek is important. If a noun is in the masculine, it must have a masculine article; and if the noun is in the feminine gender, it must have a feminine article.

The text of Mat 16:18-19 in the Greek shows that Petros [Peter, pebble] is in the masculine, and petra [a Rock] is in the feminine; thus PROVING that they are two distinct words; and each one has a distinctly different meaning.

Now the question is, on which of the two, Petros [Peter] or Petra [Christ the Rock] , did Christ establish His church?

Was it on [Peter] the petros, a movable stone, a small pebble, or is the Ekklesia built on the immovable Petra [the huge immovable Rock of Christ]?

Let us quote the text again: "I say also unto thee [to Peter], That thou art Peter [petros, masculine gender, small pebble], and upon this Rock [petra, feminine gender, unmovable mountain (Dan 2)] I will build My church; and the gates of hell [the grave] shall not prevail against it" (Mat 16:18).

The text indicates clearly that the Ekklesia is built on Petra the ROCK of our Salvation and not on Petros [the tiny pebble Peter].

Now, who is this Petra or Great ROCK on which the Ekklesia is built?

Let the Holy Bible again give the answer. If the Bible gives the answer, we make no mistake in accepting it; because the definition is authentic.

Who is sovereign; God or some man?

Psalm 98:1 O come, let us sing unto the Lord: let us make a joyful noise **to the rock** [Jesus Christ] **of our salvation**. **98:2** Let us come before his presence with thanksgiving, and make a joyful noise unto him with psalms.

The Rock is God [the Rock is a member of the YHVH (eternal) family of Elohim (Mighty Ones)] and is the very Implementing Creator

98:3 For the Lord is a great God, and a great King above all gods. **98:4** In his hand are the deep places of the earth: the strength of the hills is his also. **98:5** The sea is his, and he made it: and his hands formed the dry land.

98:6 O come, let us worship and bow down: let us kneel before the Lord our maker.

Here is the Roman Catholic Church's own Douay Version defining the Rock as being Christ and not Peter:

1 Corinthians 10:4 They drank of that spiritual Rock that followed them: and that Rock [petra, in the Greek] was Christ

The Ekklesia is to be founded on the chief corner stone [Jesus Christ the Rock of Salvation]!

Ephesians 2:20 Jesus Christ Himself being the chief Cornerstone

Deuteronomy 32:1 Give ear, O ye heavens, and I will speak; and hear, O earth, the words of my mouth. **32:2** My doctrine shall drop as the rain, my speech shall distil as the dew, as the small rain upon the tender herb, and as the showers upon the grass: **32:3 Because I will publish the name of the Lord: ascribe ye greatness unto our God.** [the Rock [Petra] is God] **32:4 He is the Rock**, his work is perfect: for all his ways are judgment: a God of truth and without iniquity, just and right is he.

Long before Jesus gave up his godhood to be made flesh, he was called the Rock and the FOUNDATION of the faithful.

Isaiah 28:16: "Therefore thus saith the Lord God, Behold, I lay in Zion for a foundation a stone, a tried stone, a precious cornerstone, a sure foundation".

Peter applies this prophecy to Christ.

1 Peter 2:6: "Wherefore also it is contained in the scripture, Behold, I lay in Sion a chief Cornerstone, elect, precious: and he that believeth on Him shall not be confounded" (1 Peter 2:6).

David said:

Psalm 61:2 Lead me to the Rock that is higher than I

Psalm 62:1 Truly my soul waiteth upon God: from him cometh my salvation. **62:2 He only is my rock and my salvation**; he is my defence; I shall not be greatly moved.

If the Ekklesia [assemblies, church] was built on Peter; then Peter would be the head of the church. However, Peter was not the head of the church; Jesus Christ is the immediate and direct HEAD of the church under God the Father.

1 Corinthians 11:3 But I would have you know, that **the head of every man is Christ**; and the head of the woman is the man; and **the head of Christ is God**.

Instead of having the disciples, apostles, and other believers call Peter pope, or Father Peter, or Holy Father Peter, Jesus said that we are not to use ecclesiastical titles which exalt any man above the Rock, Jesus Christ; and God the Father:

Matthew 23:8 But be not ye called Rabbi: for **one is your Master, even Christ**; and all ye are brethren **23:9** And call no man your father upon the earth: **for one is your Father, which is [God] in heaven**. **23:10** Neither be ye called masters: **for one is your Master, even Christ.**

If Jesus had delegated Peter to be the head of the church, why did the other disciples quarrel among themselves as to who would be the greatest?

Luke 9:46 Then there arose a reasoning among them, which of them should be greatest.

And again even at the last Passover?

Luke 22:24 And there was also a strife among them, which of them should be accounted the greatest.

If a decision had already been made by Christ to exalt Peter above the others, why should the others continue to fret about who would be the greatest?

The disciples would have accepted the decision of their Master. Thus it seems evident that no such appointment had been made by Jesus.

Neither Peter nor any of his successors [whether Roman Catholic or in the Ekklesia] were heads of the true church. Paul explains this when he says the religious head of men is Jesus Christ under God the Father: "The head of every man is Christ" (1 Cor. 11:3); NOT Peter and not James,

Jesus Christ was made the HEAD of the Ekklesia and no man is the head of the church of God, the spiritual; body of Christ! No man is the head of the Ekklesia under Jesus Christ, but every person is to live by every Word of God!

Men may head corporate churches for the sake of a certain degree of corporate organization; but no man is the head of the spiritual Ekklesia.

Yes God provides a ministry to help the brethren to focus on and learn about God, but their authority is limited to living by and teaching every person to live by every Word of God; they have absolutely no authority to depart from the Word of God in any way.

Jesus teaches that the Ekklesia [assembly or spiritual body of the faithful] is NOT built upon Peter or some man; the Ekklesia is built upon Jesus Christ the Rock of our salvation and on every Word of God!

The brethren of the true Ekklesia would NEVER follow any man contrary to anything in the Word of God! They follow God the Father and Jesus Christ; and would only follow men, if and as such men are passionately faithful to God the Father and Jesus Christ the Son, and live by every Word of God.

How does Jesus Christ exercise his Head-ship?

By living in the faithful through the agency of the Holy Spirit and leading the faithful to live by every Word of God as Jesus did and does!

We are responsible for what we know and we are responsible to continually learn and grow spiritually. If we reject spiritual growth in the truth of God's Word, we are rejecting the lead of the Holy Spirit and rejecting the Head-ship of Jesus Christ and God the Father.

If we follow any person contrary to the Word of God we are rejecting the Head-ship of the authors who inspired that Word; God the Father and Jesus Christ!

Binding and Loosing

Were Peter and his successors given the authority to bind and loose what God has said in his Word?

Did Peter really have authority to change God's Word or to interpret the Word of God according to his own wishes? And do his heirs and descendants ecclesiastically, really have such authority? Or is this a misreading of the scriptures?

Is it a twisting of the Word of God? Jesus must have known that His words would be twisted; therefore, He went on to explain what He was getting at in Matthew 18:15 where he said:

Matthew 18:15 Moreover if thy brother shall trespass against thee, go and tell him his fault between thee and him alone: if he shall hear thee, thou hast gained thy brother. **18:16** But if he will not hear thee, then take with thee one or two more, that in the mouth of two or three witnesses every word may be established.

Here we are commanded to do our best to work out our problems with each other.

If we are offended in any person; we are to go directly to the person and seek to resolve the matter privately in humility. Do not go and say: "you evil man, you did such and such;" no, rather go to him and say "there is a matter that I do not understand, why did you do this?" Speak softly and seek peace.

Do not delay and allow the matter to fester and grow out of all proportion in your imagination; go immediately.

18:17 And if he shall neglect to hear them, tell it unto the church [properly Ekklesia]: but if he neglect to hear the church, let him be unto thee as an heathen man and a publican.

If he/she will not respond to a personal petition, then go to the elders of the Ekklesia [older wise men experienced in the faith] for a judgment; and if sin be found let the sinner be accounted wicked and rejected until he/she repents.

Binding and loosing; has nothing to do with binding and loosing God's Word! Quite the contrary, it is referring to binding and loosing or judging DISPUTES among the brethren; based on God's Word! The context above is clearly about disputes among the brethren!

18:18 Verily I say unto you, **Whatsoever ye** [whatever dispute you bind according to the Word of God will be backed up by God] **shall bind on earth shall be bound in heaven: and whatsoever** [whatever dispute you loose according to the Word of God will be backed up by God] **ye shall loose on earth shall be loosed in heaven**. **18:19** Again I say unto you, That if two of you [the faithful followers and zealous keepers of God's Word] shall agree on earth as touching any thing that they shall [lawfully and according to scripture] ask, it shall be done for them of my Father which is in heaven.

Jesus is instructing us about settling disputes between brethren; and one responsibility of the elders is to properly apply the Word of God to such disputes!

The context of this matter is that when those in the faith agree based on God's Word, concerning a matter of dispute among brethren; God will bind that decision.

Such a decision MUST be a matter of legitimate POOF based on God's Word. This is about making decisions based on God's Word; it is NOT about making decisions contrary to, or outside of, or changing God's Word.

Any decision made by those faithful to and zealous to live by every Word of God; which is based on God's Word and consistent with God's Word; will be bound and backed up by God Almighty.

This "binding and loosing" instruction is about the responsibility of the Called Out, to be faithful and loyal to God's Word; which is the whole Word of God, and to make binding decisions BASED upon God's Word: This issue has nothing whatever to do with men having the right to change God's Word.

The Ekklesia, has the authority to make decisions based on the whole Word of God; there is no authority whatever to change the Word of God; as some have done in changing God's Biblical Sabbath to Sunday or in changing the Biblical Festival Calendar!

The instructions of Jesus Christ are to do our best to work out our own problems and if we fail, we are to ask for a judgment based on God's Word from the Ekklesia of the Called Out.

If some are gathered together in Christ's name, and are acting faithfully according to God's Word; He WILL back them up.

If they are acting contrary to God's Word; God WILL NOT, NO NEVER, back anyone up in such a sin!

If we are the servants of God the Father and Jesus Christ: we will be faithfully living by every Word of God!

If we are not living by every Word of God and teaching men to do likewise: we are NOT God's servants!

It's just that simple!

Romans 6:16 Know ye not, that to whom ye yield yourselves servants to obey, his servants ye are to whom ye obey; whether of sin unto death, or of obedience unto righteousness?

This friends, is talking about the responsibility to be faithful and loyal to God's Word and to make binding decisions based upon every Word of God!

Jesus Christ WAS NOT conferring upon Peter any kind of authority to change God's Word; or to change God's laws; or to bind, or to loose, or to sit in judgment of the will and the Word of Almighty God!

Jesus Christ was informing his disciples that their authority – like the authority of the Mosaic priesthood - is to faithfully teach and properly apply God's Word in all disputes which are appealed to him. That is the limit of the authority of priesthood and ministry.

When we have disputes, we should try our best to resolve them; and if we cannot do so; we can appeal to older more experienced brothers in the faith for a decision which is to be based upon God's Word.

Was Jesus saying anything new here?

Of course not, He was merely quoting the law given to Moses.

Deuteronomy 17:8 If there arise a matter too hard for thee in judgment, between blood and blood, between plea and plea, and between stroke and stroke, being matters of controversy within thy gates: then shalt thou arise, and get thee up into the place which the LORD thy God shall choose;

Mosaic Israel was to go to the priests for just judgment because the priests were to know God's Word and to judge fairly based on every Word of God; and the elders of today's New Covenant Ekklesia have the same authority to make judgments based on God's Word today.

All teachings and decisions are to be based solidly on every Word of God; and when the priests or New Covenant ministry go astray, they are NOT to be obeyed contrary to the Word of God, for they have departed from the only source of their authority; and when the elders and priests are zealous for the Word of God there is justice.

17:9 And thou shalt come unto the priests the Levites, and unto the judge that shall be in those days, and enquire; and they shall shew thee the sentence of judgment:

17:10 And thou shalt do according to the sentence, which they of that place which the LORD shall choose shall shew thee; and thou shalt observe to do according to all that they inform thee:

All judgments MUST be made, based on and consistent with, and according to; every Word of God.

17:11 According to the sentence of the law [the priests and ministry are to teach and judge by every Word of God] which they shall teach thee, and according to the judgment which they shall tell thee, thou shalt do: thou shalt not decline from the sentence which they shall shew thee, to the right hand, nor to the left.

17:12 And the man that will do presumptuously, and will not hearken unto the priest that standeth to minister there before the LORD thy God, or unto the judge, [any person who will not be subject to the Word of God] even that man shall die: and thou shalt put away the evil from Israel. **17:13** And all the people shall hear, and fear, and do no more presumptuously.

There is authority in the ministry and in the priesthood to make decisions based upon God's Word. That authority and power is to teach men about the things of God and to make judgments according to the Word of God.

They have no authority to deviate from the Word of God in any way. For it is written in Deuteronomy 13 that even miracles and fulfilled predictions are not proof of godliness or of being a messenger from God. God's messengers often do foretell events and do perform miracles by the power of God, but Satan's agents also can do these things.

No person has any authority whatsoever, except the innate authority of the Word of God which is the truth itself.

When a person departs from the Word of God he has departed from the truth and he forfeits the authority of the Word which he has departed from.

There is absolutely NO moral authority in any person; the moral authority is in the truth itself, which is every Word of God; and if a person departs from the Word of God he has forfeited all moral authority. A person who teaches differently from the Word of God has absolutely NO moral authority whatsoever!

The faithful are subject to the authority of Jesus Christ and God's Word; the priesthood and ministry have no right whatsoever to bind or loose anything contrary to the Word of God.

Deuteronomy 12:32 **What thing soever I command you, observe to do it: thou shalt not add thereto, nor diminish from it.**

We are not to follow anyone to make an idol of them and obey them in place of obeying God; and we are not to conceal those who seek to deceive the brethren into following themselves, but we are commanded by Almighty God to reveal this wickedness and warn the brethren.

Man is nothing before God; man has neither the wisdom, nor the understanding, nor the knowledge, nor the ability, nor the right, nor the power, nor the authority to sit in judgment of God's Word; and decide for himself what men should or should not do.

What did Jesus really say to Peter in Matthew 16?

He said: Caiaphas, you are Peter, a petros, a pebble, a tiny stone, but it is upon this Rock [the great mountain, being Jesus Christ himself, the Chief Cornerstone, the Foundation Stone] that I will build my people and you must bind and loose according to God's Word from heaven and you must settle disputes and make decisions based upon every Word of God.

The foundation of the Ekklesia is the Rock [Petra], Jesus Christ; not the pebble Peter, and not the pebble of any other man who claims to be an heir of Peter or James etc. No man has the right to exalt himself above God and God's Word.

No man should be looked to as an ultimate moral authority in place of God the Father and Jesus Christ the Faithful High Priest of our Salvation.

All men whether they be popes or prophets or apostles or ministers or evangelists or whoever they claim to be; should be tested according to every Word of God.

1 Thessalonians 5:21 Prove all things; hold fast that which is good.

Speaking of the people of Berea:

Acts 17:11 These were more noble than those in Thessalonica, in that they received the word with all readiness of mind, and **searched the scriptures daily, whether those things were so.**

As Paul said, **1 Corinthians 11:1** Be ye followers of me, even as I also am of Christ.

We are to follow God the Father and Jesus Christ and live by every Word of God, regardless of what any man says.

No man, no human being; has any power whatsoever to change the smallest part of the Word of God;

Matthew 5:17 Think not that I am come to destroy the law, or the prophets: I am not come to destroy, but to fulfil [to keep, and to make full by revealing the spirit and intent of the Word of God].

Christ came to keep and complete the Word of God by revealing the spirit and intent of God's Word, making it full; and making it binding in the letter and in the spirit!

Jesus Christ did NOT come to destroy his Father's commandments, but to reveal their spiritual intent: and to set an example that we are to follow, by personally zealously keeping the Whole Word of God in the letter and in the spirit and in its full intent!

5:18 For verily I say unto you, Till heaven and earth pass, one jot or one tittle [the tiniest point] shall in no wise pass from the law, till all be fulfilled.

No part of God the Father's Word will ever pass away, and ultimately all living human beings will be passionately living by every Word of God in BOTH the letter and the spirit. Then the law and Word of God will be written on our hearts and not on tables of stone (Jeremiah 31).

As long as the Heavens and the Earth exist, all the commandments, all the law must be fulfilled [fully kept]. No man can change it ever.

5:19 Whosoever therefore shall break one of these least commandments, and shall teach men so, he shall be called the least in the kingdom of heaven [and he will only be there if he sincerely repents]: but whosoever shall do and teach them, the same shall be called great in the kingdom of heaven.

If anyone says that this or that is just physical, or only a "little thing"; consider these words.

To break the law in any one point, is to break the whole law, therefore such a person will not even be in God's Kingdom unless he repents, then he will be the least.

Many, who think they are great now, may not even be chosen, or will be accounted least in the Kingdom of God; and they will not even be there unless they repent.

5:20 For I say unto you, That except your righteousness shall exceed the righteousness of the scribes and Pharisees [who make God's Word of no effect by their false traditions of men], ye shall in no case enter into the kingdom of heaven.

We were told that those who teach contrary to any part of the Word of God are wicked.

Daniel 7:25 shall speak great words against the most high and think to change times [including the Sabbath Day and the Biblical Calendar] and laws.

It is the sons of wickedness who seek to change the Word of God, claiming authority to decide for themselves what is right and wrong.

Remember how in the Garden of Eden the serpent beguiled Eve; telling her that she should decide for herself what is right and what is wrong; and that in so doing, she would become a god unto herself.

Man has been trying to do this ever since; trying to decide for himself what is right and wrong shoving God's Word aside for their own false ways.

Men do not have the wisdom, or the right; to change the law of their Creator.

The Eternal is God; not any man.

The Eternal is the Sovereign Ultimate Moral Authority in the universe.

If we say that we need only keep the Ten Commandments we condemn ourselves with our own lips for the commandment requires:

Deuteronomy 5:16 Honour thy father and thy mother, as the Lord thy God hath commanded thee; that thy days may be prolonged, and that it may go well with thee, in the land which the Lord thy God giveth thee.

If we want long [eternal] life, we must obey God the FATHER and keep his commandments and live by every Word of God; for only those who live by every Word of God will have access to the tree of life and the right to eternal life.

No one has any authority to change or to teach people to act contrary to any part of the Word of God. All men including Peter are to bind and loose in physical disputes or doctrinal controversies according to and completely consistent with every Word of God!

The Keys and Door of Eternal Life

Jesus Christ the ultimate Good Shepherd; is the New Covenant High Priest, the Mediatorial DOOR between the flock and God the Father.

The key to the kingdom of heaven given to Peter and the disciples is the Gospel of the DOOR of Salvation, Jesus Christ; who is the Way to Reconciliation with the owner of the flock, God the Father!

The gospel of warning, repentance, the washing away of sin and the commitment to sin no more at baptism, and the application of the sacrifice of Christ; is the gospel of salvation; the gospel of the Door to God the Father which Door is Jesus Christ!.

Jesus Christ is the ONLY Door, the ONLY Intercessor and the ONLY Mediator, the ONLY High Priest between humanity and God the Father.

> **1 Timothy 2:5 For there is one God, and one mediator between God and men, the man Christ Jesus; 2:6 Who gave himself a ransom for all**, to be testified in due time.

Jesus Christ is the DOOR to God the Father, the DOOR to salvation.

Sincere repentance to "Go and sin no more," the gift of the Holy Spirit and absolute fidelity to live by Every Word of God, the Holy Scripture, are the KEYS to the DOOR of SALVATION!

We must use those KEYS to open the DOOR to Salvation, Jesus Christ our High Priest and the perfect effectual sacrifice for all sincerely repented sins!

We must follow Jesus Christ unwaveringly to live by every Word of God the Father; or we have NO access to God the Father, and we have NO Salvation.

Anyone, who teaches us to compromise with the Word of God; knows neither Christ nor God the Father and is of the Adversary the devil.

John 10:1 Verily, verily, I say unto you, He that entereth not by the door into the sheepfold [any shepherd who is not zealous for Christ and diligent to live by every Word of God the Father is a false shepherd and seeks to steal God's sheep], but climbeth up some other way, the same is a thief and a robber.

10:2 But he that entereth in by the door [of Christ] is the shepherd [He who is zealous to live by Christ and by every Word of God, is a true shepherd from God the Father.] of [for God's flock] the sheep.

Those reconciled to God the Father by entering to him through the DOOR of Christ, are given the key of the Holy Spirit; which leads us to live by every Word of God in Christ-like zeal. The Holy Spirit sensitizes us to the things of God, giving us an understanding of spiritual things and empowering us to live by every Word of God.

The Holy Spirit, opens the DOOR of Christ to God the Father! It teaches the sheep the voice of the Father and leads them to follow God the Father.

10:3 To him [Christ leads the flock to God the Father] the porter openeth; and the sheep hear his voice: and he calleth his own sheep by name, and leadeth them out. **10:4** And when he putteth forth his own sheep, he goeth before them, and the sheep follow him: for they know his voice.

The truly converted who are close to God and filled with God's Spirit will not be led astray! because they are diligent in prayer, study and in doing the Word of God, and in FOLLOWING the lead of the Holy Spirit, Jesus Christ and God the Father!

It is those who have gotten lax and turned to following idols of men and false traditions instead of faithfully following God who will fall away.

10:5 And a stranger will they not follow, but will flee from him: for they know not the voice of strangers. **10:6** This parable spake Jesus unto them: but they understood not what things they were which he spake unto them.

The parable explained

10:7 Then said Jesus unto them again, Verily, verily, I say unto you, **I am the door of the sheep**.

All those who do not teach a zeal to live by evwery Word of God, are false teachers!

10:8 All that ever came before me are thieves and robbers: but the sheep did not hear them. **10:9 I am the door: by me if any man enter in, he shall be saved, and shall go in and out, and find pasture** [the spiritual food of sound doctrine].

False teachers who misrepresent Christ and teach a false love, based on emotion and not based on law; and who justify willful unrepentant sin; are NOT of Jesus Christ!

They are trying to steal the sheep of God the Father for themselves, getting the sheep to follow themselves for their personal advantage! They seek to enslave the sheep for themselves, while Christ [The DOOR to God the Father] has given himself for the sheep to reconcile them to God the Father!

Following false teachers who use the name of Christ to deceive people into following themselves will bring us to destruction. Why will we follow the spiritually blind to our own destruction?

10:10 The thief cometh not, but for to steal, and to kill, and to destroy: I am come that they might have life, and that they might have it more abundantly.

A new parable of Jesus Christ: The Good Shepherd!

10:11 I am the good shepherd: the **good shepherd giveth his life for the sheep.**

He who serves for position, money, or for any other reason, except out of a deep dedication to live as Christ lived, is a hireling; he is not zealous to keep God's Word and will not be faithful in the end.

10:12 But he that is an hireling, and not the shepherd, whose own the sheep are not, seeth the wolf coming, and leaveth the sheep, and fleeth: and the wolf catcheth them, and scattereth the sheep. **10:13** The hireling fleeth, because he is an hireling, and careth not for the sheep.

The true sheep of God know God their Father and Jesus Christ their Good Shepherd and will follow them!

10:14 I am the good shepherd, and know my sheep, and am known of mine.

Jesus Christ and God the Father are one in full complete unity with each other, and the sheep who are faithful to them, will be in full unity with them!

10:15 As the Father knoweth me, even so know I the Father: and I lay down my life for the sheep.

Christ alludes to the Gentiles being called out along with Israel

10:16 And other sheep I have, which are not of this fold: them also I must bring, and they shall hear my voice; and there shall be one fold, and one shepherd.

Christ gave his life to be a DOOR to God the Father for ALL humanity, who would come to him in sincere repentance to "Go and sin NO more!"

10:17 Therefore doth my Father love me, because I lay down my life, that I might take it again.

Jesus reveals that no man could kill him, and that he has voluntarily given his life to do God the Father's will.

10:18 No man taketh it from me, but I lay it down of myself. I have power to lay it down, and I have power to take it again. This commandment have I received of my Father.

The carnally minded cannot understand these things:

> **Romans 8:6** For to be carnally minded is death; but to be spiritually minded is life and peace. **8:7** Because the carnal mind is enmity against God: for it is not subject to the law of God, neither indeed can be.

John 10:19 There was a division therefore again among the Jews for these sayings. **10:20** And many of them said, He hath a devil, and is mad; why hear ye him? **10:21** Others said, These are not the words of him that hath a devil. Can a devil open the eyes of the blind? **10:22** And it was at Jerusalem the feast of the dedication, and it was winter.

Now the people, not understanding the previous claims of Jesus, ask him again if he is Messiah.

10:23 And Jesus walked in the temple in Solomon's porch. **10:24** Then came the Jews round about him, and said unto him, How long dost thou make us to doubt? If thou be the Christ, tell us plainly.

Jesus says that his works bear witness of him, but they could not believe because they had not been called to enter God's flock.

10:25 Jesus answered them, I told you, and ye believed not: the works that I do in my Father's name, they bear witness of me. **10:26** But **ye believe not, because ye are not of my sheep,** as I said unto you.

The true sheep of God the Father and Jesus Christ the Good Shepherd are full of God's Spirit through diligent study, prayer and diligently internalizing the nature [Word] of God! They KNOW what is godly and what is not godly; therefore they hear, they understand and they are responsive to the Word of God [the Holy Scriptures]!

If we compromise with the teachings of Christ [for example; buying on God's Sabbath as so many do] we are NOT of Christ the Good Shepherd and we are NOT a part of the flock of God the Father. I did not say that, Jesus Christ said that!

10:27 My sheep hear my voice, and I know them, and they follow me: 10:28 And I give unto them eternal life; and they shall never perish, neither shall any man pluck them out of my hand.

Today's assemblies are full of tares and false teachers trying to lead the sheep away from the Door of reconciliation to God the Father, which is Jesus Christ, to follow themselves; but the true sheep will follow ONLY Christ and God the Father!

10:29 My Father, which gave them me, is greater than all; and no man is able to pluck them [the zealous truly converted] out of my Father's hand.

Jesus Christ and God the Father are ONE in FULL UNITY with each other; and we are to become ONE in FULL UNITY with them!

We are obligated by our baptismal commitment to Jesus Christ and God the Father, to become ONE in FULL UNITY with THEM, by zealously keeping their Word: That is our obligation!

We MUST NEVER compromise with our UNITY with Jesus Christ and God the Father in the name of a false organizational unity.

Organizational unity apart from UNITY with Christ and God the Father: Separates us from Christ and God the Father!

Those organizations that revel in their member's unity with each other as a substitute for UNITY with God through living by every Word of God are most foolish.

To compromise with Christ-like zeal to live by every Word of God for the sake of organizational unity; is to separate ourselves from Christ the DOOR of salvation and from any possibility of reconciliation with God the father.

How very, very sad that so many have been seduced away from God and have cast aside crown of eternal life for a sense of belonging to a social club entity!

10:30 I and my Father are one.

The Jews understood that Jesus was claiming to be one with God; that is, they thought he was claiming to be equal with God the Father.

10:31 Then the Jews took up stones again to stone him.

10:32 Jesus answered them, Many good works have I shewed you from my Father; for which of those works do ye stone me? **10:33** The Jews answered him, saying, For a good work we stone thee not; but **for blasphemy; and because that thou, being a man, makest thyself God.**

10:34 Jesus answered them, Is it not **written in your law, I said, Ye are gods?** [Psalm 82]

> **Psalm 82:6** I have said, Ye are gods; and all of you are children of the most High.

Jesus asks them if they think the scripture that calls men gods is wrong, especially when the person does the works of God.

John 10:35 If he called them gods, unto whom the word of God came, and the scripture cannot be broken; **10:36** Say ye of him, whom the Father hath sanctified, and sent into the world, Thou blasphemest; because I said, I am the Son of God? **10:37** If I do not the works of my Father, believe me not.

Believe that Christ's works are godly, and believe that godly works come from God and that Christ is ONE in FULL UNITY with God the Father.

10:38 But if I do, though ye believe not me, **believe the works: that ye may know, and believe, that the Father is in me, and I in him.**

Jesus again goes to the Jordan just north of the Dead Sea.

10:39 Therefore they sought again to take him: but he escaped out of their hand, **10:40** And went away again **beyond Jordan into the place where John at first baptized;** and there he abode. **10:41** And many resorted unto him, and said, **John did no miracle: but all things that John spake of this man were true.**

10:42 And many believed on him there.

Jesus Christ is the good shepherd. He is the Door; NOT some man.

Christ is the Door to the sheepfold and the door to the Kingdom of Heaven. It is through that Door that we can enter the Kingdom of God. The Door is the way to reconciliation with God the Father and eternal life in the Kingdom of God. That Door is Christ.

It is the sacrifice of Jesus Christ paying the penalty for our sincerely repented PAST sins that opens the door to reco09nciliation with God the Father and eternal life.

> **Romans 2:13** (For not the hearers of the law are just before God, but the doers of the law shall be justified [by the application of the sacrifice of Christ].

The sacrifice of Jesus Christ, the Lamb of God, is applied ONLY to those who sincerely repent of sinning, who are aggrieved with their past behavior and sorry enough to stop doing what they have been doing, to stop breaking the commandments of God, and to start living by every Word of God.

This is what repentance is. It means a change, a change from doing wrong to start doing right. It means to stop sinning. And what is sin?

> **I John 3:4** Whosoever commits sin transgresses also the law: for sin is the transgression of the law.

We must repent of breaking God's law, of breaking His commandments; and the commandment tells us to honor our father; which means physical fathers but even more, it means that we are to honor and to live by every Word of God our Father in heaven.

We must sincerely repent of not living by every Word of God; and when we do sincerely repent and STOIP sinning, the sacrifice of Jesus Christ will be applied to us. This is exactly what Peter said on the official birth of the New Covenant church.

We find this in **Acts 2:37** Now when they heard this, they were pricked in their hearts, and said unto Peter and to the rest of the apostles, Men and brethren, what shall we do? Then Peter said unto them, **repent and be baptized every one of you in the name of Jesus Christ for the remission of sins, and you shall receive the gift of the Holy Spirit**.

These people were told to repent, to turn away from sin which is the transgression of God's law, **1 John 3:4** Whosoever committeth sin transgresseth also the law: for sin is the transgression of the law.

We must sincerely repent from breaking any part of God's Word and we must turn away from all sin to embrace and live by every Word of God, to embrace the Word, Will and Law of God; for Jesus himself tells us in **Matthew 5:18** Truly I say unto you, till heaven and earth pass away, one jot or one tittle, one punctuation mark; shall in no wise pass from the law until all be fulfilled [kept by all].

The law will exist as long as matter exists. As long as the heavens and the earth exist, the commandments of God will exist and must be obeyed.

In **Matthew 19:17** our Lord also said, "Why callest me good? There is none good but one, that is, God". Even Jesus Christ [when in the flesh] said, "Only God is good".

Only the Father in heaven is good, not any man; and to enter into life, last part of the verse; "if you will enter into life; keep the commandments".

What commandments? Every Word of God the Father!

We are even told to pray to God the Father, "Thy will be done". And what is his will? It is his will that we do what he tells us, that we do what He says!

We are to keep his commandments and we are to pray that his commandments be kept by all that exists. We are to pray, "Thy will be done" and then we are to DO his will ourselves just as we have prayed, or we are hypocrites.

Repentance does not mean simply saying you are sorry in order to avoid punishment.

Repentance means to actually be sorry enough to stop doing the offensive thing.

If you were a parent and every time you had a problem with your child, and your child said, "Sorry" and ran off, and you knew very well he was not sorry and will continue to do those things. And that child ignored everything you said and went out and did whatever he wanted, and did a great many very bad and evil things. And every time you call him on, and he would say, "Oh I'm sorry and I'll do better", and he went away and did the same things again; it wouldn't be long before you would throw up your hands in frustration and say, "What am I supposed to do with this child? How can I get him to stop hurting others, and stop stealing, or lying, or fighting, or abusing others or whatever it is".

How it is that people think God is so very different? That God is just going to tolerate and put up with whatever we do, put up with us ignoring Him, with us ignoring His commandments, with us cheating, and stealing, and lying, and abusing, and hurting His other children.

That somehow God is going to put up with all that; and tolerate that; and smile on us; just because we say that little word "sorry;" and do we think that God will say, "Bless you child, go on and do what you want to do and inherit my kingdom".

How do we think that we can get away with rebellion against our heavenly Father? Do we think that God doesn't care? Don't we realize that our behavior in the Kingdom of God, in the Kingdom of Heaven; is going to be exactly the same as our behavior now? That we are practicing NOW to be in God's Kingdom; and how we behave at this time is how we will continue to behave in the future.

What we are doing now needs to be corrected before it becomes a permanently ingrained habit, a permanently ingrained pattern of behavior. We have to learn to do things right. We have to learn to stop hurting one another, to stop doing evil and to develop the habit of living by every Word of God; now!

People go around with this attitude, "Well I can do anything I want now and in Heaven or in eternity, things will somehow be different, there everyone is going to be so nice and so great".

So they go and they make war, and they maim and kill people, and they think, "I hate these people. They are my enemies. I will slaughter them. And somehow we are all going to be in the Kingdom of God, we are all going to be buddy-buddy there".

It doesn't work that way. We have to learn to behave now while we are physical, before we become spiritual adults. When we are spiritual adults, when we are mature in the things of God, when we are living by every

Word of God, that is when we will be allowed into God's kingdom; and not before.

If we are NOT living by every Word of God, if we are not repentant of sin; if we are NOT repenting and turning away from living by every Word of God: The sacrifice of Jesus Christ, which is the key to opening the Door to God's Kingdom and letting us in will NOT be applied to us and we will not be allowed entry into God's eternity. For it is written:

Revelation 22:14 Blessed are they that do His commandments, that they may have a right to the tree of life, and may enter in through the gates into the city [New Jerusalem].

Only those who live by every Word of God will have the right to enter that Holy City, the eternal Jerusalem, the New Jerusalem and will inherit the gift of ETERNAL LIFE.

The apostle Paul tells us this in **I Corinthians 7:19** Circumcision is nothing, and uncircumcision is nothing, but the commandments of God [are everything].

It is the keeping of every Word of God which is important. If we have a mark in our flesh, it doesn't mean anything unless we live a godly life.

If we are splashed or immersed in water; it means NOTHING unless we also obey our God, and live by every Word of God with enthusiastic zeal!

We need to repent of living contrary to God's Word and we need to start living by every Word of God, we need to start listening to God our Father in heaven and to start doing what He says in his Word we need to start doing the Father's will.

When our hearts are turned towards our heavenly Father our Father's heart will be turned toward us.

The prophecy of Elijah in Malachi chapter 4:6 will be fulfilled, and he shall turn the hearts; speaking of the Elijah to come. "Behold I will send you Elijah the prophet before the coming of the great and dreadful day of the Lord: And he shall turn the heart of the fathers [properly God the Father Luk 1:76] to the children, and the heart of the children to their fathers [properly God the Father Luke 1:76], lest I come and smite the earth with destruction".

The only way to peace between men is for all to first be reconciled to and to be at peace with God! The foundation to peace between men, including parents and children is to bring both physical parents and children into sincere repentance from all sin, so that all will then turn to live by every Word of God; thereby reconciling both physical fathers and their children to God the Father in heaven.

Living by every Word of God is the foundation of peace between men, therefor Elijah will turn parents and children to each other by calling all men to God the Father, and thereby building the only true foundation to peace between men; which is peace between mankind and God!

this is about turning the hearts of the children of men toward God the Father, for we are told in another place that John the Baptist was a type of the Elijah to come. And it is written in **Luke 1:76** And thou, child [speaking of John] shall be called the prophet of the highest for you shall go before the face of the Eternal to prepare His ways; **to give knowledge of salvation unto His people for the remission of their sins** [Elijah will preach the true Gospel of Salvation], through the tender mercy of our God; whereby the days spring from on high hath visited us, to give light to them that sit in darkness, and in the shadow of death, **to guide our feet into the way of peace.**

It is the job of Elijah the prophet to turn men toward God the Father and to turn them toward repentance, to give them knowledge of salvation, to shine the light of God's Word in the darkness of this world, and to show us the way to peace, which comes through living by every Word of God.

It is God's Word and laws which lead us to proper harmonious peaceful coexistence with one another through reconciliation with God the Father.

Jesus is recorded by John in **John 15** I am the true vine, and my Father is the husbandman. Every branch in me that bears not fruit He takes away: and every branch that bears fruit, He purges it, that it may bring forth more fruit.

Abide in me, and I in you. As the branch cannot bear fruit of itself, except it abide in the vine, the trunk of the tree; no more can you, except you abide in me. I am the vine, you are the branches: He that abides in me, and I in him, the same brings forth much fruit: for without me you can do nothing. If a man does not abide in me, he is cut forth as a branch, and is withered and then gather them and cast them into the fire, and they are burned up.

There are NOT many paths to the same God. That is a damnable LIE.

The ONLY path to God our Father in heaven is through his son, Jesus Christ, for he is the ONLY Mediator between mankind and God.

1 Timothy 2:5 For there is one God [the Father], and one mediator between God [the Father] and men, the man Christ Jesus [The one who became Jesus Christ gave up his Godhood, and as a physical man came and gave his life for us, after which he was resurrected to spirit and returned to God-hood as the ONLY Intercessor between men and God the Father.]; **2:6** Who gave himself a ransom for all, to be testified in due time.

This is talking about the second death, the lake of fire. Anyone who does not abide in Christ, that is, who has not sincerely repented and has not been covered by the atoning sacrifice of Christ; cannot be reconciled to God the father, cannot bear godly fruit and will be cast into the fire.

John 15:7 If you abide in me, and my words abide in you, you shall ask whatsoever you will, and it shall be done unto you. Herein is my Father glorified, that ye bear much fruit; so shall ye be my disciples.

To be a disciple of Jesus Christ, we must abide in him. We must be like a branch grafted into a tree, which bears fruit, not by its own ability or power, but through the power and the ability and the strength given to it from the trunk of that tree the main foundation, which is Jesus Christ.

And in order to have a relationship with Jesus Christ, we must sincerely repent of all sin.

Then He will apply His atoning sacrifice to us, opening the door to reconciliation with God the Father and opening the door to the resurrection to eternal life. **Revelation 12:17** "And the dragon was wroth with the woman, and went to make war **with the remnant of her seed, which keep the commandments of God, and have the testimony of Jesus Christ**".

When the tribulation begins very many of today's spiritually lax will repent and Satan will vigorously persecute them.

Keeping the Father's commandments makes the Dragon, the devil, Satan, very angry. He doesn't like it because he doesn't like God. He is jealous of God and he wants to replace God in our lives. Because he wants to replace God in our lives, he doesn't like it when we live by God's Word. Satan wants us to keep his ways in rebellion against our Creator and God the Father in heaven.

This verse also shows that there is a difference between the commandments of God and the testimony of Jesus Christ.

You cannot come and say, "Well, this is referring to some vague commandment by Christ to love one another". The testimony of Jesus Christ and the commandments of God are different yet they are the same, for the testimony of Jesus Christ is His example and His instruction.

Christ's testimony, His instruction is to live by every Word of God the Father [Mat 4:4] in Christ-like zeal as Jesus did and does. We see this again in **Revelation 14:12** Here is the patience of the saints: Here are they that keep the commandments of God, and the faith of Jesus.

The faith of Jesus Christ is deeply involved with living by every Word oif God. If we love Jesus Christ, if we follow the testimony, the example, of Jesus Christ, we will be living by every Word of God as Christ did. For he himself said, "I have kept my Father's commandments".

At this time in history, one can look around and find very many different groups calling themselves God's people.

The truth is that most of these people don't have a clue what godliness is.

It is human nature to want to think well about ourselves. People want to feel comfortable with themselves, they want to think that they are pretty good folks, that God has no criticism for them. And so they just read through the Bible and they say, "Wherever there is a good guy, that must be us. Wherever there is a good group, that must be our group".

Most people tend to overlook any criticism and reject it as only applying to others. This was never the intention of Scripture. Scripture was intended to be a mirror of ourselves to show us what we are really like in the eyes of God

What is important is that we read all of these messages and apply every single one to ourselves and say, "Could we be doing better? Could we be learning more? How can we be closer to God?" And apply every one of these messages to ourselves and strive to be closer and more God-like, to have a better relationship with God.

Because, in the ultimate end of things, it doesn't matter a grain of dust what we label ourselves. God will call us what we really are in His eyes.

We can go around patting ourselves in the back and saying, "We are good Christians, we are righteous and good people". But God may call us something very different indeed. God calls things what they are. Unfortunately, people do not.

We need to look at all the Scriptures, apply them all to ourselves and profit from all of them, for they are all written for our instruction, and our profit; all of them, not just the good things, every Word of God.

What does God or Jesus Christ really have to say about who can save us?

Let us read in **Revelation 3 :7** And to the angel of the church in Philadelphia write; these things sayeth he that is holy, he that is true, he that hath the key of David, he that opens, and no man shuts; and shuts, and no man opens.

WHO shuts and no man opens? And WHO opens and no man shuts? WHO has the keys to the Kingdom of Heaven?

Is it Peter? Is it some apostle? Is it some prophet? Is it some minister? Is it some man somewhere? Is it a man, or woman, or a Pope?

Or is it Jesus Christ of Nazareth, the son of the Most High God the Father in Heaven?

Read it in verse seven of Revelation 3. It is Jesus Christ who has the keys to eternal life; and the keys are; on our part, repentance, and diligently living by every Word of God the heavenly Father, and all the instructions of Jesus Christ; and a diligent following of the example of Chrit in pleasing the heavenly Father in all things.

And on God's part forgiveness, and the application of Christ's sacrifice; that is the key to the Kingdom of Heaven.

Without sincere repentance the Door of salvation door will be shut tight and no man can get through it.

But with sincere repentance, which is the STOPPING of our sin and rebellion against God, the STOPPING of deciding for ourselves what is right and wrong and instead relying on our Father to direct our paths: Jesus Christ will open that door, applying His sacrifice, blessing us with loving forgiveness, and reconciliation with God the Father in heaven. And he goes continues in verse eight, "I know your works [the works of faith of the sincerely repentant]: behold, I have set before you an open door that no man can shut".

The Door of Christ has been opened giving access to God the Father for those who know and use the Keys to The Kingdom Heaven; and the keys which unlocked that Door to Reconciliation with God the Father and eternal life are wholehearted repentance from sin, and diligently living by every Word of God from that time onward.

A Great Falling Away

1 Thessalonians 2:1 Now we beseech you, brethren, by the coming of our Lord Jesus Christ, and by our gathering together unto him, **2:2** That ye be not soon shaken in mind, or be troubled, neither by spirit, nor by word, nor by letter as from us, as that the day of Christ is at hand. **2:3** Let no man deceive you by any means: for that day shall not come, except there come a falling away first, and that man of sin be revealed, the son of perdition.

Let us consider Paul's words.

He begins by saying that we are not to be shaken or disturbed by words that the end is near, because certain things must happen first. These things are our warning signs.

The first point is that there will be a general "falling away" from God.

There was a great falling away during the days of Constantine and there has been a great apostasy through to these latter days when many in today's Ekklesia apostatized and adopted the false teaching that some man or organization has the right to bind or loose the Word of God.

This putting of anyone or anything between us and God is the SIN OF IDOLATRY. This was the beginning of a GREAT falling away of the early church from God, and a great falling away of today's Church of God organizations as men began to focus on other men and not directly on God.

TODAY, those who claim to be the called out Ekklesia have fallen into idolatry; for they are loyal to the teachings of men and are not loyal to the teachings of Holy Scripture.

Today most of the various groups of the called out Ekklesia calling themselves the Church of God, have fallen very far away from the Eternal Father God. Right now there are only scattered individuals who are being faithful to the Great God.

Only those who prove all things and hold fast to that which is good (1 Thes 5:21); by the Word of God, are being faithful to the Eternal.

A GREAT and TREMENDOUS and GENERAL falling away; has already happened!

Paul tells us that those who do not love the truth of God, which is every Word of God enough to rely on and live by every Word of God, who do not prove all things by God's Word; WILL BE DECEIVED.

2 Thessalonians 2:9: Even him, whose coming is after the working of Satan with all power and signs and lying wonders, **2:10** And with all deceivableness of unrighteousness in them that perish; because they received not the love of the truth, that they might be saved. **2:11** And for this cause God shall send them strong delusion, that they should believe a lie: **2:12** That they all might be damned [judged, punished and corrected in tribulation, and eternally damned if they will not repent] who believed not the truth, but had pleasure in unrighteousness.

Yes, those who do not love the truth of God above the words and false traditions of men; will be deceived and conned, taken advantage of, led about, and eventually they will be destroyed for their wilful ignorance.

As it is written:

Hosea 4:6 My people are destroyed for lack of knowledge: because thou hast rejected knowledge, I will also reject thee, that thou shalt be no priest to me: seeing thou hast forgotten the law of thy God, I will also forget thy children. **4:7** As they were increased, so they sinned against me: therefore will I change their glory into shame

Those who swell with pride, calling themselves God's people because they are faithful to the teachings of some man; have already been deceived and turned away from God.

Because they have allowed some person to come between them and God, they have gone astray. They are really spiritually blind, and wretched and spiritually naked; and they know it not.

The Mark of the Beast

Some have said that this mark of the beast is Sabbath pollution and the observance of Sunday; yet if one breaks one point of the law, one has broken the whole law.

The mark of the Beast is the mark of Satan who is the arch rebel and the father of rebellion against God.

Every person who does not obey God fully and makes excuses for sin, or compromises with God's Word, is like Satan in his attitude of mind and his actions of rebellion against God.

This mark of rebellious attitude and action against God was first applied to mankind in the garden when Eve and then Adam rebelled against God and sought to become gods unto themselves, deciding right and wrong for themselves.

To bind and loose God's Word according to our own pleasure or to follow those who do so, is to decide for ourselves what is right and wrong! All who do so have the MARK OF THE BEAST [Satan].

ONLY those who are faithful to God the Father and Jesus Christ; who follow the Lamb whithersoever he goeth; and who are passionately loyal, living by every Word of God; only those who refuse and reject the very idea of deciding for themselves what is right or wrong and who rely totally on God as their moral authority; will be in the resurrection to spirit!

This is so very vital!

To say that Jesus Christ will understand if we sin and will forgive wilful sin, because he knows men are weak; and to say that we should tolerate sin, out of a misguided false idea of "love'; or to say that we can compromise with the Word of God: Is to exalt the supposed authority of some person or organization above the Word of God and IS THE MARK OF THE BEAST!

Those who do such things; WILL NOT be in the resurrection to spirit!

Brethren, all organizations and persons who obey idols of men, and are not zealous to live by every Word of God: Have the Mark of the Beast!

People have been deceived into believing and doing what false religious leaders say, following idols of men contrary to believing and living by every Word of God.

All humanity except for a few overcoming faithful has been deceived in their foreheads [the beliefs of their minds] to follow Satan in their deeds [the deeds of their hands]; into rejecting any zeal to live by every Word of God.

This deception and mark of the beast has overwhelmed most of mankind since Adam, and today the vast majority of the spiritual Ekklesia has also fallen away from any zeal to live by every Word of God in order to follow idols of men and corporate entities; and we have the Mark of the Beast stamped upon us as well.

Following idols of men in the assemblies is exactly the same thing as following the final man of sin; the only difference is the name of the person being followed contrary to the Word of God.

Revelation 13:16 And he causeth all, both small and great, rich and poor, free and bond, to receive a mark in their right hand [referring to actions and deeds], or in their foreheads [referring to what is believed in the mind]:

The mark of the beast is the mark of Satan; it is compromising with and rebellion against God and the Word of God; it is a rejecting of any zeal to live by every Word of God.

It is what Satan taught Eve to do in the garden; to decide for ourselves what is right and wrong, instead of standing on God's Word and doing as God commands.

The Mark of God is to obey and follow God in all things; which only comes by sincere repentance and being sealed with the Holy Spirit! One can only live by the Word of God through the indwelling presence of

God's Holy Spirit which is given to those who have committed to Obey him in all things (Acts 5:32).

When we have been called by God the Father in heaven to have a part in the collective bride for the Son, and we respond positively to that call washing away past sin and committing to remain sinless through the power of God at our baptism, then the atoning sacrifice of Christ the Lamb of God is applied to us and God the Father pours out his Holy Spirit upon us.

God's Spirit is in complete unity with God the Father in heaven and with the Son, and will bring US into complete unity with God the Father in heaven if we follow its lead when we are sealed with that Spirit of Promise.

Ephesians 1:12 That we should be to the praise of his glory, who first trusted in Christ. **1:13** In whom ye also trusted, after that ye heard the word of truth, the gospel of your salvation: in whom also after that ye believed, **ye were sealed with that holy Spirit of promise,**

Those sealed with God's Spirit will learn and follow the things of God and will grow into a full unity of mind, spirit and deeds with God; IF they endure and follow the lead of the Spirit of God.

God's elect will become like God in all things, and will diligently work to internalize the very nature of the Father in heaven through a passionate love for him and his will and Word; loving God the Father as Jesus loved God the Father.

For if we are of God we will have Jesus Christ dwelling within us through God's Spirit, and we will love the things that Christ loved, and we will do those things that Christ did and does.

1 John 2:3 And hereby, we do know that we know Jesus Christ, if we keep his commandments. 2:4 He that sayeth, I know him, and keeps not his commandments, is a liar, and the truth is not in him.

2:5 But whoso keepeth his word [Yes, we are to keep zealously the whole Word of God], **in him truly is the love of God perfected** [Don't let yourselves be deceived, godly love is to keep the whole Word of God; true godly love is not some false human imagined emotional feel good that tolerates sin]**: hereby know we that we are in him**. **2:6** He that sayeth he abides in Christ ought himself also so to walk [live or behave,] even as Christ walked [lived and lives or behaved].

If we are in Christ and he is in us, we will be doing the things that he did; and what did he do? He kept every Word of God the Father with enthusiastic passion (Mat 4:4).

John 15:10: **If ye keep my commandments, ye shall abide in my love; even as I have kept my Father's commandments, and abide in his love.**

If Christ is dwelling in us, he will be keeping the Father's Word in us! And if we are residing in him, dwelling in him and he in us; if our branch is plugged into the trunk of the tree, (see John 15), if we are plugged into Jesus Christ then we will be doing what he did: Which is to live by every Word of God in Christ-like zeal to the very end!

1 John 2:7 Brethren, I write no new commandment unto you, but an old commandment [the Old Testament] which you had from the beginning. The old commandment is the word [to keep the whole Word of God] which you have heard from the very beginning [the Old Testament]. **2:8** Again, a new commandment I write unto you, which thing is true in him and in you: because **the darkness is past, and the true light** [godliness is the letter and spirit of the whole Word of God] **now shines.**

We ARE to keep the OLD commandment[s], in a new way! In their fullest spirit and intent as well as in the letter: In a full and passionate zeal to live by every Word of God with all our beings, going beyond just the letter and keeping the spirit of the Word as well.

The sign of God's people is that they are filled with love for God and diligently live by every Word of God, and that they live by every Word of God's without compromise or tolerance for any sin because the law is love for God and man.

The Mark of God is zealous faithfulness to our heavenly Father and all his Word and Will through the Holy Spirit.

The Mark of Satan [The Mark of the Beast] is to follow Satan into his spiritual rebellion against and compromise with the Word, Will and Nature of Almighty God!

For those who think that this mark is only Sunday observance; what about the billions who do not observe Sunday and are still rejecting the practical application of God's Word? What about those who observe God's Sabbath and break God's Word in other ways?

Remember that breaking any one point of the law is breaking the whole law, no matter which point you have broken. Breaking ANY law is rebellion against God and is just as sinful as breaking the Sabbath which sin is universal in the Ekklesia today. Today the Ekklesia call the Sabbath holy as they shamelessly pollute it!

Many are even rejecting the ONLY Mediator between man and God the Father, our High Priest and ONLY Intercessor Jesus Christ.

1 Timothy 2:5 For there is one God, and **one mediator between God and men, the man Christ Jesus**; **2:6** Who gave himself a ransom for all, to be testified in due time.

There is ONLY ONE Intercessor, ONLY ONE Mediator between men and the heavenly Father, Jesus Christ ALONE! NOT Mary, or Buddha, or Mohammed, or your corporate church leadership and elders, or ANY other!

There is ONLY one sacrifice for sin, and ONLY one High Priest that mediates for the sincerely repentant before God the Father!

For Jesus Christ ascended to the Father as our Wave Sheaf to be accepted as a sacrifice for us and to be made a High Priest for our salvation.

Hebrews 4:14 Seeing then that **we have a great high priest, that is passed into the heavens, Jesus the Son of God, let us hold fast our profession.**

Paul reveals that Jesus Christ is now our High Priest and that He has passed up into the heavens. Therefore, let us hold fast our profession, our belief, our faith, our works of faith.

4:15 For we have not an high priest which cannot be touched with the feeling of our infirmities; but was in all points tempted like as we are, yet without sin. **4:16** Let us therefore come boldly unto the throne of grace, that we may obtain mercy, and find grace to help in time of need.

Yes, we have a High Priest who gave up his God-hood to be made flesh and who was tempted in the flesh and experienced the weaknesses of the flesh and suffered in the flesh and gave his life for us. Therefore, he has empathy for us and he understands the things we have to endure and the things we go through and the problems we have. He will support and succor the faithful who believe and DO as he commands; while he will reject the faithless who will not keep all of God's Word with righteous zeal.

He is not going to justify wilful rebellion and sins and our faults, if we do not sincerely repent of them. But if we are repentant and sincerely trying to live by every Word of God, we can then go to God the Father through our High Priest and ask for help, ask for the power to overcome, and He will give us that power through His Holy Spirit.

We can endure. We can overcome.

We can beat sin and we can beat Satan through the power of God and through the power of God's Spirit and the Spirit of Jesus Christ DWELLING IN US. But we have to ask for that Spirit. We have to diligently seek it and we have to allow it to dwell within us. We have to follow where it leads and we have to do what it guides us to do. And how does it guide us? It inspires us with an understanding of the Holy Scriptures of God and a passionate zeal to live by every Word of Almighty God.

Paul writes in another place that the law is holy and just and good. And we know that God's Spirit is holy, therefore it will do nothing against the Scripture, it will do nothing against the Word of God. It will empower us to live by every Word of God!

Any man or spirit who says, "Oh, don't keep this commandment or that commandment," or this is only physical, or this is insignificant and not important, or God will understand my need to do this sin: IS NOT THE SPIRIT OF GOD!

It is a spirit of antichrist and of Satan!

God's Spirit will always point you to God, because it is God's Spirit. It is the Spirit of God: It will point you to God; and it will never ever turn you aside from zeal to live by every Word of God. It will always point you to God and always point you toward and empower you to keep the whole Word of God!

The Mark of Satan [Mark of the Beast]; is to decide for ourselves what is right and wrong instead of relying on, honouring and obeying our Father in heaven.

The "Primacy of Peter or James" heresy is the Mark of the Beast and the Mark of Satan, for it exalts men above God as judges of God's Word and the Will of Almighty God!

This Mark of the Beast applies to ALL of mankind who are doing their own thing and not enthusiastically keeping the whole Word of God in its fullness; and that includes the Ekklesia.

Brethren, this applies to the church of God today: it applies to all those who are lukewarm for the practical application of every Word of God.

Nearly all people in the world today and throughout history have had or have the Mark of the Beast, as they do what they think is right, instead of zealously doing what God says is right!

Do not be deceived into thinking that you have the Mark of God and do not have the Mark of the Beast just because you have been baptized and follow the teachings of some man!

All of the major corporate church of God leaders and brethren have the mark of the beast, as is self-evident by their rejection of truth and large parts of the Word of God.

The time of great tribulation is fast approaching when the mark of the beast [which is living contrary to the Word of God] will be in full ascendency, and anyone who sincerely repents and turns to live by every Word of God will face intense persecution and will suffer very greatly.

During the coming 42 month tribulation all those who reject the mark of the beast, which is rebellion against the Word of God; and who sincerely repent to live by every Word of God; will be persecuted greatly and will very probably die physically.

Revelation 13:17 And that no man might buy or sell, save he that had the mark, or the name of the beast, or the number of his name.

Legitimate Ministerial Authority

The Mosaic priesthood was intended to be the moral leaders of the physical nation, and today the ministry is to be the moral leaders of the brethren, the spiritual nation.

The very first responsibility of the ministry or priesthood is to set a proper godly example through living by every Word of God.

Their second responsibility is to diligently teach the brethren to live by every Word of God.

> **Physical Israel was to live by all the words that God had given Moses to teach the people; and spiritual Israel is to do the same, living by every Word of God in both the letter and the spiritual intent of God's Word.**

> **Deuteronomy 4:1** Now therefore hearken, O Israel, unto the statutes and unto the judgments, which I teach you, for to do them, that ye may live, and go in and possess the land which the LORD God of your fathers giveth you.

God gave his Word to Moses who in turn taught the priesthood of Aaron and the entire congregation the entire Word of God. The concept that there is some hidden or secret word from God which Moses did not tell the people, is a fiction intended to enable the use of Hellenic reasoning to justify departing from God's Word as given to Moses

4:2 Ye shall not add unto the word which I command you [the Word of God which Moses was given to teach the people was not to be added to or diminished by some non existent oral tradition], **neither shall ye diminish ought from it**, that ye may keep the commandments of the LORD your God which I command you.

Deuteronomy 4:39 Know therefore this day, and consider it in thine heart, that **the LORD he is God in heaven above, and upon the earth beneath: there is none else.** **4:40 Thou shalt keep therefore his statutes, and his commandments, which I command thee this day** [Moses gave the entirety of the commandments of God to the people in writing and there is no such thing as an oral tradition from God or from Moses]**,** that it may go well with thee, and with thy children after thee, and that thou mayest prolong thy days upon the earth, which the LORD thy God giveth thee, for ever.

Deuteronomy 5:29 O that there were such an heart in them, that they would fear me, and keep all my commandments always, that it might be well with them, and with their children for ever!

Israel is sent away while Moses hears the Word of the LORD, which Moses then gives to Israel. These are not the laws of Moses; they are the Word of Almighty God given through the messenger, the intermediary, Moses.

5:30 Go say to them, Get you into your tents again. **5:31** But as for thee, stand thou here by me, and **I will speak unto thee all the commandments, and the statutes, and the judgments, which thou shalt teach them, that they may do them in the land which I give them to possess it.**

5:32 Ye shall observe to do therefore as the LORD your God hath commanded you: ye shall not turn aside to the right hand or to the left. 5:33 Ye shall walk in all the ways which the LORD your God hath commanded you, that ye may live, and that it may be well with you, and that ye may prolong your days in the land which ye shall possess.

Brethren, no man has any right to change add to or diminish anything from the Word, commandments, laws, statutes, ordinances, precepts and judgments that God gave us through Moses!

Neither the pope nor the Rabbinate nor ANY other person has the right to loose the Word of God!

The priesthood and the ministry are to bind and loose judgments in human disputes ACCORDING to the Word of God: They are NEVER to try to change God's Word according to their own opinions.

Jesus also said:

Matthew 28:19 Go ye therefore, and teach all nations, baptizing them in the name of the Father, and of the Son, and of the Holy Ghost: **28:20** Teaching them to observe all things whatsoever I have commanded you [and Jesus commanded us to live by every Word of God the Father Matthew 4:4]: and, lo, I am with you always, even unto the end of the world. Amen.

The third responsibility of the priesthood or ministry is to enforce the Word of God and reprove all evil doers especially all evil doers in the congregations.

2 Timothy 4:2 Preach the word; be instant in season, out of season; reprove, rebuke, exhort with all long suffering and doctrine.

1 Timothy 5:20 Them that sin rebuke before all, that others also may fear [to sin].

The fourth responsibility of the priesthood or ministry is to pass godly judgment in disputes between brethren, judging all things by the Word of God.

Deuteronomy 17:8 If there arise a matter too hard for thee in judgment, between blood and blood, between plea and plea, and between stroke and stroke, being matters of controversy within thy gates: then shalt thou arise, and get thee up into the place which the LORD thy God shall choose;

We are to go to the priests for just judgment because they are to know God's Word and they are to judge fairly by the Word of God. When the priests go astray, justice departs from the land; and when the elders and priests are zealous for the Word of God there is justice.

17:9 And thou shalt come unto the priests the Levites, and unto the judge that shall be in those days, and enquire; and they shall shew thee the sentence of judgment:

17:10 And thou shalt do according to the sentence, which they of that place which the LORD shall choose shall shew thee; and thou shalt observe to do according to all that they inform thee:

The priests were the ultimate judges in Israel; as the overcomers in spiritual Israel shall teach and judge humanity when they are resurrected to become the priesthood of Jesus Christ in the Kingdom of God.

ALL judgments MUST be made based on, consistent with, and according to; the whole Word of God.

Jesus taught the same thing for the New Covenant assemblies

Matthew 18:15 Moreover if thy brother shall trespass against thee, go and tell him his fault between thee and him alone: if he shall hear thee, thou hast gained thy brother. **18:16** But if he will not hear thee, then take with thee one or two more, that in the mouth of two or three witnesses every word may be established.

Here we are commanded to do our best to work out our own problems.

If we are offended by any person; we are to go directly to them, and seek to resolve the matter privately in humility. Do not go and say: "you evil man, you did such and such;" no, rather go to him and say "there is a matter that I do not understand, why did you do this?" Speak softly and seek peace.

It is better to cool off a little if angry and then think the matter through while taking the matter to God in prayer first, and then do not delay and allow the matter to fester and grow out of all proportion in your imagination but work to resolve the issue quickly.

18:17 And if he shall neglect to hear them, tell it unto the church [the elders of the Assemblies]: but if he neglect to hear the church [rejects the scripture based instructions of the ministry], let him be unto thee as an heathen man and a publican.

If he/she will not respond to a personal entreaty, then go to the Ekklesia for a judgment; and if a scripture based judgment is rejected, let the offender be accounted wicked and rejected until he repents.

The authority of the Priesthood and ministry is limited to:

1. To live by every Word of God, setting an example for others,

2. Teaching, expounding and explaining the truth of the Word of God; and when any teacher departs from the Word of God they have departed from the source of their authority, and therefore that authority is forfeit! If people do not speak the truth of the Word of God they have absolutely NO moral authority!

3. Making judgments based on the Word of God

4. Rebuking any departure from the Word of God and rejecting willful sinners from the assemblies. Justice must be seen to be done and hearings on disputes or willful sin are to be open to the brethren: No secret courts. **1 Timothy 5:20** Them that sin [including elders] rebuke before all, that others also may fear [to sin]. **Titus 3:10** A man that is an heretick after the first and second admonition [warning] reject; For reasons of mercy a person should first be warned in private as per Matthew 18 and if he is persistent in sin, he or she is to be brought to a public hearing before the congregation and publicly rebuked.

To help perfect the brethren certain offices were established in the New Covenant ministry for this time. These offices are primarily difference of responsibilities, divisions of labor so that different people could make best use of their particular talents and gifts for the building up of the brethren.

Ephesians 4:11 And, he gave some apostles and some prophets and some evangelists and some pastors and teachers **4:12** for the perfecting of the saints for the work of ministry, for the edifying of the body of Christ. **4:13** Till we all come in the unity of the faith and of the knowledge of the Son of God unto a perfect man and to the measure of the stature of the fullness of Christ.

God has given us teachers and helpers and guides to help us to become perfect; to help us to become like God the Father and Jesus Christ.

They are older brothers in the faith whose job is to focus us on God the Father and Jesus Christ, to teach us God's ways and to help us to internalize every Word of God; which defines what God is; so that we can internalize the very nature of God and become just like God is in our own attitudes, words and actions!

The minute anyone says "tolerate sin", or "a little compromise doesn't matter Christ understands and will overlook it": Such men have ceased to be men of God; and HAVE BECOME FALSE PROPHETS AND FALSE

TEACHERS; seeking to steal our lives and lead us into the path of destruction!

It is our calling to become FULLY like God the Father and Jesus Christ: "unto **a perfect man and to the measure of the stature of the fullness of Christ**".

We are not to seek excuses for failing to become like Christ, who lived by every Word of God; we are to diligently WORK to achieve our goal and seek that Christ would fully dwell within us and lead and strengthen us to overcome, all evil as HE overcame.

What did Christ do? He KEPT HIS FATHER'S COMMANDMENTS! Without a shadow of compromise! To be like him we must do what he did!

John 15:10 **If ye keep my commandments, ye shall abide in my love; even as I have kept my Father's commandments, and abide in his love.**

Christ said, I have kept the Father's commandments; I have kept my Father's law. And, we are to become like Christ: We are to "fulfill the measure of the stature of the fullness of Christ".

We are to keep God's commandments as Christ kept them in both the letter and the spirit.

Jesus Christ kept the whole Word of God as our example; so, that we can learn from his example and fill up the measure of the stature of the fullness of Christ: So that we can become like him. And, therefore, we can be good children to God the Father, as Jesus Christ was [and is] a good Son. And being good children we would also be acceptable to God the Father.

The various offices and gifts given to members of the body are merely responsibilities to be helps in various areas, to better assist the brethren to become LIKE God the Father and like Jesus Christ.

People in such positions are to be respected as our helps; they are not to be exalted as some kind of grand idol or little god above God our Father and his Word! And they are to be followed ONLY as they faithfully follow God the Father and Jesus Christ. If they do not live by every Word of God, they forfeit all moral authority; and are to be rejected as anathema from God.

Apostles, prophets, evangelists, pastors and teachers are offices of responsibility and not necessarily a hierarchical system of authority.

Yes, the offices do have some authority as long as the holders are acting and teaching according to the whole Word of God and are not departing from God's Word; but the authority resides in God and the Word of God and not in the person.

If any religious leader departs from God's Word, then his authority has departed from him!

True apostles, prophets, evangelists, pastors and teachers will stand firmly upon the whole Word of God. False leaders will claim to be godly as they try to deceive us away from any zeal for the whole Word of God to follow themselves.

We are not to be foolish and follow the cunning craftiness of false teachers into every false way like ignorant spiritual children, we are to be filled with and stand unshakably on the whole Word of God.

Ephesians 4:14 That we henceforth be no more children, tossed to and fro, and carried about with every wind of doctrine, by the sleight of men, and cunning craftiness, whereby they lie in wait to deceive;

The true people of God speak the TRUTH of the Word of God, and stand on God's Word, to internalize the very nature of God the Father and grow to become holy as God is holy (Lev 11:45, 1 Pet 1:16); to become like Jesus Christ our espoused Husband and God our Father in heaven.

4:15 But **speaking the truth** [which is the Word of God]: **in love, may grow up into him** [Jesus Christ and God the Father] **in all things, which is the head** [the head of the Ekklesia under God the Father], **even Christ:**

The way to avoid being tricked and deceived by cunning men and by the tares sowed amongst the wheat, is to stand on the solid foundation of the whole Word of God and the Chief Cornerstone Jesus Christ.

We must test the words of all men against the words of the scriptural apostles, and prophets and Jesus Christ. And by the apostles and prophets, I am referring to the written Holy Scriptures. I am not referring to some fellow, who comes along saying;" I am an Apostle" and is doing that to get your attention and excite your admiration so that he can deceive you with cunning craftiness to follow himself. Remember that God calls things what they are: men seldom do.

Some people are truly sent by God **But, if they are, they will be utterly consistent with the Word of God** and they will have no fear of, and no concern about anyone testing what they say against the Word of God.

The only reason for a fellow not to like you testing what he says, is because he is not consistent with the Word of God. Such false men who say "Questioning me is questioning God;" are liars: for we are commanded not to blindly follow men, and instructed to question all men by the whole Word of God.

1 Thessalonians 5:21 Prove all things; hold fast that which is good.

If we hold men up to the standard of God's Word: We are NOT questioning God at all! We are questioning the man to discern his faithfulness to God!

A true man of God will say; go ahead and check up on me. Absolutely, I will be consistent with the Word of God and if I am not, then there is a problem and you better believe the Word of God, first.

All elders and leaders are charged to be faithful to live by every Word of God; and to faithfully teach, apply and enforce the whole Word of God

2 Timothy 4:1 I charge thee therefore before God, and the Lord Jesus Christ, who shall judge the quick and the dead at his appearing and his kingdom; **4:2 Preach the word; be instant in season, out of season; reprove, rebuke, exhort with all longsuffering and doctrine.**

John 17:17 Sanctify them through thy truth: thy word is truth.

The Mosaic Priesthood

The function of the priesthood is to work to reconcile all persons to God the Father by:

Setting a godly example in living by every Word of God,

Teaching all persons to live by every Word of God,

Judge all issues according to the Word of God,

Sternly rebuking all sin and any departure from any part of the Word of God, and

Offering sacrifices for repented sin.

No priest has the right to act or tech contrary to the whole Word of god, and if he does he is in rebellion against God and has forfeited all authority and is NOT to be listened to.

The New Covenant Ministry

After the Mosaic Covenant and priesthood ended with the death of the Husband of Israel, the ONLY priesthood remaining is the spirit High Priest Jesus Christ [Melchisedec].

There is no physical priesthood today, however all of God's called out are in training to become spirit priests of the priesthood of Melchisedec under Jesus Christ at the resurrection to spirit.

The entire Ekklesia is in training to become priests at the resurrection and to assist them to grow in godliness God has given us "HELPS" in the form of various offices of responsibilities. These offices will last until the resurrection when the faithful will be resurrected to spirit and added to the priesthood of Melchisedec under the High Priest Jesus Christ.

At that time the chosen will dwell on the earth and will fulfill the functions of priests teaching the righteousness of every Word of God and reconciling all humanity to God through the Door of Salvation, the Lamb of God, Jesus Christ.

No human being especially one who claims to be a priest or minister of Jesus Christ or of God the Father, has any authority to change any part of the Word of God. It is the divine duty of every priest and minister and called out person to live by every Word of God and to teach others to do likewise.

Deuteronomy 13

Miracles and fulfilled predictions are not proof of godliness or of anyone being a messenger from God. God's messengers often foretell events and do perform miracles by the power of God, but Satan's agents also can do these things. God tells Moses and tells us, how to discern the difference between the true man of God and Satan's counterfeits.

Deuteronomy 13:1 If there arise among you a prophet, or a dreamer of dreams, and giveth thee a sign or a wonder [makes a prediction, or performs a miracle], **13:2** And the sign or the wonder come to pass, whereof he spake unto thee, saying, Let us go after [exalts anything including any person, rather than the Eternal] other gods, which thou hast not known, and let us serve them;

13:3 Thou shalt not hearken unto the words of that prophet, or that dreamer of dreams: for the LORD your God proveth [is testing us] you, **to know whether ye love the LORD your God with all your heart and with all your soul.**

God Tests His People!

God wants to know just how much we really love HIM! Do we truly love God enough to do what God says? or will we be turned aside by every person who claims to be of God?

13:4 Ye shall walk after the LORD your God, and fear him, and keep his commandments, and obey his voice, and ye shall serve him, and cleave unto him.

Those who seek to dominate the brethren and cause people to follow after themselves and their false traditions in place of the Word of Almighty God will be destroyed by the Eternal if they do not sincerely repent.

Brethren, that means that nearly every church of God leader and elder is facing rejection by Jesus Christ (Rev 3:15-22), and stern correction in the soon coming great tribulation.

13:5 And that prophet, or that dreamer of dreams, **shall be put to death; because he hath spoken to turn you away from the LORD your God,** which brought you out of the land of Egypt, and redeemed you out of the house of bondage, to thrust thee out of the way which the LORD thy God commanded thee to walk in. So shalt thou put the evil away from the midst of thee.

Miracles and fulfilled prophecy are not proof of whether a man is of God or not: the proof that a person is godly is their zeal and faithfulness to live by and teach others to live by every Word of God.

Anyone who waters down or diminishes, or adds to God's commandments; is to be rejected as if he did not exist for you, as if he is dead. We are not to make idols of any person or thing to put them before God, not even a member of our own family.

Matthew 10:37 He that loveth father or mother more than me is not worthy of me: and he that loveth son or daughter more than me is not worthy of me.

Deuteronomy 13:6 If thy brother, the son of thy mother, or thy son, or thy daughter, or the wife of thy bosom, or thy friend, which is as thine own soul [body], entice thee secretly, saying, Let us go and serve other gods, which thou hast not known, thou, nor thy fathers;

We are not to follow anyone to make an idol of them and obey them in place of obeying God; and we are not to conceal those who do seek to deceive the brethren into following themselves or anything other than the

Eternal, but we are commanded by Almighty God to make this wickedness known and to warn the brethren.

We have become softhearted about wickedness and evil deceitful men! Almighty God is outraged at such misguided pity for those who would steal our crowns and our potential eternal lives!

13:7 Namely, of the gods of the people which are round about you, nigh unto thee, or far off from thee, **from the one end of the earth even unto the other end of the earth; 13:8** Thou shalt not consent unto him, nor hearken unto him; neither shall thine eye pity him, neither shalt thou spare, **neither shalt thou conceal him**:

13:9 But thou shalt surely kill him; thine hand shall be first upon him to put him to death, and afterwards the hand of all the people. **13:10** And thou shalt stone him with stones, that he die; because he hath sought to thrust [or to deceive] thee away from the LORD thy God, which brought thee out of the land of Egypt, from the house of bondage.

13:11 And all Israel shall hear, and fear, and shall do no more any such wickedness as this is among you.

In the New Covenant such people are to be publicly brought before the people with proof and then they are to be rejected by all the brethren (Titus 3:10).

Do you dabble in Astrology, or celebrate birthdays in the pagan manner, or go to Christmas or Easter etc celebrations? Do you allow crosses or pictures of Saturn falsely labeled Christ in your home? How much do we compromise with the thing that Almighty God, our God, hates?

How can we claim to love God when we do what God hates?

See how serious God is about apostasy! God commands us not to even keep the property of the apostates who are destroyed!

13:12 If thou shalt hear say in one of thy cities, which the LORD thy God hath given thee to dwell there, saying, **13:13** Certain men, the children of Belial, are gone out from among you, and have withdrawn the inhabitants of their city, saying, Let us go and serve other gods, which ye have not known; **13:14** Then shalt thou enquire, and make search, and ask diligently; and, behold, if it be truth, and the thing certain, that such abomination is wrought among you;

The New Covenant called out, are to reject all false teachers who would demand that we exalt them above the Word of God; and we are to reject all those who would commit idolatry by following such wicked men.

13:15 Thou shalt surely smite the inhabitants of that city with the edge of the sword, destroying it utterly, and all that is therein, and the cattle thereof, with the edge of the sword.

13:16 And thou shalt gather all the spoil of it into the midst of the street thereof, and shalt burn with fire the city, and all the spoil thereof every whit, for the LORD thy God: and it shall be an heap for ever; it shall not be built again. **13:17** And there shall cleave nought of the cursed thing to thine hand: that the LORD may turn from the fierceness of his anger, and shew thee mercy, and have compassion upon thee, and multiply thee, as he hath sworn unto thy fathers;

13:18 When thou shalt hearken to the voice of the LORD thy God, to keep all his commandments which I command thee this day, to do that which is right in the eyes of the LORD thy God.

Church Government

Many leaders and organizations make a big thing about their corporate government; the gist of which is that they insist that the brethren obey them no matter what they do.

In reality God's government in the Ekklesia is very simple;

1 Corinthians 11:3 But I would have you know, that the head of every man is Christ; and the head of the woman is the man; and the head of Christ is God.

God the Father is the head of all things and he is to be obeyed unconditionally, being our Father in heaven,

Jesus Christ is the head of the brethren under God the Father, and he tells us to live by every Word of God the Father and works to reconcile us to God the Father,

Certain brethren are tasked with responsibility to HELP us to focus on God and on living by every Word of God. They are to be respected and listened to, ONLY as long as they are faithfully living and teaching others to live by every Word of God.

The moment they fall away from an enthusiastic Christ-like zeal to live by and to teach all persons to live by every Word of God, sternly rebuking all sin; they forfeit their authority and are NOT to be followed, obeyed or listened to!

The ONLY authority which is to be unconditionally obeyed is every Word of God the Father. Men can be a great help in focusing us on God, but men have ABSOLUTELY NO authority to demand that men be followed and obeyed contrary to any part of the whole Word of God!

God's Sabbath and Calendar

Almighty God commanded all humanity to keep the seventh day [Friday sunset to Saturday sunset] Holy. Yet many professing Christians refuse to live by the Word of God in this matter, refusing to set apart and dedicate the seventh day Sabbath to God.

Almighty God commanded that we begin our months by the first visible light of the new moons. Yet today's Rabbins insist on beginning their months by the darkness of conjunctions [molads].

No human being especially one who claims to be a priest or minister of Jesus Christ or of God the Father, has any authority to change any part of the Word of God. It is the divine duty of every priest and minister and called out person to live by every Word of God and to teach others to do likewise.

The next section is about the change of God's Sabbath to man's Sunday, by human religious leaders in defiance of God's command.

The last section is about the change from the Biblical Calendar which God gave to Moses by human religious leaders in defiance of God's command.

God's Sabbath Day

God's Holy Sabbath

Genesis 1 shows that the universe was created first and then later all the work of preparing the earth for humanity from the time that the earth was covered with water was completed in six days.

Genesis 2:1 Thus the heavens and the earth were finished, and all the host of them.

The Creator then rested from his activity of preparing the earth for man and making man; and sanctified [Set Apart] the seventh day for man to also rest from his physical activities and join with his Creator in learning of his ways.

Here we see that the seventh day Sabbath was a memorial that God created all things; and a time for Adam and all humanity to rest and take time out from physical activities to spend that time with God.

The Sabbath had nothing to do with being Jewish and was made for Adam the father of all humanity and for ALL of his descendants!

2:2 And on the seventh day God ended his work which he had made; and he rested on the seventh day from all his work which he had made. **2:3** And God blessed the seventh day, and sanctified it [Set it Apart from other days]: because that in it he had rested from all his work which God created and made.

The Creator then rested from his activity of preparing the earth for man and making man; and sanctified the seventh day for man to also rest from his physical activities and join with his Creator in learning of his ways.

It was the Creator of mankind who made the Sabbath in order that he might have a Set Aside Time to be with and teach his creation, Adam and Eve and all of their descendants.

The seventh day was sanctified [made holy], and was to be a time set aside for man to rest from his physical activities and learn of God in the presence of man's Creator.

Since Adam was the father of all humanity and Judah did not even exist for about two thousand years after creation; the seventh day Sabbath is NOT Jewish and was created by the Creator for ALL of Adam's descendants! For all of humanity!

This six days of physical creation followed by a weekly seventh day Sabbath is a memorial of the physical creation and the awesome power and greatness of the Creator God. It is also a day to set aside physical pursuits to come to and learn the ways of God and which bring peace and eternal life.

No man has any authority to change this perpetual seven day cycle of remembrance of Almighty God, acknowledging Him as the Creator who created humanity and all things.

2:2 And on the seventh day God ended his work which he had made; and he rested on the seventh day from all his work which he had made. **2:3** And God blessed the seventh day, and sanctified it [Set it Apart for Holy Use]: because that in it he had rested from all his work which God created and made.

The very Creator of all things, the one who gave up his God-hood to become flesh, Jesus Christ [Hebrew: Yeshua Messiah]; also created the seventh day Sabbath! Therefore he could rightly claim that he was the Lord of the Sabbath!

Matthew 12:8 For the Son of man is Lord even of the sabbath day.

Jesus Christ on that occasion reminded us that the seventh day Sabbath was created for all mankind! The seventh day Sabbath was created for Adam and Eve and for ALL of their descendants at the first week of creation! The seventh day Sabbath was NOT made two thousand years after the creation, just for the Jews!

In saying **Mark 2:27** And he said unto them, The sabbath was made for man, and not man for the Sabbath: Jesus revealed that the Sabbath was made for all men at the Creation!

Which day is God's Holy Sabbath Day?

Why the very seventh day of creation, the Creator made the Sabbath by the majesty of his authority: The seventh day of the week which is sunset Friday to sunset Saturday! How do we know this? Because in the flesh Jesus Christ the very Creator of the weekly Sabbath kept the seventh day Sabbath from Friday sunset to Saturday sunset, the same as the Jews of his day!

How do we know that the biblical days run from sunset to sunset? Go to Genesis one and you will see that every day of the creation week is described as beginning and ending in the evening and includes the evening and the morning.

Some professing Christians actually reject the seventh day Sabbath that Jesus Christ created and kept, thinking that they honor Christ by disobeying him and observing the first day of the week, Sunday; instead of the day which Jesus Christ created and commanded his people to observe. This is rebellion against Jesus Christ.

What do the prophets say?

In the millennium when Jesus Christ rules the earth as King of kings; he will require ALL humanity to keep HIS seventh day, Friday sunset to Saturday sunset Holy Biblical Sabbath Day.

Isaiah 66:23 And it shall come to pass, that from one new moon to another, and **from one sabbath to another, shall all flesh come to worship before me, saith the Lord.**

The very Implementing Creator [under the Executive Creator, God the Father] of the universe and of humanity also created the weekly Sabbath for Adam and Eve and for ALL their descendants, ALL of humanity!

The Creator commanded all humanity to rest from their labors and spend the seventh day Sabbath, from Friday Sunset to Saturday sunset; with God learning to live by every Word of God.

The seventh day Sabbath is a gift of love to all humanity so that we might have rest from our labors and time to commune with God to learn about God and the way to life eternal in peace and harmony with God and with each other.

As the Implementing Creator of the entire universe; this Being of incredible power and glory who made man and all things, set aside the weekly seventh day Sabbath for man; and most men today reject this incredible opportunity to learn the habit of obeying the Creator and the way to eternal life.

The Sabbath was instituted by our Creator on the seventh day after the completion of six days of physical creative activity. (Gen 2:2-3). The Sabbath was made for man (Mark 2:27) so that man could follow the example of his Creator and rest from his labors. It is not reasonable to think that God should need to rest; therefore he rested as an example for us that we should rest from our physical activities to spend time on learning the spiritual things of God.

Thus was the history of creation explained by Moses: First the creation of the universe in Genesis 1:1, followed by God coming to a water covered earth and then preparing the earth and creating living creatures and placing physical plants, animals and man upon it, in the subsequent verses.

2:4 These are the generations of the heavens and of the earth when they were created, in the day that the LORD God made the earth and the heavens, **2:5** And every plant of the field before it was in the earth, and every herb of the field before it grew:

Then God watered the earth by means of evaporation and then condensing dew, and there was no rain with its rainbow until the days of Noah.

for the LORD God had not caused it to rain upon the earth, and there was not a man to till the ground. **2:6** But there went up a mist from the earth, and watered the whole face of the ground.

Quickly after creation the woman and the man sinned and cut themselves off from God by refusing to obey God. From that time forward only a tiny few were faithful to live by the Word of God, until in bondage as slaves in Egypt the children of Jacob also forgot God's Holy Sabbath Day.

Then God delivered physical Israel from bondage in Egypt and at Mount Sinai reminded the people to REMEMBER God's Holy Sabbath Day!

The word "remember" implies restoring something that once existed and has been forgotten or fallen into disuse.

The weekly Sabbath day was not given to Israel as some new thing, rather they were reminded of something that already existed and had been forgotten during the time of seven day a week slavery in Egypt; they were being REMINDED that God had created the Sabbath Day for all of humanity from the very beginning!

Exodus 20:8 Remember the sabbath day, to keep it holy. **20:9** Six days shalt thou labour, and do all thy work: **20:10** But the seventh day is the sabbath of the LORD thy God: **in it thou shalt not do any work, thou, nor thy son, nor thy daughter, thy manservant, nor thy maidservant, nor thy cattle, nor thy stranger that** [anyone that you are responsible for] **is within thy gates: 20:11** For in six days the LORD made heaven and earth, the sea, and all that in them is, and rested the seventh day: wherefore the LORD blessed the sabbath day, and hallowed it.

1. God's Holy Sabbath Day was Set Apart from all other days at creation,
2. The weekly Sabbath Day is the seventh day of a weekly seven day cycle,
3. The weekly Sabbath is from sunset Friday evening to sunset Saturday evening
4. The weekly Sabbath day was made for Eve and Adam and ALL of their descendants; All of humanity,
5. When Jesus Christ comes he will require all humanity to observe the weekly Friday sunset to Saturday sunset Sabbath,
6. The Weekly Sabbath Day is one of the Ten Commandments, and must be obeyed forever.

Deuteronomy 4:39 Know therefore this day, and consider it in thine heart, that the Lord he is God in heaven above, and upon the earth beneath: there is none else. 4:40 Thou shalt keep therefore his statutes, and his commandments, which I command thee this day, that it may go well with thee, and with thy children after thee, and that thou mayest prolong thy days upon the earth, which the Lord thy God giveth thee, **for ever.**

A New Covenant will be extended to all Israel; and to all nations as they are grafted into spiritual Israel. All people will be repentant and spiritually circumcised; with the whole Word of God written on their hearts through the indwelling of God's Holy Spirit.

A major part of the New Covenant is the gift of the Holy Spirit to enable an understanding and to empower people to live by every Word of God.

All repentant nations and peoples will be grafted into a Spiritual Israel of a New Covenant!

Jeremiah 31:31 Behold, the days come, saith the LORD, that I will make a new covenant with the house of Israel, and with the house of Judah: **31:32** Not according to the covenant that I made with their fathers in the day that I took them by the hand to bring them out of the land of Egypt; which my covenant they brake, although I was an husband unto them, saith the LORD:

The whole Word of God, IS the law of God; it is the constitution of the Kingdom of God

If we are called and accept the call into the New Covenant, then we will have the Law and Word of God written on our hearts through the Holy Spirit of God and we will be keeping and living by every Word of God (Mat 4:4), including God's Holy Sabbath day from Friday sunset to Saturday sunset!

31:33 But this shall be the covenant that I will make with the house of Israel; After those days, saith the LORD, I will put my law in their inward parts, and write it in their hearts; and will be their God, and they shall be my people. 31:34 And they shall teach no more every man his neighbour, and every man his brother, saying, Know the LORD: for they shall all know me [All will be at ONE in spiritual unity with God the Father and Jesus Christ through zealously living by every Word of God.]**, from the least of them unto the greatest of them, saith the LORD: for I will forgive their iniquity, and I will remember their sin no more.**

The Mighty One of Jacob declares that the Law of God and the whole Word of God are permanent and will last forever. This was quoted by Jesus Christ.

Matthew 5:18 For verily I say unto you, Till heaven and earth pass, one jot or one tittle shall in no wise pass from the law, till all be fulfilled [the Word and Law of God will be fulfilled (that is KEPT) forever!].

As long as Israel [including New Covenant spiritual Israel] exists [and the faithful will be given the gift of eternal life]; the whole Word or God will be kept in enthusiastic zeal! And all those who depart from any part of the Word of God will be corrected, and if they will not repent, they shall be destroyed forever.

Jeremiah 31:35 Thus saith the LORD, which giveth the sun for a light by day, and the ordinances of the moon and of the stars for a light by night, which divideth the sea when the waves thereof roar; The LORD of hosts is his name: **31:36** If those ordinances depart from before me, saith the LORD, then the seed of Israel also shall cease from being a nation before me for ever.

31:37 Thus saith the LORD; If heaven above can be measured [by physical man], and the foundations of the earth searched out beneath, I will also cast off all the seed of Israel for all that they have done, saith the LORD.

Sabbath Activities

It is lawful to do those things which God has commanded us to do on the Sabbath, since God is also the maker of the Sabbath and can therefore tell us what he wants us to do on HIS Sabbath; for this reason the Priests may fulfill their God commanded duties on the Sabbath.

Matthew 12:5 Or have ye not read in the law, how that on the sabbath days the priests in the temple profane the Sabbath **[by doing the work commanded by God]**, and are blameless?

Since the Sabbath was made for the good of man, we may also do acts of compassion and mercy; however we are NOT to use the "ox in the ditch" emergency excuse, to justify and excuse habitual Sabbath breaking.

We are not to travel on the Sabbath to the extent that it becomes a tiring labor, nor are we to buy gas, food, drink and lodgings on the Sabbath day.

We are to use the Preparation Day to properly prepare for the Sabbath Day.

We are not to do any cooking on the Sabbath (Ex 16:22-24) nor are we to do our own things, speak our own words, or to even think our own thoughts. We are to be totally dedicated to our God on his Holy Sabbath Day (Is 56 and Is 58).

We are to do no work at all on God's Holy Sabbath, except for that which God himself commands to be done, instead we are to focus on studying God's Word, discussions of godliness, teaching and learning godliness and prayer, and acts of mercy for the health of others; nor shall we be responsible for any other person or creature being required to do any work on the Sabbath Day.

To pay others to serve us in a restaurant is no different than to pay others to work at any other service. To pay anyone else to do what we would not do ourselves is HYPOCRISY! We are to avoid all appearance of evil (1 Thess 5:22).

Exodus 20:10 But the seventh day is the sabbath of the LORD thy God: **in it thou shalt not do any work, thou, nor thy son, nor thy daughter, thy manservant, nor thy maidservant, nor thy cattle, nor thy stranger that is within thy gates** [subject to our responsibility]:

Cooking, Buying and Work on the Weekly Sabbath and Annual Holy Days

This scripture is often used by unlearned persons to justify cooking on God's Holy Sabbaths.

Speaking of the very first Feast of Unleavened Bread when Israel was leaving Egypt, God allowed food preparation on the Holy Days as an extraordinary emergency measure.

Exodus 12:15 And in the first day there shall be an holy convocation, and in the seventh day there shall be an holy convocation to you; no manner of work shall be done in them, **save that which every man must eat, that only may be done of you**.

This statement that food may be prepared during that first Feast of Unleavened Bread when Israel was marching out of Egypt, has been used to justify food preparation on all subsequent and all other Holy Days and Sabbaths by some. Is that a valid assumption?

This verse actually refers to the very First "Feast of Unleavened Bread" and its two High Holy Days ONLY, allowing food to be prepared and eaten on that very FIRST Feast of Unleavened Bread ONLY.

Some extrapolate from this verse that food may also be prepared and eaten on all subsequent Feasts of ULB Holy Days and all other High Holy Days.

It is necessary to understand that this particular scripture is a history of Israel coming out of Egypt.

After that FIRST Passover, all leftovers had been burned and there was no prepared food available when Israel began the march out of Egypt; later when they had been crossing the Red Sea throughout the sixth day - just before the seventh and Holy Day - of that Feast there was also not time to prepare food ahead of the seventh day High Holy Day.

Because the people were engaged in an arduous journey out of Egypt and had no food prepared, God as a singular emergency act of mercy, permitted food to be prepared and eaten on this one emergency "ox in the ditch" occasion.

Remember that even the journey itself was not ordinarily lawful on Holy Days, but on that one occasion the people were being led directly by God to leave Egypt on those days.

As a singular emergency act of mercy, God permitted food to be prepared and eaten on this one emergency "ox in the ditch" occasion.

Nowhere else in all scripture is such a liberty [to prepare food on a Sabbath or High Day] permitted. This is simply a record of a special allowance, a special act of mercy; made for a special situation.

This one time act of mercy is an act of merciful exception to the rule, and does NOT justify breaking the commandments for the weekly Sabbath and subsequent annual High Day Sabbaths!

To cook or buy food or drink on God's weekly and annual Sabbaths, except for a very special and extreme extraordinary emergency is SIN!

We must quickly repent and turn from this sin of using Holy Time for our own purposes and pleasures, before we are corrected as physical Israel / Judah were corrected anciently and will be corrected again for the same sin!

The fact that the Passover was the preparation day for the first annual Sabbath of the Feast of Unleavened Bread, on which it was well understood that no work including cooking was to be done; is made clear by the faithful who rushed to entomb Jesus BEFORE the High Day of Unleavened Bread began at sunset that evening.

John 19:31 The Jews therefore, **because it was the preparation** [the preparation day for the first Holy Day of the Feast of Unleavened Bread], that the bodies should not remain upon the cross on the sabbath day, (for **that sabbath day was an high day,**) besought Pilate that their legs might be broken, and that they might be taken away.

Servile Work

In Leviticus 23 the statements regarding the High Holy Days refer to commands not to do any servile work. This has been taken to mean something different than the "do NOT do ANY work" of the Sabbath command; and has been used to try and justify cooking and doing other work on the Annual High Days.

The word "abodah" is translated in the KJV as "servile". The related word "abidah" refers to "work of any kind".

In reality, far from justifying some types of work like cooking; the term "servile work" is a redoubling of the command to do no work of ANY kind at all; for emphatic emphasis!

No work of any kind, including food preparation and purchasing is permitted to be done on any weekly or annual Sabbath! Only acts of mercy for health and safety and anything specifically commanded by God to be done on the weekly and annual Sabbaths may be done.

We are to properly prepare on the preparation day so that everyone might rest from physical duties, and engage in spiritual pursuits learning about God on God's Holy Time

The Weekly Sabbath and the Annual Holy Days are Holy Time. No work of any kind is to be done on them. That means no food preparation or cooking and no buying of food or drink.

Food and drink are to be prepared on the previous day which is the Preparation Day for the Weekly and Annual Sabbaths.

On the weekly and annual Sabbaths we are to do what God has specifically commanded us to do on those days; in addition, acts of mercy are to be done and the days are to be observed by convoking with God as Adam and Eve did and by doing so with other like-minded persons.

The Sabbaths are God's time, not our time; and the Sabbaths are for our good to teach us the way to peace and life eternal.

All mankind is obligated to obey their Creator Father and to spend time with him, and that time is specified by our Creator to be the seventh day; Friday sunset to Saturday sunset! Which seventh day is to be observed week by week FOREVER as time to be spent with God in peace and in physical rest; learning of Him and acknowledging God as Sovereign Creator in a memorial of the completion of creation in six days, the seventh being a rest from that creation and a memorial of that creation.

Exodus 20:8 Remember the sabbath day, to keep it holy. **20:9** Six days shalt thou labour, and do all thy work: **20:10** But the seventh day is the sabbath of the LORD thy God: **in it thou shalt not do any work, thou, nor thy son, nor thy daughter, thy manservant, nor thy maidservant, nor thy cattle, nor thy stranger that** [anyone that you are responsible for] **is within thy gates: 20:11** For in six days the LORD made heaven and earth, the sea, and all that in them is, and rested the seventh day: wherefore the LORD blessed the sabbath day, and hallowed it.

We are not to work on that day and we are not to require or force anyone else to work on the seventh day Sabbath. No one; Not an employee, a slave, a servant, an animal, or even a beast shall be required to do any work on the Sabbath Day, for God Almighty has decreed that the seventh day shall be a rest for all living things forever!

In **Exodus 31:12**, zeal for keeping the Sabbath is emphasized as one sign between God and his people. This sign is for us, so that we may have this weekly time to spend with God and learn of him: **"that ye may know that I am the LORD that doth sanctify you."**

Exodus 31:12 And the LORD spake unto Moses, saying, **31:13** Speak thou also unto the children of Israel, saying, **Verily my sabbaths ye shall keep: for it is a sign between me and you throughout your generations; that ye may know that I am the LORD that doth sanctify you.**

Today the Assemblies proclaim the Set Apartness of the Sabbath, and then go out to pollute it on a weekly basis: FOR SHAME! We cook, do menial work around the home and pay others to cook and work for them! For Shame, that the brethren for the most part, speak their own words about business and gossip, and do not discuss the Word of the Eternal!

For this sin, God proclaims that we are cut off from HIM, and from being accounted among his people as a part of his collective bride!

31:14 Ye shall keep the sabbath therefore; for it is holy unto you: **every one that defileth it shall surely be put to death: for whosoever doeth any work therein, that soul shall be cut off from among his people.**

The Called Out of Spiritual Israel wo defile God's Sabbaths will surely be rejected by Christ (Rev 3:14-22) and vomited out into great tribulation, where they will be strongly corrected for defiling the sanctity of God's Sabbath and Holy Days.

31:15 Six days may work be done; but **in the seventh is the sabbath of rest, holy to the LORD: whosoever doeth any work in the sabbath day, he shall surely be put to death.** **31:16** Wherefore the children of Israel shall keep the sabbath, to observe the sabbath throughout their generations, for a perpetual covenant.

Keeping the Sabbath, New Moons, the Annual Sabbaths and Festivals on God's schedule in the way that God has said; acknowledges the absolute authority of God and His Word.

31:17 It is a sign between me and the children of Israel for ever: for in six days the LORD made heaven and earth, and on the seventh day he rested, and was refreshed.

This was a sign between Israel and God; and we must become Israel in the spiritual sense through living by every Word of God (Jer 31).

All of the commandments that God gave to physical Israel are equally applicable to all those of the spiritual Israel of the New Covenant; not only in their physical keeping, but in the keeping of the spirit and full intent of those commandments. For Jesus commanded that we are to live by every Word of God the Father (Mat 4:4).

Even as physical Israel was called out of bondage to become the people of God; so the spiritual New Covenant called out people, have been called out of bondage to sin to become a spiritual people of God. Just as physical Israel was required to obey God, spiritual Israel is also required to obey the same God and to keep the same commandments.

If we are to be God's people, just as physical Israel was called to be God's people, we must absolutely obey and live by every Word of the same God and do the will of God. The Sabbath was commanded to be observed by Adam and by ALL humanity as Adam's descendants! Not just the Jews.

What does God want us to do on His Sabbaths?

Isaiah 58:13

Those who make the seventh day Sabbath [Friday sunset to Saturday sunset] their delight and are zealous to keep it in its full sanctity; those who reject doing their own pleasure, like participating in sin by buying food and services in restaurants; those who do not cook or do any work or pay others to work [except for doing what God has commanded to be done on his Sabbaths, and acts of mercy to care for man and beast]; are honoring God their Father in heaven according to the commandments and will reap a blessing for doing so.

Brethren, we pollute the Sabbath Day by even speaking of business! We are to speak of the scriptures and holy things and we are NOT to speak of worldliness and our own words; and yes, we are not to gossip about family things either. Save your own words for other times, and use God's time to speak of him.

58:13 If thou turn away thy foot from the sabbath, from doing thy pleasure on my holy day; and call the sabbath a delight, the holy of the LORD, honourable; and shalt honour him, not doing thine own ways, nor finding thine own pleasure, nor speaking thine own words:

What we speak about - especially on God's Sabbaths - reveals to God what is in and on our minds; the Word of God or our own matters.

> **Luke 6:45** A good man out of the good treasure of his heart bringeth forth that which is good; and an evil man out of the evil

treasure of his heart bringeth forth that which is evil: for of the abundance of the heart his mouth speaketh.

When we think about, listen to and speak of the whole Word of God; we learn of the wondrous perfection of all God's ways; and by following God the Father and Jesus Christ and longing to be with them: learning from them both and keeping all the ways of God, doing all we can to please God and become like God our Father and our espoused Husband on HIS Sabbath Day; they will bless us for learning and keeping the whole Word of God.

To go to a service and then do our own thing, and speak our own words the remainder of the day; is to pollute the Sabbath and is SIN! It is dishonoring God our Father and it is STEALING God's time, which is NOT our time, to do as we want with!

To do our own thing and to speak our own words on God's Sabbaths; is to demonstrate to Christ and to God the Father that we are only attending for social purposes and to experience an emotional feeling of righteousness and thinking of ourselves as pretty good godly people!

That is SELF-righteousness and NOT godly righteousness; for godly righteousness would be focusing on the whole Word of God and not on our own pleasures on GOD'S DAY!

Isaiah 58:14 Then shalt thou delight thyself in the LORD; and I will cause thee to ride upon the high places of the earth, and feed thee with the heritage of Jacob thy father: for the mouth of the LORD hath spoken it.

On the Sabbath day we are not to do our own pleasure. We are rather to seek out and make the things of God our pleasure; and we are not to speak our own words.

How many times can you remember going to a Sabbath service where you heard a sermon and then you or your friends talked about nothing except recipes and babies and business and weather, and didn't even discuss the sermon? You were speaking your own words and not discussing the scriptures as God commands us. You were polluting God's Sabbath Day!

Now obviously it wouldn't be wrong to say it's a nice day, isn't it? But to do that and to speak of other mundane things and completely neglect discussing the Word of God is sin! It is using God's time for our own purposes.

Brethren, I am not saying that we must speak exclusively of scripture, I am saying that our focus should be on God on God's Day; and today we have gotten so far out of balance, that we discuss our own affairs virtually exclusively, and completely neglect discussing the Word of God on HIS Sabbaths today.

A sermon should be given and then we should search the Scriptures, discuss the sermon, sharpen each other by discussing these things and try to learn more and understand better. And we should be able to ask our minister to expound things a little more thoroughly on this point or that point, which we may not have fully grasped. And we should be able to go to our home or perhaps to the homes of our friends and continue to discuss God's Word and the things of God.

If we are spending more time discussing our own things and doing our own pleasure than we are spending on the things of God, it is not right.

Isaiah says in verse 13, we should not be finding our own pleasure, nor speaking our own words. We should be thinking of and speaking about the things of God.

The truth is that; what comes out of our mouth is a reflection of what's going on in our mind. And if we are not talking about the things of God, chances are about 95 percent that we are not thinking about the things of God and our mind is not on holy things on God's holy Sabbath Day.

In Exodus 16:2 the people complained against God instead of seeking his deliverance, and instead they longed for the bondage of Egypt.

This is a lesson that Satan tries his best to discourage us to give up the fight against sin, but if we are faithful to live by every Word of God, God will deliver us.

God tests Israel as to whether they were zealous for his Sabbath or not.

Exodus 16:2 And the whole congregation of the children of Israel murmured against Moses and Aaron in the wilderness: **16:3** And the children of Israel said unto them, Would to God we had died by the hand of the LORD in the land of Egypt, when we sat by the flesh pots, and when we did eat bread to the full; for ye have brought us forth into this wilderness, to kill this whole assembly with hunger.

Then the Eternal rained Bread down from heaven; this being an obvious analogy of the spiritual Bread of Life [Jesus Christ and the Word of God], given to men from God in the spiritual wilderness of this world.

16:4 Then said the LORD unto Moses, Behold, I will rain bread from heaven for you; and the people shall go out and gather a certain rate every day, **that I may prove [test] them, whether they will walk in my law, or no.**

God did not prepare food for the people on the Sabbath, revealing that we should also follow the example of God and NOT prepare food on the Sabbath as per God's example. We are to prepare our food on the day BEFORE the Sabbath and Holy Days and we are not to cook on God's Sabbaths and High Days.

16:5 And it shall come to pass, that **on the sixth day they shall prepare that which they bring in; and it shall be twice as much as they gather daily.**

16:6 And Moses and Aaron said unto all the children of Israel, At even, then ye shall know that the LORD hath brought you out from the land of Egypt: **16:7** And in the morning, then ye shall see the glory of the LORD; for that he heareth your murmurings against the LORD: and what are we, that ye murmur against us? **16:8** And Moses said, This shall be, when the LORD shall give you in the evening flesh to eat, and in the morning bread to the full; for that the LORD heareth your murmurings which ye murmur against him: and what are we? your murmurings are not against us, but against the LORD.

Christ then appears to all Israel in his glory [in a bright cloud].

16:9 And Moses spake unto Aaron, Say unto all the congregation of the children of Israel, Come near before the LORD: for he hath heard your murmurings. **16:10** And it came to pass, as Aaron spake unto the whole congregation of the children of Israel, that they looked toward the wilderness, and, behold, the glory of the LORD appeared in the cloud.

Christ promises Israel quails in the evening and heavenly bread in the morning.

16:11 And the LORD spake unto Moses, saying, **16:12** I have heard the murmurings of the children of Israel: speak unto them, saying, At even ye shall eat flesh, and in the morning ye shall be filled with bread; and ye shall know that I am the LORD your God. **16:13** And it came to pass, that at even the quails came up, and covered the camp: and in the morning the dew lay round about the host.

In the morning Israel found small grains: What's this? They asked and Moses told them that it was the food that God had supplied.

16:14 And when the dew that lay was gone up, behold, upon the face of the wilderness there lay a small round thing, as small as the hoar frost [a grainy pebbly material] on the ground. **16:15** And when the children of Israel saw it, they said one to another, It is manna: for they wist not what it was. And Moses said unto them, This is the bread which the LORD hath given you to eat.

Moses commanded the people to gather up this "Bread" according to the needs of each person every morning, with double on the sixth day to be used on the Sabbath as well as the sixth day. Thus teaching us to use the day before a Sabbath or High Day to properly prepare for the approaching Sabbath or High Day.

16:16 This is the thing which the LORD hath commanded, Gather of it every man according to his eating, an omer for every man, according to the number of your persons; take ye every man for them which are in his tents. **16:17** And the children of Israel did so, and gathered, some more, some less. **16:18** And when they did mete it with an omer, he that gathered much had nothing over, and he that gathered little had no lack; they gathered every man according to his eating.

If the regular daily gathering was left overnight until the following morning it would rot and breed worms [maggots].

16:19 And Moses said, Let no man leave of it till the morning.

Yet some could not follow even these simple instruction to prepare the day before the Sabbath Day.

16:20 Notwithstanding they hearkened not unto Moses; but some of them left of it until the morning, and it bred worms [maggots, flies], and stank: and Moses was wroth with them. **16:21** And they **gathered it every morning**, every man according to his eating: and when the sun waxed hot, it melted [evaporated on the open ground in the sun like the dew].

On the sixth day they were to prepare for the Sabbath by collecting one portion for the sixth day and one extra portion for the Sabbath day.

This was to teach us that we are to follow the example of God and we are NOT to cook and prepare food on any Sabbath or High Day, and that we are NOT to pay others to do this for us!

16:22 And it came to pass, that on the sixth day they gathered twice as much bread, two omers for one man: and all the rulers of the congregation came and told Moses. **16:23 And he said unto them, This is that which the LORD hath said, To morrow is the rest of the holy sabbath unto the LORD: bake that which ye will bake to day, and seethe that ye will seethe; and that which remaineth over lay up for you to be kept until the morning.**

16:24 And they laid it up till the morning, as Moses bade: and it did not stink, neither was there any worm therein. **16:25 And Moses said, Eat that to day; for to day is a sabbath unto the LORD: to day ye shall not find it in the field.**

16:26 Six days ye shall gather it; but on the seventh day, which is the sabbath, in it there shall be none.

Yet some did not prepare and went out to gather food to cook on the Sabbath Day; as is too often done in today's Ekklesia as well.

16:27 And it came to pass, that there went out some of the people on the seventh day for to gather, and they found none.

Then Jesus Christ was very angry with those people who refused to obey him regarding the Sabbath and Holy Days. Later he sent Israel and then Judah into captivity mainly for breaking his Sabbaths. How much more is he angry with those of spiritual Israel who are supposed to love and to live by every Word of God?

16:28 And the LORD said unto Moses, **How long refuse ye to keep my commandments and my laws? 16:29 See, for that the LORD hath given you the sabbath, therefore he giveth you on the sixth day the bread of two days; abide ye every man in his place,**

Jesus Christ told the people that they are not to bake, or seethe [simmer, boil]: We are not to do any kind of cooking on God's Holy Sabbaths.

Exodus 16:23 And he said unto them, This is that which the Lord hath said, To morrow is the rest of the holy sabbath unto the Lord: bake that which ye will bake to day, and seethe that ye will seethe; and that which remaineth over lay up for you to be kept until the morning.

The preparation day is Friday up until sunset: And the Sabbath, God's seventh day Sabbath runs from sunset Friday to sunset Saturday: And on God's Sabbaths we are not to do any cooking.

We are not to do any work. We are not to do any traveling. We are simply to take the day off and relax. Spend it with God in prayer, in study, in reading, in thinking about Him, and in discussing the words of God with others, and in teaching our mates and our families, and spending the day totally focused on God, and of course also resting on that day, taking it easy.

One should have the attitude of saying, "This is my day off, I'm glad I don't have to do this or that."

It is wrong to have the bad attitude that "Oh, I can't do this and I shouldn't do that" and taking a negative approach.

Take a positive approach and say, "It's my day off, it's my break. I don't have to go out and mow the lawn. I don't have to get up early and go to work. I don't have to bake bread today. I can take it easy and relax."

Now, what about the lady who says, "Cooking relaxes me, I enjoy it." Or the man who says "Working on my car relaxes me, or I enjoy it."

We are to make the things of God our pleasure and we are not to seek out and do our own pleasures, even if we enjoy those things.

After all, why would they be our pleasures if we didn't enjoy them? Of course we enjoy our own pleasures. But we are not to do our own pleasures on God's Sabbath or on a High Holy Day. We are to dedicate that time to the things of God.

On the Sabbath Day, we are not to work, we are not to cook, we are not to engage in travel; and we are not to pay others to serve us either!

What about the person who has to drive 30 or 40 miles to attend a service? The time to walk from the outskirts of the camp to the tabernacle in the wilderness was probably about an hour and one should not spend much more than an hour driving to services on a Sabbath. Be sure to fill up your gas tank before sunset on Friday and prepare a boxed lunch on Friday. Do your preparation on Friday.

If you have to drive a few miles to associate with the brethren and hear a message, that's fine. Only don't decide you're going to fly to Australia from Britain on a Sabbath, or that you are going to take a bus trip across the continent on a Sabbath.

No, absolutely not. No extensive travel and no travel for personal reasons. Travel should be for Godly reasons and should be very, very limited in scope and duration; and should not involve any expense. If you have to buy an extra tank of gas on a Sabbath, the trip is too far. Don't go. Make some kind of other arrangement. It can be done. Things can be worked out. You can work around these things and truly make God's Sabbath a delight.

If you have to drive for four or five hours in each direction to attend the service, such a trip is not a Sabbath rest and is not appropriate. Perhaps it could be arranged to travel on Friday before sunset and to stay with some of the brethren in the town where the service is being held.

Conference Type Zoom or Skype sermons which allow interaction and discussion for small groups after the presentation might be considered.

There are different things that can be arranged, especially in today's world.

Perhaps one can alternate and one can go one week and then people can come to your town the next week. There are lots of ideas that an inquiring and motivated mind can come up with. But we are not to travel, or do any work or do our own pleasure on the Sabbath Day.

Nehemiah on the Sabbath

In the time of Nehemiah, some of the Jewish people who had returned to Jerusalem from Babylon had strayed very far from God.

In Nehemiah 10:31 they were told by Nehemiah that if the people of the land brought ware [goods] or victuals [food] on the Sabbath Day to sell, we should not buy it of them on a Sabbath or on a Holy Day.

We should also be willing to forgive debts especially on the seventh year, which is the Land Sabbath. But on the Sabbath Day, people shall not buy or sell. And the people agreed to that instruction from God in Nehemiah 10:31.

Then after returning from visiting the king, Nehemiah saw a great evil being done with many people working and buying on the Sabbath; this same wickedness is openly practiced in the major Groups calling themselves God's people today.

It was for this major sin [among other sins] that Israel and Judah went into captivity, and it is for the sin of calling the Sabbath holy and then openly polluting it for their own pleasure, that today's Church of God will go into the captivity and correction of the Great Tribulation in the very near future.

Nehemiah 13:15 In those days saw I in Judah some treading wine presses on the sabbath, and bringing in sheaves, and lading asses; as also wine, grapes, and figs, and all manner of burdens, which they brought into Jerusalem on the sabbath day: and I testified against

them in the day wherein they sold victuals [food and drink on the Sabbath].

13:16 There dwelt men of Tyre also therein, which brought fish, and all manner of ware, and **sold on the sabbath** unto the children of Judah, and in Jerusalem.

13:17 Then I contended with the nobles of Judah, and said unto them, **What evil thing is this that ye do, and profane the sabbath day? 13:18 Did not your fathers thus, and did not our God bring all this evil upon us, and upon this city? yet ye bring more wrath upon Israel by profaning the Sabbath.**

Nehemiah then enforces the Sabbath.

13:19 And it came to pass, that when the gates of Jerusalem began to be dark before the sabbath, I commanded that **the gates should be shut, and charged that they should not be opened till after the sabbath: and some of my servants set I at the gates, that there should no burden be brought in on the sabbath day.**

13:20 So the merchants and sellers of all kind of ware lodged without Jerusalem once or twice.

Then Nehemiah threatened the sellers. Today we cannot threaten physical violence, but we certainly can warn the brethren to avoid the sin of buying food and drink [or anything else] on the Sabbath, and remind them that Almighty God will reject them into the great correction and violence of tribulation if they will not sincerely repent.

13:21 Then I testified against them, and said unto them, Why lodge ye about the wall? if ye do so again, I will lay hands on you. From that time forth came they no more on the sabbath.

Nehemiah as a leader used force to keep the sellers out of the city on the Sabbath; Jesus Christ will use force to correct the wickedness of Sabbath pollution in the very near future.

13:22 And I commanded the Levites that they should cleanse themselves, and that they should come and keep the gates, to sanctify the sabbath day.

Remember me, O my God, concerning this also, and spare me according to the greatness of thy mercy.

Nehemiah writes that he is very zealous for the holy Sabbath Day of the Eternal Creator God. And he asked God to be merciful to him because of his zeal for the Sabbath in keeping out those who would buy and sell on the Sabbath Day.

Brethren

- ❖ We are not to buy or sell on God's Sabbaths.
- ❖ We are not to pay others to serve us on the Sabbath Day.
- ❖ We are not to go in the stores and buy things.
- ❖ We are not to go into restaurants to buy goods and services or order catered meals.
- ❖ We are not to travel.
- ❖ We are not to do any cooking.
- ❖ We are not to any work.
- ❖ We are not to be responsible for any person or animal having to work on God's Sabbath Day:
- ❖ We are to enjoy a real day off to spend in learning godliness and the way to eternal life.

The sixth day is the day of PREPARATION for the Sabbath. On the sixth day we are to do all our cooking, cleaning and household labor in preparation for the Sabbath rest.

We are NOT to COOK or PREPARE FOOD (Ex 16:23) on the Sabbath, or to travel (Ex 16:29). We are not to do any work or even to bear burdens on penalty of death and destruction (Jer 17:21-27).

The Sabbath is God's time, not our time, it is HOLY TIME, it is NOT our own. To do our own pleasures is to STEAL from God something that belongs to Him.

It is lawful to seek the things of God on the weekly and annual Sabbaths; to pray and study God's Word, to meet together in holy convocation (Lev 23:3) with like-minded believers. To do good (Luk 6:9), by healing or visiting the sick and elderly and to alleviate the suffering of man and beast.

It is lawful to cope with genuine emergencies, like fire, broken pipes or the ox in the ditch (Luk 14:5) emergency, but beware of using the excuse "this is an emergency" to justify habitual Sabbath breaking.

If an ox falls into a ditch many times, one should perhaps repair one's fence! That is to say, most of these so called emergencies come through a simple LACK OF PROPER PREPARATION.

It is also not wrong to find a beautiful or peaceful place to meditate (Acts 16:13) and relax, enjoying God's creation, but we must not meet in the buildings - high places - of false religions.

A convocation is ONLY holy if it is God centered! If you go to a service to hear a sermon and then talk ONLY about work and business, the weather, clothes and babies; you have PROFANED that convocation and God's Sabbath.

Out of one's mouth come those things that are dearest to one's heart (Mat 12:34). If your heart and mind are not on the things of God, your mouth will reveal this. We should be thinking deeply and discussing the things of God on the Sabbath. How do you ever expect to begin to UNDERSTAND the things of God, if you do not think and talk about them?

God will preserve those who think upon His name and make it their pleasure to do God's will (Ezek 9:4-6, Mal 3:16-18).

It is NOT LAWFUL to buy goods and services in restaurants or other establishments. To say that we may buy, because they are going to work anyway, makes a mockery of God's way. For that excuse justifies ALL SIN; because there is NO SIN that men are not going to do ANYWAY! Shall we use the whore because she will do it anyway. Why not have our enemy murdered, for the killer will kill anyway. This is a juvenile and pathetic excuse to justify SIN.

If we say that we are not paying restaurant employees directly, we must admit that we are paying the establishment that hired them. So we are admitting that we are paying the establishment to induce people to sin!

We have CONDEMNED OURSELVES with our own mouths! If we would not work for them on the Sabbath in order to obey God and WE PAY THEM TO HIRE OTHERS ON THE SABBATH, WE ARE HYPOCRITES. There is no other word for it. If we pay others to do what we would not do ourselves on moral grounds; WE HAVE BECOME HYPOCRITES!

Some say that because they have to cross a toll bridge on the Sabbath to attend a service, that; that somehow justifies them buying goods and services in restaurants! This excuse is also ridiculous! THE ONE DOES NOT JUSTIFY THE OTHER!

Some may think that proper Sabbath observance is some kind of burden that God's people should not have to bear. Yet these same people say to the poor man. You must tithe, have FAITH and God will work things out for you.

Where is Our Faith?

If we make an HONEST EFFORT TO PLEASE GOD, don't you think that He WILL HELP us? Most problems involving Sabbath pollution through buying and selling can be resolved simply and easily, with a little forethought, planning and effort. I have avoided this sin for forty years and it has been difficult at times but God has always provided a way.

If we lose a job, God will provide, and if he chooses to test us and does not provide; it is better to die serving the God who is able to raise us up; than to live serving wickedness and be cast into the fire of eternal death!

As for meals, some bread and cheese and fruit, together with each other and our God would make for an uplifting evening.; and probably a healthier one than gorging in a restaurant!

For far too long. the church has been more of a social club then an Ekklesia of GOD! It's time we became more GOD CENTERED and less concerned with social activities. Yes social things are important but the central thing should be OUR GOD. How we impress Him is far more important than how much we impress each other!

Did you think that God created the Sabbath for our hurt? It was made for our benefit, the benefit of all mankind. We should enjoy the Sabbath, but we should not infringe upon the potential enjoyment of this blessing by others. Remember that the burden of Christ is light and His yoke is easy Mat 11:30, it is Satan who comes along and tries to make the burden SEEM HEAVY by persecuting us.

When you can fully understand that Satan is the true source of all our heavy burdens, the true source of the SIN which causes our sufferings; and that God's way is really liberating us from that burden, you will have no problem in keeping ALL GOD'S COMMANDMENTS!

It is by the doing that we learn! By the proper observance of the Sabbath, we may learn many things and we will show our God how very much we LOVE HIM and HIS WAYS! On the other hand, by not keeping the Sabbath in the commanded manner, are we really keeping it at all?

What can we learn? Why FAITH and TRUST in GOD, as well as all those things that we learn in our studies, meditations and talks. Remember that the Holy Spirit is given to those who obey Him (Acts 5:32) and that it is that Spirit which shall lead you into the truth (Joh 16:13). If you want to know the things of God, you must learn and live by every Word of God and be pleasing to HIM (1 Joh 3:22).

Because of the complete lack of zeal in today's assemblies, to live by every Word of God including God's Sabbaths; God has withdrawn his Spirit from many today. It is those who claim to have the Holy Spirit the most, who probably have the least; because of their sins against the Word of God.

God's day is a day of rest for all His creation, for all the creation of God. It is a time of rest and it is sanctified to be holy time so that every person could spend time with God.

If all people did observe the Sabbath Day, and did rest on that day, and did seek the Eternal with all their hearts, believe me, they would find the way to peace, which at the present time they know not.

Common Excuses for Sinning Against God's Sabbath

Some people try to argue that the New Testament allows cooking, food preparation and other work on the Sabbath; here are the few common arguments.

1. Jesus and his disciples ate grain on the Sabbath
2. David ate the Bread of Presence
3. Peter's mother in law served on the Sabbath

Matthew 12:1 At that time Jesus went on the sabbath day through the corn [grain, in 1611 English corn meant a kernel, as of grain]; and his disciples were an hungred, and began to pluck the ears of grain and to eat.

Notice: They gleaned a few heads of grain as one might take an apple to munch; they gleaned and did not pay for this, they did not cook it and they did not take a basket to harvest, nor did they bear any burden in removing anything to their homes.

12:2 But when the Pharisees saw it, they said unto him, Behold, thy disciples do that which is not lawful to do upon the sabbath day.

There is NOTHING WRONG with eating on the Sabbath, as long as the cooking and preparation is done before Sabbath. These men did NOT cook, pay for, or in any way do any amount of work beyond grabbing a handful of grain and eating it.

Actually Sabbath preparation is easy and takes little time. The term "preparation day", does not mean that it takes the whole day to prepare; it means that all necessary preparation is to be done on that day. Simply having ones clothes ready, shining ones shoes, filling the gas tank and making sure there is enough food ready, is all that is really needed.

12:3 But he said unto them, Have ye not read what David did, when he was an hungred, and they that were with him; **12:4** How he entered into the house of God, and did eat the shewbread, which was not lawful for him to eat, neither for them which were with him, but only for the priests? **12:5** Or have ye not read in the law, how that on the sabbath days the priests in the temple profane the sabbath, and are blameless? **12:6** But I say unto you, That in this place is one greater than the temple.

Of course David and his men were fainting with hunger and fleeing for their lives for three days; this act of mercy towards David was a genuine emergency "Ox in the ditch" situation.

The Sabbath was made for people to rest and enjoy; and suffering, even of hunger is to be relieved, this is done through proper preparation, but one may grab a handful of grain or an apple off a tree to serve an immediate need, as one is walking along!

Genuine emergency situations are an exception to the rule and such rare exceptions are not an excuse for habitually failing to properly prepare, or by deliberately defying God's Word by making a big dinner on God's Sabbath.

12:7 But if ye had known what this meaneth, I will have mercy, and not sacrifice, ye would not have condemned the guiltless.

It is certainly permissible to do the commanded Sabbath activities, to relieve suffering and to eat on the Sabbath; however we are to properly prepare for the Sabbath and Holy Days on the preparation day. We are not to buy or sell or to do any regular work, including food preparation and cooking on Sabbath or Holy Days.

Matthew 8 and serving

Some claim that because Christ healed Peter's mother in law on a Sabbath and she rose up to serve him, it means that she cooked on the Sabbath.

Of course to "minister" could have been as simple as offering them some wine or a glass of water, or a bit of food that had already been prepared on the preparation day; therefore this idea that she cooked on the Sabbath is imaginary.

The scripture and its companions

Matthew 8:14 And when Jesus was come into Peter's house, he saw his wife's mother laid, and sick of a fever. **8:15** And he touched her hand, and the fever left her: **and she arose, and ministered unto them.**

Mark 1:21 and they went into Capernaum; and straightway on the sabbath day he entered into the synagogue, and taught. . . . .

Mark 1:29 And forthwith, when they were come out of the synagogue, they entered into the house of Simon and Andrew, with James and John. **1:30** But Simon's wife's mother lay sick of a fever, and anon they tell him of her. **1:31** And he came and took her by the hand, and lifted her up; and immediately the fever left her, **and she ministered unto them**.

Luke 4:31 And came down to Capernaum, a city of Galilee, and taught them on the sabbath days. . . .

Luke 4:38 And he arose out of the synagogue, and entered into Simon's house. And Simon's wife's mother was taken with a great fever; and they besought him for her. **4:39** And he stood over her, and rebuked the fever; and it left her: and immediately **she arose and ministered unto them.**

We can see in all three versions that Peter's mother in law was healed of a fever in the privacy of their home with a few disciples present. This was AFTER Jesus had finished teaching on the Sabbath; had walked to the house, had healed the lady, and she would have rested for a short space. It is a gross assumption to say that she had served them by cooking on the Sabbath day before the sun had set!

This is jumping to the false conclusion that "ministering" meant cooking, or a likely false conclusion that the sun had not set on that Sabbath before she began serving them.

To say that someone "ministered" to Christ on the Sabbath is an assumption; since the sun could have already set, and serving on the Sabbath would have had nothing to do with cooking anyway.

This is nothing more than a shallow attempt to justify polluting the Sabbath by claiming something that is just NOT there.

Ministering is serving, yes; yet she was most likely serving them AFTER the sun had set; and could easily have served their needs completely and entirely WITHOUT cooking, being faithful and therefore having properly prepared the previous day. For all we know, all they needed was a little water!

To pollute the Sabbath based on a personal assumption, is indicative of a desire to justify doing what one wants to do contrary to the scriptures; and it reveals that the self-justifying person does NOT want to please God, but wants to seek their own pleasures on God's time.

Jesus Christ is the same yesterday, today and forever; the scriptures are filled with admonitions to keep the Sabbath Holy and condemnations for polluting it.

We are clearly told NOT to buy food and drink, or to work, or to do our own pleasures on God's Sabbaths and Holy Days.

Just as physical Israel went into captivity for their lack of respect for the laws of God and for polluting the Sabbath and doing their own thing; today we are also at the very point of going into captivity for the same reasons.

We have the record of the past for our instruction and we are supposed to have God's Spirit: WE ARE SUPPOSED TO KNOW BETTER!

1. Each day ends and a new day begins at sunset local time.
2. The Sabbath is the seventh day, Friday evening to Saturday evening; and being a day, begins and ends at sunset.
3. Genuine emergencies or care for the sick and injured excepted; no ordinary work of any kind including buying food and drink or cooking is to be done on any weekly or annual Sabbath.
4. God's seventh day Sabbath is a Holy Convocation, meaning that on that day we are to meet with God. Whenever possible we are to meet with like-minded persons who seek to live by every Word of God; we are not to meet with just anyone to have a social gathering. The emphasis is on meeting and focusing on Almighty God, to learn and internalize the Word of God; not on a social feel good experience.

Please do study the word Sabbath in the Holy Scriptures with a good concordance; to learn of the great anger of God against those who pollute his Sabbaths; and of the great blessings that come from faithfully and zealously keeping God's Holy Sabbath Day!

The Biblical Sabbath to Sunday Change

The Eternal Almighty God created mankind and then he created the weekly Sabbath to be observed forever for all of humanity. Later when God called Israel out of Egypt God reminded Israel concerning the Sabbath as one of the Ten Commandments.

Mankind is commanded to forgo our own activities and devote the seventh day - Friday sunset to Saturday sunset - to remembering God our Creator and focusing on spiritual things.

The weekly seventh day Sabbath was created for man by God Almighty and to observe it is to acknowledge God as our Creator.

To refuse to observe God's seventh day Sabbath from Friday sunset to Saturday sunset, or to observe any other day in its place, is to disobey God and denies the authority of Almighty God our Creator.

Jesus Christ observed the seventh day Sabbath from Friday sunset to Saturday sunset as an example that we should do likewise, and he taught us to live by every Word of God (Mat 4:4) who commanded us to keep the weekly Sabbath.

How did Sunday come to replace God's commanded Sabbath Day in the professing Christian world?

Jesus Christ always kept God's commanded Holy Sabbath day from sunset Friday to sunset Saturday and the early church followed Christ's instructions and example.

Up until after the time of the Emperor Constantine, the church was scattered throughout the world and particularly across the Mediterranean area of the Roman Empire, each major city looking to its own Bishop. At the same time the vast majority in the empire had their many gods with the most popular being the sun god.

The Sun Worshiper Constantine is reported to have seen a vision of a cross and the words "in this sign conquer". At that time the cross was considered a symbol of Tammuz the founder of Sun Worship; and Constantine used this vision, real or not, to gather the masses of pagans who worshiped the sun under the names of Jupiter, Saturn, Apollo, Baal etc, around his cause.

Achieving victory, he then began the arduous task of attempting to unify his empire.

Finding the sect of the Christians a divisive influence and finding many of them already lukewarm for the practical aspects of their religion; he entered into talks with the Bishop of Rome; Sylvester.

Constantine agreed to legalize Christianity if the Bishop would support him as Emperor and in return Constantine would also support Sylvester as supreme bishop of the Christian church, and make the other bishops bow to him, and declare Christianity the official religion of Rome.

Conferences of Bishops were then called to standardize teachings and secure the loyalty of the Bishops to Sylvester and Constantine. This was accomplished at the Councils of Nicaea and Laodicea as well as in many other meetings.

They took the "ends justifies the means" approach to unify the empire and the church and the Bishop of Rome were called to the Council of Nicaea and there Constantine commanded that all the bishops would now observe the venerable day of the invincible sun and could no longer observe the Biblical Sabbath, which runs from sunset Friday to sunset Saturday on the grounds that it was Jewish.

Constantine wanted the people to worship on the day of the sun god, passing an edict that all people would worship on the day of the invincible sun. And this edict by the Emperor and the Bishop of Rome was to be enforced by the power of Rome, the armies and police of the Roman Empire.

At these meetings the sun worshiper Constantine forced the already passive, permissive professing Christians to apostatize and accept the observation of the "Venerable Day of the Invincible Sun" as a day of rest and worship; instead of the Biblical Sabbath observed by Jesus Christ, His apostles and disciples.

Those who refused this change were forced to flee beyond the borders of the Empire, or be turned over to the authorities for punishment and often torture and execution. That is how the Sunday of the pagan sun worshippers came to be called "Christian" instead of the Sabbath commanded by God; which falls on Saturday.

The observance of the Sunday of the sun worshipers which was already accepted by most in the empire was then forced on all people - including the professing Christians - by the power of the sword of Rome, as a part of the process of unifying the Empire under one religion.

Compromise after compromise was made until the now apostate professing "Christian" Church, became a new organism; A new faith, looking nothing like the faith of Christ and the early church.

Constantine remained a confirmed Sun Worshipper until the day of his death. On his deathbed, when he was too ill to resist; some water was sprinkled on him and he was pronounced a Christian.

Constantine was always a sun worshiper and was never a convert. He was sprinkled on his deathbed in 337 A.D. and declared a "Christian."

Changing God's Biblical Sabbath to Sunday

Constantine forced the professing Christians to stop obeying God and abandon God's scriptural Friday sunset to Saturday sunset Sabbath, in favor of the day of the invincible sun god.

Roman Emperors portrayed Sol Invictus on their official coinage, with a wide range of legends, such as SOLI INVICTO COMITI, claiming the Unconquered Sun as a companion to the Emperor. This inscription was used with particular frequency by Constantine

Statuettes of Sol Invictus, carried by the standard-bearers, appear in three places in reliefs on the **Arch of Constantine**. Constantine's official coinage continues to bear images of Sol until 325/6.

A solidus of Constantine as well as a gold medallion from his reign depict the Emperor's bust in profile twinned (jugate) with Sol Invictus, with the legend INVICTUS CONSTANTINUS

Constantine decreed (March 7, 321) *dies Solis*—day of the sun, "**Sunday**"—as the Roman day of rest (Codex Justinianus 3.12.2):

> "On the venerable day of the Sun let the magistrates and people residing in cities rest, and let all workshops be closed. In the country however persons engaged in agriculture may freely and lawfully continue their pursuits because it often happens that another day is not suitable for grain-sowing or vine planting; lest by neglecting the proper moment for such operations the bounty of heaven should be lost."

Constantine's triumphal arch was carefully positioned to align with the **colossal statue of Sol** by the **Colosseum**, so that Sol formed the dominant backdrop when seen from the direction of the main approach towards the arch.

The Roman Catholic Church and the Papacy as we know it today, was born in the fourth and fifth centuries. Massive and awesome changes were made to bring this birth about.

The primacy of Peter, an Authoritarian form of Church Government system exalting men above the Word of God was brought in, placing the priests and popes between the people and God.

I suggest that those who wish to dispute these findings do some inquiring and searching into history for themselves. These findings are certainly NOT unique to me. Take the time to do some serious research on your own and discover the roots of modern Roman Catholic / Protestant Christianity.

Jesus Christ NEVER changed God's Sabbath to Sunday; nowhere in all the Holy Scriptures is God's seventh day Friday sunset to Saturday sunset weekly Sabbath changed to Sunday.

The papacy changed God's Sabbath to Sunday with the public excuse that they were doing so to honor the resurrection of Christ on a Sunday. This begs the question; is it honoring a person to reject his instructions in order to do something different? or is it rebellion against the clear command of our Lord?

The ONLY authority which exists for observing Sunday in place of God's Holy Sabbath Day is that of the sun worshipper Constantine and the

Roman Pope. Ask the pope and he will tell you the same thing, on this matter there is no dispute.

The life and death question is: Will you obey Almighty God the Supreme Moral Authority in the Universe, and receive eternal life; or will you rebel against the plain Word of God to idolize and exalt a mere man above the Word of God, which brings death?

Catholics and Protestants on Sunday and the Sabbath

Today the professing Christian world rejects God's command to observe the seventh day Sabbath, which is from sunset Friday to sunset Saturday; in open defiance of the Word of God. Instead they have decided to observe a different day as their Sabbath, and they observe their Sabbath by attendance at religious service while otherwise doing their own thing.

Today the vast majority of professing Christian churches teach the observance of Sunday, the first day of the week, as a time for worship in place of God's commanded seventh day Sabbath. Yet it is generally known and freely admitted by them that the early Christians observed the seventh day as the Sabbath.

How did this change come about?

History reveals that it was decades after the death of the apostles that a politico-religious system repudiated the Sabbath of Scripture and substituted the observance of the first day of the week. The following quotations, all directly from Roman Catholic or Protestant sources, freely acknowledge that there is no Biblical authority for the observance of Sunday as the weekly Sabbath, and that it was the Roman Church that rebelled against the Word of God to change the Sabbath to the first day of the week.

The Catholic Cardinal Gibbons, in *Faith of Our Fathers*, pg. 111, said, "You may read the Bible from Genesis to Revelation, and you will not find a single line authorizing the sanctification of Sunday. The Scriptures enforce the religious observance of Saturday, a day which we (the Roman Catholic Church) never sanctify.

The Catholic Mirror (a publication by Cardinal Gibbons) Sept. 2, 1893- **"...the Redeemer, during His mortal life, never kept any other day than Saturday."**

The Catholic Mirror Sept. 9, 1893- "Nor can we imagine any one foolhardy enough to question the identity of Saturday with the Sabbath or seventh day, seeing that the people of Israel have been keeping the Saturday from the giving of the Law, A.M., 2514 to A.D. 1893 (to the present day)..."

The Catholic Mirror Sept.9, 1893- **"We deem it necessary to be perfectly clear on this point....The Bible- the Old Testament- confirmed by the living tradition of weekly practice for 3383 years by the chosen people of God, teaches, then, with absolute certainty, that God had, Himself, named the day "to be kept holy to Him"- that the day was Saturday, and that any violation of that command was punishable with death."**

Peter Geiermann, C.S.S.R., *The Converts Catechism of Catholic Doctrine* Third Edition"1). **Question: Which is the Sabbath day? "Answer: Saturday is the Sabbath day.** 2). "Question: Why do we observe Sunday instead of Saturday?"Answer. "We observe Sunday instead of Saturday because the Catholic Church in the Council of Laodicea, transferred the solemnity from Saturday to Sunday."

Martin J. Scott- *Things Catholics Are Asked About* (1927) **"Nowhere in the Bible is it stated that worship should be changed from Saturday to Sunday** .... Now the Church ... instituted, by God's authority, Sunday as the day of worship. This same Church, by the same divine authority, taught the doctrine of Purgatory long before the Bible was made. We have, therefore, the same authority for Purgatory as we have for Sunday."

John Laux- *A Course in Religion for Catholic High Schools and Academies* (1 936) "Some theologians have held that God likewise directly determined the Sunday as the day of worship in the New Law, that He Himself has explicitly substituted the Sunday for the Sabbath. But this theory is now entirely abandoned. It is now commonly held that God simply gave His Church the power to set aside whatever day or days she would deem suitable as Holy Days. The Church chose Sunday, the first day of the week, and in the course of time added other days as holy days."

Peter R. Kraemer- Catholic Church Extension Society (1975), Chicago, Illinois. "Regarding the change from the observance of the Jewish Sabbath to the Christian Sunday, I wish to draw your attention to the facts:"1) That Protestants, **who accept the Bible as the only rule of faith and religion, should by all means go back to the observance of the Sabbath.** The fact that they do not, but on the contrary observe the Sunday, stultifies them in the eyes of every thinking man."2) We Catholics do not accept the Bible as the only rule of faith. Besides the Bible we have the living Church, the authority of the Church, as a rule to guide us. We say, this Church, instituted by Christ to teach and guide man through life, has the right to change the ceremonial laws of the Old Testament and hence, we accept her change of the Sabbath to Sunday. **We frankly say, yes, the Church made this change, made this law, as she made many other laws**, for instance, the Friday abstinence, the unmarried priesthood, the laws concerning mixed marriages, the regulation of Catholic marriages and a thousand other laws. "It is always somewhat laughable, to see the Protestant churches, in pulpit and legislation, demand **the observance of Sunday, of which there is nothing in their Bible."**

"It seems to have been customary in the Celtic churches of early times, in Ireland as well as Scotland, to keep Saturday, the Jewish Sabbath, as a day of rest from labour. They obeted the fourth commandment literally upon the seventh day of the week." - **Professor James C. Moffat,** DD., Professor of Church History at Princeton.; from *The Church in Scotland, pp140.*

Dr. Hefele, *Concilliengesch 3, 512, sec. 362* about the Council of Liftinae, Belgium AD 745 (attended by Boniface)- "The third allocution of this council warns against the observance of the Sabbath, referring to the decree of the council of Laodicea"

Dr. Hefele, *Concilliengesch 4, 346-352, sec 478* quoting Pope Nicholas I answer to a question from Bogaris the prince of Bulgaria- "One is to cease from work on Sunday, but not also on the Sabbath" /On the subject of the same letter- "The head of the Greek Church , offended at the interference of the papacy, declared the Pope ex-communicated"- *Truth Triumphant pp 232*

"They worked on Sunday, but kept Saturday in a sabbatical manner...These things Margaret abolished" - *A History of Scotland from the Roman Occupation*, speaking of Queen Margaret's (a Catholic) decree.

"During the first crusade, Pope Urban II decreed at the council of Clermont (AD 1095) that the Sabbath be set aside in hounour of the Virgin Mary."- *History of the Sabbath p 672*

"There is much evidence that the Sabbath prevailed in Wales universally until AD 1115, when the first Roman bishop was seated at St. David's. The old Welsh Sabbath-keeping churches did not even then altogether bow the knee to Rome, but fled to their hiding places." - Lewis, *Seventh Day Baptists in Europe and America, Vol 1, p 29*

Josephus, first century Historian, says : "There is not any city of the Grecians, nor any of the barbarians, nor any nation whatsoever, whither our custom of resting on the seventh day hath not come!" M'Clathie, *Notes and Queries on China and Japan.* (edited by Dennys),Vol.4, Nos. 7,8, p.100.

"It was the practice generally of the Easterne Churches; and some churches of the west..For in the church of Millaine [Milan];.. it seemes the Saturday was held in farre esteeme ..Not that the Easterne churches, or any of the rest which observed that day, were inclined to Iudaisme [Judaism]; but that they came together on the Sabbath day, to worship Iesus [Jesus] Christ the Lord of the Sabbath." , **Dr. Heylyn's**- *History of the Sabbath* Part 2, pp. 73,74, London: 1636

"The primitive Christians did keep the Sabbath of the Jews; therefore the Christians for a long time together, did keep their conventions on the Sabbath, in which some portion of the Law were read: and this continued till the time of the Laodicean council." ***The Whole Works of Jeremey Taylor****, Vol. IX*, p416 (R. Heber's Edition, Vol.XII, p.416)

"The gentile Christians observed also the Sabbath." *Gieseler's Church History*, Vol.1, ch.2, par.30, p.93.

"The first matter concerned a keeping holy of Saturday. It had come to the earth of the archbishop that people in different places of the kingdom had ventured the keeping holy of Saturday. **It is strictly forbidden- it is stated- in the Church-Law, for any one to keep or adopt holy-days. outside of those which the pope, archbishop, or bishops appoint.**" - speaking of the Church Council held at Bergen, Norway in the year 1435, ***The History of the Norwegian Church under Catholicism,*** R. Keyser, Vol II, p 488. Oslo: 1858.

"It will surely be far safer to observe the seventh day, according to express commandment of God, than on the authority of mere human conjecture to adopt the first [day]."- John Milton, *Sab. Lit.* pp 46-54.

"Thus we see Dan. 7, 25, fulfilled, the little horn changing 'times and laws'. Therefore it appears to me that all who keep the first day for the Sabbath are Pope's Sunday-keepers and God's Sabbath-breakers."- American **Elder T.M. Preble**, Feb 13 1845.

James Cardinal Gibbons, THE FAITH OF OUR FATHERS, 88th ed., pp. 89.

"But you may read the Bible from Genesis to Revelation, and you will not find a single line authorizing the sanctification of Sunday. The Scriptures enforce the religious observance of Saturday, a day which we never sanctify."

Stephen Keenan, A DOCTRINAL CATECHISM 3rd ed., p. 174.

"Question: Have you any other way of proving that the Church has power to institute festivals of precept?

"Answer: Had she not such power, she could not have done that in which all modern religionists agree with her-she could not have substituted the observance of Sunday, the first day of the week, for the observance of Saturday, the seventh day, a change for which there is no Scriptural authority."

John Laux, A COURSE IN RELIGION FOR CATHOLIC HIGH SCHOOLS AND ACADEMIES (1 936), vol. 1, P. 51.

"Some theologians have held that God likewise directly determined the Sunday as the day of worship in the New Law, that He Himself has explicitly substituted the Sunday for the Sabbath. But this theory is now entirely abandoned. It is now commonly held that God simply gave His Church the power to set aside whatever day or days she would deem suitable as Holy Days. The Church chose Sunday, the first day of the week, and in the course of time added other days as holy days."

Daniel Ferres, ed., MANUAL OF CHRISTIAN DOCTRINE (1916), p.67.

"Question: How prove you that the Church hath power to command feasts and holy days?

"Answer. By the very act of changing the Sabbath into Sunday, which Protestants allow of, and therefore they fondly contradict themselves, by keeping Sunday strictly, and breaking most other feasts commanded by the same Church.'

James Cardinal Gibbons, Archbishop of Baltimore (1877-1921), in a signed letter.

"Is Saturday the seventh day according to the Bible and the Ten Commandments? I answer yes. Is Sunday the first day of the week and did the Church change the seventh day -Saturday - for Sunday, the first day? I answer YES . Did Christ change the day'? I answer NO!

"Faithfully yours, J. Card. Gibbons"

THE CATHOLIC MIRROR, official publication of James Cardinal Gibbons, Sept. 23, 1893.

"The Catholic Church, . . . by virtue of her divine mission, changed the day from Saturday to Sunday."

CATHOLIC VIRGINIAN Oct. 3, 1947, p. 9, art. "To Tell You the Truth."

"For example, nowhere in the Bible do we find that Christ or the Apostles ordered that the Sabbath be changed from Saturday to Sunday. We have the commandment of God given to Moses to keep holy the Sabbath day, that is the 7th day of the week, Saturday. Today most Christians keep Sunday because it has been revealed to us by the[Roman Catholic] church outside the Bible."

Peter Geiermann, C.S.S.R., THE CONVERTS CATECHISM OF CATHOLIC DOCTRINE (1957), p. 50.

"Question: Which is the Sabbath day?

"Answer: Saturday is the Sabbath day.

"Question: Why do we observe Sunday instead of Saturday?

"Answer. We observe Sunday instead of Saturday because the Catholic Church transferred the solemnity from Saturday to Sunday."

Martin J. Scott, THINGS CATHOLICS ARE ASKED ABOUT (1927),p. 136.

"Nowhere in the Bible is it stated that worship should be changed from Saturday to Sunday .... Now the Church ... instituted, by God's authority, Sunday as the day of worship. This same Church, by the same divine authority, taught the doctrine of Purgatory long before the Bible was made. We have, therefore, the same authority for Purgatory as we have for Sunday."

Peter R. Kraemer, Catholic Church Extension Society (1975),Chicago, Illinois.

"Regarding the change from the observance of the Jewish Sabbath to the Christian Sunday, I wish to draw your attention to the facts:

"1) That Protestants, who accept the Bible as the only rule of faith and religion, should by all means go back to the observance of the Sabbath. The fact that they do not, but on the contrary observe the Sunday, stultifies them in the eyes of every thinking man.

"2) We Catholics do not accept the Bible as the only rule of faith. Besides the Bible we have the living Church, the authority of the Church, as a rule to guide us. We say, this Church, instituted by Christ to teach and guide man through life, has the right to change the ceremonial laws of the Old Testament and hence, we accept her change of the Sabbath to Sunday. We frankly say, yes, the Church made this change, made this law, as she made many other laws, for instance, the Friday abstinence, the unmarried priesthood, the laws concerning mixed marriages, the regulation of Catholic marriages and a thousand other laws.

"It is always somewhat laughable, to see the Protestant churches, in pulpit and legislation, demand the observance of Sunday, of which there is nothing in their Bible."

Enright, C.S.S.R., in a lecture at Hartford, Kansas, Feb. 18,1884.

"I have repeatedly offered $1,000 to anyone who can prove to me from the Bible alone that I am bound to keep Sunday holy. There is no such law in the Bible. It is a law of the holy Catholic Church alone. The Bible says, 'Remember the Sabbath day to keep it holy.' The Catholic Church says: 'No. By my divine power I abolish the Sabbath day and command you to keep holy the first day of the week.' And lo! The entire civilized world bows down in a reverent obedience to the command of the holy Catholic Church."

> **All scholars and religions agree** that the Sabbath of the Old and New Testaments was the seventh-day of the week [Friday sunset to Saturday sunset] and not the first day [Sunday].

Here are some more quotes.

"Down even to the fifth century the observance of the Jewish [God's Biblical Sabbath] Sabbath was continued in the Christian church." **Ancient Christianity Exemplified**, Lyman Coleman, Ch.26, sec. 2, p.527.

"**Our Saturday.** The custom to call the Lord's day Sabbath did not commence until a thousand years later." Adamnan's *Life of Columba* p.230, Dublin, 1857

"According to the Assyrian-Babylonian conception, the particular stress lay necessarily on the number seven...The whole week pointed prominently towards the seventh day, the feast day, the rest day, in this day it collected, in this day it also consumated. 'Sabbath' is dervied from both 'rest' and 'seven'. With the Egyptians it was the reverse...for them on the contrary the sun-god was the beginning and origin of all things. The day of the sun, Sunday, became necessarily for them the feast day...The holiday was transferred from the last to the first day of the week." *Daglige Liv i Norden*, Vol.XIII, pp.54,55.

"The seven planetary names of the days were at the close of the second century A.D., prevailing everywhere in the Roman Empire...This astrology originated in Egypt, where Alexandria now so loudly proclaimed it to all... 'The day of the sun' was the Lord's day, the chiefest and first of the week. The evil and fatal Saturn's day was the last of the week on which none could celebrate a feast.. *Daglige Liv i Norden*, Vol.XIII, pp.91,92

"This Sunday law constituted no real favoratism to Christianity..... It is evident from all his statuatory provisions that the Emperor during the time 313-323 with full consciousness has sought the realisation of his religeous aim: the amalgamation of heathenism and Christianity." -Dr. **A.Chr. Bang - Kirken og Romerstaten** (The Church and the Roman State) p.256. Christiania, 1879

Enright, C.S.S.R., in a lecture at Hartford, Kansas, Feb. 18, 1884. "I have repeatedly offered $1,000 to anyone who can prove to me from the Bible alone that I am bound to keep Sunday holy. There is no such law in the Bible. It is a law of the holy Catholic Church alone. The Bible says, 'Remember the Sabbath day to keep it holy.' **The Catholic Church says: 'No. By my divine power I abolish the Sabbath day and command you to keep holy the first day of the week.'** And lo! The entire civilized world bows down in a reverent obedience to the command of the holy Catholic Church."

"The seventh-day Sabbath was...solmenised by Christ, and primitive Christians, till the Laodicean Council did in a manner quite abolish the observations of it." - **Dissertation on the Lord's Day** pp. 33, 34, 44

"Because the Third Commandment (which is really the fourth commandment but Catholicism does away with the second commandment so they do not have to acknowledge their idolatry which to them makes the Sabbath the third~kh) depends upon the remembrance of God's saving works and because Christians saw the definitive time inaugurated by Christ as a new beginning, they made the first day **after** the Sabbath a festive day, for that was the day on which the Lord rose from the dead."- **Pope John Paul II-DIES DOMINI-Dies Hominis v.18, May 31, 1998**

Augsburg Confession of Faith art. 28; written by Melanchthon, approved by Martin Luther, 1530; as published in The Book of Concord of the Evangelical Lutheran Church "They [Roman Catholics] refer to the Sabbath Day, as having been changed into the Lord's Day, contrary to the Decalogue, as it seems. Neither is there any example whereof they make more than concerning the changing of the Sabbath Day. Great, say they, is the power of the Church, since it has dispensed with one of the Ten Commandments!"

"The distinction of Sunday from the Jewish Sabbath grew ever stronger in the mind of the Church, even though there have been times in history when, because the obligation of Sunday rest was so emphasized, the Lord's Day tended to become more like the Sabbath. Moreover, there have always been groups within Christianity which observe both the Sabbath and Sunday as "two brother days"."-(v.23)**Pope John Paul II-DIES DOMINI-Dies Hominis, May 31, 1998**

"The ancient Christians were very careful in the observation of Saturday, or the seventh-day...It is plain that the Oriental churches, and the greatest part of the world, observed the Sabbath as a festival...Anthanasius likewise tells us that they held religious assemblies on the Sabbath, **not because they were infected with Judaism, but to worship Jesus, the Lord of the Sabbath**, Epiphanius says the same." - **Antiquities of the Christian Church**, Vol II, Book XX

"'And on the seventh day God rested from the work he had done. ... He blessed the seventh day and hallowed it'. The 'shabbat', the biblical sabbath is tied to this mystery of God's rest. If we Christians celebrate the Lord's day on Sunday, it is because on that day the Resurrection of Christ occurred." **Pope John Paul II**-July 12 1998

Stephen Keenan- A Doctrinal Catechism Third Edition "Question: Have you any other way of proving that the Church has power to institute festivals of precept? "Answer: Had she not such power, she could not have done that in which all modern religionists agree with her-she could not have substituted the observance of Sunday, the first day of the week, for the observance of Saturday, the seventh day, **a change for which there is no Scriptural authority.**"

Daniel Ferres- ed., Manual of Christian Doctrine (1916) "Question: How prove you that the Church hath power to command feasts and holy days? "Answer. By the very act of changing the Sabbath into Sunday, which Protestants allow of, and therefore they fondly contradict themselves, by keeping Sunday strictly, and breaking most other feasts commanded by the same Church.'

The Catholic Press said, "Sunday is a Catholic institution, and its claims to observation can be defended only on Catholic principles . . . From beginning to end of Scripture there is not a single passage that warrants the transfer of week public worship from the last day of the week to the first."- CATHOLIC PRESS, (Sydney, Australia), Aug. 25, 1900.

James Cardinal Gibbons, Archbishop of Baltimore (1877-1921), in a signed letter. "Is Saturday the seventh day according to the Bible and the Ten Commandments? I answer yes. Is Sunday the first day of the week and did the Church change the seventh day - Saturday- for Sunday, the first day? I answer yes. **Did Christ change the day'? I answer no!**" Faithfully yours, J. Card. Gibbons"

"The Catholic Church, . . . by virtue of her divine mission, changed the day from Saturday to Sunday."- The Catholic Mirror, official publication of James Cardinal Gibbons, Sept. 23, 1893.

Catholic Virginian Oct. 3, 1947- "To Tell You the Truth." "For example, nowhere in the Bible do we find that Christ or the Apostles ordered that the Sabbath be changed from Saturday to Sunday. We have the commandment of God given to Moses to keep holy the Sabbath day, that is the 7th day of the week, Saturday. Today most Christians keep Sunday because it has been revealed to us by the [Roman Catholic] church outside the Bible."

"Wise pastoral intuition suggested to the Church the christianization of the notion of Sunday as "the day of the sun", which was the Roman name for the day and which is retained in some modern languages.(29) This was in order to draw the faithful away from the seduction of cults which worshipped the sun, and to direct the celebration of the day to Christ, humanity's true "sun "-**Pope John Paul II**-DIES DOMINI-Dies Hominis, May 31, 1998

"They despise our sun-god, Did not Zoroaster, the sainted founder of our divine beliefs, institute Sunday one thousand years ago in honour of the sun and supplant the Sabbath of the Old Testament. <u>Yet these Christians have divine services on Saturday.</u> - O'Leary, The Syriac Church and Fathers, pp 83,84

Protestant theologians and preachers from a wide spectrum of denominations have been quite candid in admitting that there is no Biblical authority for observing Sunday as a sabbath.

Protestant Admissions

Canon Eyton,- *The Ten Commandments* "There is no word, no hint, in the New Testament about abstaining from work on Sunday .... into the rest of Sunday no divine law enters .... The observance of Ash Wednesday or Lent stands exactly on the same footing as the observance of Sunday."

Episcopal - 'The Bible commandment says on the seventh day thou shalt rest. That is Saturday. Nowhere in the Bible is it laid down that worship should be done on Sunday." Philip Carrington, *Toronto Daily Star*, October 26, 1949.

Baptist - Harold Lindsell, former editor of Christianity , said, **'There is nothing in Scripture that requires us to keep Sunday rather than Saturday as a holy day."** *Christianity Today*, November 5, 1976.

Baptist Dr. Edward T. Hiscox,-a paper read before a New York ministers' conference, Nov. 13, 1893, reported in *New York Examiner*, Nov. 16, 1893. "<u>There was and is a commandment to keep holy the Sabbath day, but that Sabbath day was not Sunday.</u> It will be said, however, and with some show of triumph, that the Sabbath was transferred from the seventh to the first day of the week .... Where can the record of such a transaction be found? Not in the New Testament absolutely not. ...."**To me it seems unaccountable that Jesus, during three years' intercourse with His disciples, often conversing with them upon the Sabbath question . . . never alluded to any transference of the day;**

also, that during forty days of His resurrection life, no such thing was intimated........ "Of course, I quite well know that Sunday did come into use in early Christian history . . . . But what a pity it comes branded with **the mark of paganism**, and **christened with the name of the sun god, adopted and sanctioned by the papal apostasy,** and bequeathed as a sacred legacy to Protestantism!"

William Owen Carver- *The Lord's Day in Our Day* "There was never any formal or **authoritative** change from the Jewish seventh-day Sabbath to the Christian first-day observance."

Dr. R. W. Dale (Congregationalist)- *The Ten Commandments* " . . . it is quite clear that however rigidly or devotedly we may spend Sunday, we are not keeping the Sabbath - - . . . the Sabbath was founded on a specific Divine command. We can plead no such command for the obligation to observe Sunday .... There is not a single sentence in the New Testament to suggest that we incur any penalty by violating the supposed sanctity of Sunday."

Congregationalist Timothy Dwight- *Theology: Explained and Defended* (1823)- " . . . the Christian Sabbath [Sunday] is not in the Scriptures, and was not by the primitive Church called the Sabbath."

First Day Observance, pp. 17, 19. "The first day of the week is commonly called the Sabbath. **This is a mistake.** The Sabbath of the Bible was the day just preceding the first day of the week. **The first day of the week is never called the Sabbath anywhere in the entire Scriptures. It is also an error to talk about the change of the Sabbath from Saturday to Sunday. There is not in any place in the Bible any intimation of such a change.**"

"*The Sunday Problem*"- United Lutheran Church (1923), "We have seen how gradually the impression of the Jewish sabbath faded from the mind of the Christian Church, and how completely the newer thought underlying the observance of the first day took possession of the church. We have seen that the Christians of the first three centuries never confused one with the other, but for a time celebrated both."

Lutheran- Dr. Augustus Neander, *The History of the Christian Religion and Church* (1843) "The festival of Sunday, like all other festivals, was always only a human ordinance, and it was far from the intentions of the apostles to establish a Divine command in this respect, far from them, and from the early apostolic Church, to transfer the laws of the Sabbath to Sunday."

John Theodore Mueller (a Lutheran) - *Sabbath or Sunday*- "But they err in teaching that Sunday has taken the place of the Old Testament Sabbath and therefore must be kept as the seventh day had to be kept by the children of Israel .... These churches err in their teaching, for Scripture has in no way ordained the first day of the week in place of the Sabbath. There is simply no law in the New Testament to that effect."

"Take the matter of Sunday. There are indications in the New Testament as to how the church came to keep the first day of the week as its day of worship, but there is no passage telling Christians to keep that day, or to transfer the Jewish Sabbath to that day." Methodist- Harris Franklin Rall, *Christian Advocate*, July 2, 1942

Methodist, Clovis G. Chappell- *Ten Rules For Living*- 'The reason we observe the first day instead of the seventh is based on no positive command. **One will search the Scriptures in vain for authority for changing from the seventh day to the first.**"

John Wesley- *The Works of the Rev. John Wesley* "But, the moral law contained in the ten commandments, and enforced by the prophets, he [Christ] did not take away. It was not the design of his coming to revoke any part of this. This is a law which never can be broken... Every part of this law must remain in force **upon all mankind, and in all ages**; as not depending either on time or place, or any other circumstances liable to change, but on the nature of God and the nature of man, and their unchangeable relation to each other." (Wesley was a Methodist)

"The Sabbath instituted in the beginning and confirmed again and again by Moses and the Prophets, *has never been abrogated*. A part of the moral law, not a part or tittle of its sanctity has been taken away."- New York Herald 1874, on the Methodist Episcopal Bishops Pastoral 1874.

Another Methodist, Dwight L. Moody- *Weighed and Wanting*, The Sabbath was binding in Eden, and it has been in force ever since. This fourth commandment begins with the word 'remember,' showing that the Sabbath already existed when God Wrote the law on the tables of stone at Sinai. **How can men claim that this one commandment has been done away with when they will admit that the other nine are still binding?"**

Anglican/Episcopal Admissions

Isaac Williams- PLAIN SERMONS ON THE CATECHISM, vol. 1, pp.334, 336.

"And where are we told in the Scriptures that we are to keep the first day at all? We are commanded to keep the seventh; but we are nowhere commanded to keep the first day .... The reason why we keep the first day of the week holy instead of the seventh is for the same reason that we observe many other things, not because the Bible, but because the church has enjoined it."

Canon Eyton, THE TEN COMMANDMENTS, pp. 52, 63, 65.

"There is no word, no hint, in the New Testament about abstaining from work on Sunday .... into the rest of Sunday no divine law enters.... The observance of Ash Wednesday or Lent stands exactly on the same footing as the observance of Sunday."

Bishop Seymour, WHY WE KEEP SUNDAY

We have made the change from the seventh day to the first day, from Saturday to Sunday, on the authority of the one holy Catholic Church."

Baptist

Dr. Edward T. Hiscox, a paper read before a New York ministers' conference, Nov. 13, 1893, reported in NEW YORK EXAMINER, Nov.16, 1893.

"There was and is a commandment to keep holy the Sabbath day, but that Sabbath day was not Sunday. It will be said, however, and with some show of triumph, that the Sabbath was transferred from the seventh to the first day of the week .... Where can the record of such a transaction be found? Not in the New Testament absolutely not.

"To me it seems unaccountable that Jesus, during three years' intercourse with His disciples, often conversing with them upon the Sabbath question ... never alluded to any transference of the day; also, that during forty days of His resurrection life, no such thing was intimated.

"Of course, I quite well know that Sunday did come into use in early Christian history .... But what a pity it comes branded with the mark of paganism, and christened with the name of the sun god, adopted and sanctioned by the papal apostasy, and bequeathed as a sacred legacy to Protestantism!"

William Owen Carver, THE LORD'S DAY IN OUR DAY , p. 49.

"There was never any formal or authoritative change from the Jewish seventh-day Sabbath to the Christian first-day observance."

Congregationalist

Dr. R. W. Dale, THE TEN COMMANDMENTS (New York: Eaton &Mains), p. 127-129.

" . . . it is quite clear that however rigidly or devotedly we may spend Sunday, we are not keeping the Sabbath - . . 'Me Sabbath was founded on a specific Divine command. We can plead no such command for the obligation to observe Sunday .... There is not a single sentence in the New Testament to suggest that we incur any penalty by violating the supposed sanctity of Sunday."

Timothy Dwight, THEOLOGY: EXPLAINED AND DEFENDED (1823), Ser. 107, vol. 3, p. 258.

" . . . the Christian Sabbath [Sunday] is not in the Scriptures, and was not by the primitive Church called the Sabbath."

Disciples of Christ

Alexander Campbell, THE CHRISTIAN BAPTIST, Feb. 2, 1824,vol. 1. no. 7, p. 164.

"'But,' say some, 'it was changed from the seventh to the first day.' Where? when? and by whom? No man can tell. No; it never was changed, nor could it be, unless creation was to be gone through again: for the reason assigned must be changed before the observance, or respect to the reason, can be changed! It is all old wives' fables to talk of the change of the Sabbath from the seventh to the first day. If it be changed, it was that august personage changed it who changes times and laws EX OFFICIO - I think his name is Doctor Antichrist.'

FIRST DAY OBSERVANCE , pp. 17, 19.

"The first day of the week is commonly called the Sabbath. This is a mistake. The Sabbath of the Bible was the day just preceding the first day of the week. The first day of the week is never called the Sabbath anywhere in the entire Scriptures. It is also an error to talk about the change of the Sabbath from Saturday to Sunday. There is not in any place in the Bible any intimation of such a change."

Lutheran

THE SUNDAY PROBLEM , a study book of the United Lutheran Church (1923), p. 36.

"We have seen how gradually the impression of the Jewish sabbath faded from the mind of the Christian Church, and how completely the newer thought underlying the observance of the first day took possession of the church. We have seen that the Christians of the first three centuries never confused one with the other, but for a time celebrated both."

AUGSBURG CONFESSION OF FAITH art. 28; written by Melanchthon, approved by Martin Luther, 1530; as published in THE BOOK OF CONCORD OF THE EVANGELICAL LUTHERAN CHURCH Henry Jacobs, ed. (1 91 1), p. 63.

"They [Roman Catholics] refer to the Sabbath Day, a shaving been changed into the Lord's Day, contrary to the Decalogue, as it seems. Neither is there any example whereof they make more than concerning the changing of the Sabbath Day. Great, say they, is the power of the Church, since it has dispensed with one of the Ten Commandments!"

Dr. Augustus Neander, THE HISTORY OF THE CHRISTIAN RELIGION AND CHURCH Henry John Rose, tr. (1843), p. 186.

"The festival of Sunday, like all other festivals, was always only a human ordinance, and it was far from the intentions of the apostles to establish a Divine command in this respect, far from them, and from the early apostolic Church, to transfer the laws of the Sabbath to Sunday."

John Theodore Mueller, SABBATH OR SUNDAY , pp. 15, 16.

"But they err in teaching that Sunday has taken the place of the Old Testament Sabbath and therefore must be kept as the seventh day had to be kept by the children of Israel .... These churches err in their teaching, for Scripture has in no way ordained the first day of the week in place of the Sabbath. There is simply no law in the New Testament to that effect."

Methodist

Harris Franklin Rall, CHRISTIAN ADVOCATE, July 2, 1942, p.26.

"Take the matter of Sunday. There are indications in the New Testament as to how the church came to keep the first day of the week as its day of worship, but there is no passage telling Christians to keep that day, or to transfer the Jewish Sabbath to that day."

John Wesley, THE WORKS OF THE REV. JOHN WESLEY, A.M., John Emory, ed. (New York: Eaton & Mains), Sermon 25, vol. 1, p. 221.

"But, the moral law contained in the ten commandments, and enforced by the prophets, he [Christ] did not take away. It was not the design of his coming to revoke any part of this. This is a law which never can be broken .... Every part of this law must remain in force upon all mankind, and in all ages; as not depending either on time or place, or any other circumstances liable to change, but on the nature of God and the nature of man, and their unchangeable relation to each other."

Dwight L. Moody

L. Moody, WEIGHED AND WANTING (Fleming H. Revell Co.: New York), pp. 47, 48.

The Sabbath was binding in Eden, and it has been in force ever since. This fourth commandment begins with the word 'remember,' showing that the Sabbath already existed when God Wrote the law on the tables of stone at Sinai. How can men claim that this one commandment has been done away with when they will admit that the other nine are still binding?"

Presbyterian

C. Blake, D.D., Theology Condensed, pp.474, 475.

"The Sabbath is a part of the decalogue - the Ten Commandments. This alone forever settles the question as to the perpetuity of the institution .... Until, therefore, it can be shown that the whole moral law has been repealed, the Sabbath will stand .... The teaching of Christ confirms the perpetuity of the Sabbath."

Episcopalian- Bishop Seymour, -Why We Keep Sunday. "We have made the change from the seventh day to the first day, from Saturday to Sunday, on the authority of the one holy Catholic Church."

Alexander Campbell,- The Christian Baptist, Feb. 2, 1824, "'But,' say some, 'it was changed from the seventh to the first day.' Where? when? and by whom? No man can tell. No; it never was changed, nor could it be, unless creation was to be gone through again: for the reason assigned must be changed before the observance, or respect to the reason, can be changed! It is all old wives' fables to talk of the change of the Sabbath from the seventh to the first day. <u>If it be changed, it was that august personage changed it who changes times and laws ex officio</u> - I think his name is Doctor Antichrist.'

"Examining the New Testament from cover to cover, critically, we find the sabbath referred to sixty-one times. We find too, that the Saviour invariably selected the Sabbath (Saturday) to teach in the synagogues and work miracles. The four Gospels refer to the Sabbath fifty-one times. In one instance , the Redeemer refers to Himself as 'Lord of the Sabbath' as mentioned by Matthew and Luke, but, during the whole record of His life, while invaribly keeping and utilizing the day, (Saturday), *He never once hinted at a desire to change it.* "- *The Catholic Mirror* Nov. 25 1893. J. Cardinal Gibbons.

"...with the Bible alone as the teacher and guide in faith and morals. This teacher *most emphatically forbids any changes in the day for paramount reasons.* The command calls for a '*perpetual covenant*'. The day commanded to be kept by the teacher (The Bible) *has never once been kept* (by the Protestant or Catholic churches), thereby developing an apostasy from an asumedly fixed principle, as self-contradictory, self-stultisfying, and consequently as suicidal as it is within the power of language to express." - *The Catholic Mirror* Nov. 25, 1893, Cardinal Gibbons

"The Sabbath is a part of the decalogue - the Ten Commandments. This alone forever settles the question as to the perpetuity of the institution . . . .

Until, therefore, it can be shown that the whole moral law has been repealed, the Sabbath will stand . . . . The teaching of Christ confirms the perpetuity of the Sabbath." Presbyterian T. C. Blake, D.D., - Theology Condensed.

All of these folks and organizations have decided to do as they please in clear defiance of the Word of God, which begs the question asked of the

Sanhedrin by Peter: **Acts 4:19** But Peter and John answered and said unto them, **Whether it be right in the sight of God to hearken unto you more than unto God, judge ye.**

The Biblical Calendar

The Biblical Calendar Explained

In the beginning God established a method of calculating time and identifying seasons by using the sun and moon. God said that men should use the setting sun to end the previous day and begin a new day; while the moon was intended to establish months and the sun was intended to establish years even before God created mankind.

God said: **Genesis 1:14** Let there **be lights** in the firmament of the heaven to divide the day from the night; and let them **[the light of the sun and moon]** be for signs, and for seasons, and for days, and for years. Thus God set in motion the means of dividing and measuring time.

This is very clear and it was understood by all people including later by Israel that God intended that the LIGHT of these bodies be used to establish days, months and years. God clearly commanded that we use the LIGHT and not the darkness of conjunctions to be used to begin the months. **1:15** And let them be for lights in the firmament of the heaven to give light upon the earth: and it was so.

We know that the sun and moon already existed since God caused the light to shine on the surface of the earth - by removing the heavy fog and setting the bodies in motion - on the first day, therefore we know that the following refers to setting the bodies in motion and is not a reference to original creation.

1:16 And God made [Strong's 6213 to make, to attend to, to put in order] two great lights; the greater light **[the sun]** to rule **[dominate]** the day, and the lesser light [the moon] to rule [dominate] the night: he made the stars [previously made the stars and now caused them to shine on the earth by removing the fog] also. **1:17** And God set them in the firmament of the heaven [caused them to be seen over all the earth by beginning the full rotation of the earth] to give light upon the earth, **1:18** And to rule over the day and over the night, and to divide the light from the darkness: and God saw that it was good. **1:19** And the evening and the morning were **the fourth day**.

Dictionaries define the word CALENDAR as; A means of measuring the passing of time by Days, Weeks, Months and Years.

God set in motion a simple astronomical calendar for all people. It was not necessary to have clocks or watches or to rely on others to determine Days, Weeks, Months and Years; one need only look and see the sun set to know that the day had ended and a new day had begun. In the same way one need only see that there was no moonlight for a day or two and then see the first new light of the moon to set the end of the old month and begin the new month.

Days

God first defined days by concluding each creation day with the phrase **Genesis 1:5** . . . And the evening and the morning were the first day. **Genesis 1:8** . . . And the evening and the morning were the second day etc. etc.

In support of this fact; the terms sunset and evening or end of the day are used synonymously in Joshua.

Joshua 8:29 And the king of Ai he hanged on a **tree until eventide: and as soon as the sun was down**, Joshua commanded that they should take his carcase down from the tree,

Joshua 10:26 And afterward Joshua smote them, and slew them, and hanged them on five trees: and they were hanging upon the trees **until the evening. 10:27** And it came to pass at the time of **the going down of the sun**, that Joshua commanded,

Weeks

Every Seventh Day was Set Apart by God for godly use and the continual cycle of sevens created the week. This is covered in detail in the Sabbath Section.

Months

Originally everything that God had made was GOOD and there were 12 thirty day months in each solar year.

From creation the biblical years were a consistent 12 thirty day months making each year 360 days long. The years during the Noachian flood and the various lives of the ancients, as well as all bible prophecy are measured in consistent 360 day years.

In the same way David and Saul [and everyone else] knew when the new moon would begin because the months were always a consistent 30 days long followed by the first visible light of a new moon.

The Biblical New Moon is NOT the same as today's astronomical new moon which is considered by astronomers to be the conjunction when there is no moonlight at all.

Conjunctions [molads] cannot be the beginning of the first light of the moon since they have NO light whatsoever; Biblically the month begins with the first visible LIGHT of the moon..

Early civilizations around the world used calendars with months of 30 days and years of 360 days. These calendars functioned well until sometime in the 8th century BC when it suddenly became necessary to change the calendars. Then civilizations around the world began to modify their calendars to allow for 5 extra days for the solar year and 6 fewer days for a lunar year of 12 full months; a modern lunar year is 354 days (12 months x 29.5 days).

The number of days in a year change was marked by the second King of Rome, Numa Pompilius, and by his Jewish contemporary, King Hezekiah. Later other civilizations adopted the new 365 day year as well. This change happened about 700-750 B.C. and are thought by some to be linked with the shadow on the sundial going back 10 degrees in the days of Hezekiah around 700-750 BC.

The change in the number of days in a solar year and in the lunar month in about the 8th century B.C. necessitated the intercalation of a 13th month every so often to keep the lunar year in line with the seasons and the solar year.

This new more complicated calendric system began about the time of Hezekiah which after that would have been needed through the days of Jesus Christ and is still needed today.

About the time of Hezekiah the Sanhedrin began to set the new moons at Jerusalem and also set the new year from Jerusalem.

God Chooses Jerusalem

God gave Moses instructions that once they had entered the land they were to be careful not to sacrifice just anywhere they wanted, but were to come before God at the place of his tabernacle or later the temple, to sacrifice and worship.

Deuteronomy 12:5 But **unto the place which the Lord your God shall choose out of all your tribes to put his name there, even unto his habitation shall ye seek, and thither thou shalt come.**

Later God chose Jerusalem during the life of David, and Solomon built the Temple where the people were to go to seek God.

2 Chronicles 7:12 And the LORD appeared to Solomon by night, and said unto him, I have heard thy prayer, and **have chosen this place to myself** for an house of sacrifice.

7:13 If I shut up heaven that there be no rain, or if I command the locusts to devour the land, or if I send pestilence among my people; **7:14** If my people, which are called by my name, shall humble themselves, and pray, and seek my face, and turn from their wicked ways; then will I hear from heaven, and will forgive their sin, and will heal their land.

7:15 Now mine eyes shall be open, and mine ears attent unto the prayer that is made in this place. **7:16** For **now have I chosen and sanctified this house, that my name may be there for ever: and mine eyes and mine heart shall be there perpetually.**

Micah 4:2 And many nations shall come, and say, Come, and let us go up to the mountain of the Lord, and to the house of the God of Jacob; and **he will teach us of his ways, and we will walk in his paths: for the law shall go forth of Zion, and the word of the Lord from Jerusalem.**

God chose Jerusalem as the place to build his Holy Temple where he would dwell among his people.

In the very near future, Messiah the Christ is coming and the new Ezekiel Temple (Ezekiel 40 - 48) will be built.

The New Moon is the Head of the Month

The Head of the month is determined by the first visible light of the new moon, and is a New Beginning and a special time to remember the Headship of God over his Creation.

We are to observe the first light of the new moon at Jerusalem to remember that the Creator is the true HEAD of the Ekklesia, remembering that it is the spiritual LIGHT of God which drives away the darkness of ignorance.

The Moon being newly visible, pictures a New Beginning of LIGHT and a monthly REMINDER to dedicate ourselves to godliness, to particularly repent of sin; and to acknowledge the Authority of God as our Sovereign King and HEAD.

God in his wisdom has given us the weekly Sabbath to worship Him, and he has given us a monthly New Moon on which to worship Him, and he has given us His annual Festivals: All for our good, as a help to keep our hearts and minds always on Him and the Word of God which brings peace and life eternal!

Isaiah 66:23 And it shall come to pass, that **from one new moon to another, and from one sabbath to another, shall all flesh come to worship before me**, saith the LORD.

In the days of Hezekiah when a calendar change was needed because of the orbital changes of the sun and moon, they did not begin to go searching across the nation looking for a place to see the first visible light of the new moon, but set the new months by the light of the moon as seen from Jerusalem in the vicinity of the Temple; because the nation was to look to Jerusalem and the Temple for guidance.

In the same way they set the new year by the maturing barley in the immediate vicinity of Jerusalem, where it would be cut when the nation was to gathered at Jerusalem for the Passover and the Feast of Unleavened Bread.

Since after Hezekiah the moon's cycle has been and still is no more than 30 days, therefore no month can be longer than 30 days; the Sanhedrin would simply count 27 days from the previous month's sighting to begin looking for the next New Moon.

Because of the necessity to declare the New Moons as soon as possible after sunset, observers watched for the first visible light of the New Moon from the immediate vicinity of the Temple in Jerusalem. Those who thought they saw the moon's first light then rushed to give witness to a Special Calendar Committee of the Mosaic 70 [Sanhedrin] established for that purpose and when two or more credible witness were heard, the committee sanctified the new month and the news was sent out across the nation by signal fires.

They could of course easily calculate the first visible light of the New Moon, but potential issues like possible cloud cover or a short lag time between sunset and moonset made actual sightings essential.

Today the first visible light of the new moon as seen by normal eyesight unaided by optical magnification [binoculars or telescopes] from Jerusalem begins each Biblical Month.

A History of Today's Rabbinic Calendar

God's Biblical Calendar is very simple; When the sun sets the day ends and a new day begins; every seventh day is the Sabbath and after the Sabbath a new cycle of seven begins making the seven day week; each new month begins with the first visible light of the new moon as seen from Jerusalem and the new year begins at the same season that Israel left Egypt. This system was used for generations.

A Brief Historical Overview

In Babylon the Jews learned of the Babylonian Calendar system, and later when Alexander swept through Egypt and the Middle East and conquered Babylon he brought Greek culture and the logic of Aristotle with him.

Many of the Pharisees who remained in Babylon after the Nehemiah / Ezra return to Judea were deeply impressed with Greek logic and began to apply the logic of Aristotle in their interpretation of the scriptures; while many others - especially those who returned to Judea - held to a literal view of the scriptures.

Both of these groups are called Pharisees and for the sake of easy identification I will call one group the "Mosaic Pharisees" and the ones influenced by Greek logic the "Hellenic Pharisees."

The Hellenic Pharisees grew very influential across the known world and in Palestine until after endless feuding, the Mosaic Pharisees asked the Romans to intervene in their support, and Judea became a Roman province.

At that point we find the Sadducees [priests] and scribes and the Mosaic Pharisees in control in Jerusalem and Judea with many Hellenized Pharisees also living there.

Then when Jerusalem and the Temple were destroyed by Prince Titus of Rome in c 70 A.D. the Mosaic Pharisees, Sadducees and Scribes went into decline and the Hellenized Pharisees already controlling Judaism in Babylon and Alexandria began to slowly gain dominance.

The Hellenized Pharisees began to use the logic of Aristotle to change Judaism, just as in the West the Roman emperor Constantine and the church leaders began to use the logic of Aristotle to change professing Christianity from a zeal to live by every Word of God, into reliance on blindly following human leaders.

In both cases the issue was the same; whether we should live by every Word of God or live by the reasoning's of men and the traditions of men.

The Hellenic Pharisees changed much in Judaism just as the professing Christian leaders changed much in professing Christianity.

This is a fascinating study of how both professing Christianity and modern Rabbinic Judaism were changed from the scriptures, but the subject at hand is the Biblical Calendar.

The Development of Today's Rabbinic Calendar

After 536 B.C. Cyrus allowed some Jews to return to Judea but the majority stayed in Babylon and the Jews in Babylon were exposed to the Babylonian Calendar which did not yet have fixed intercalated months. At the same time those Jews who had returned to Judea continued to keep the Biblical Calendar of observing the moon and spring from Jerusalem under the leadership of Nehemiah and Ezra.

In 503 B.C. Darius I the Great (if not earlier) established a fixed system of intercalation which contained 7 leap years in a 19-year calendrical cycle. An extra month called "Addaru II" was added in the 3rd, 6th, 8th, 11th, 14th, 17th and 19th years of a 19-year calendrical cycle. This accounted for 7 leap years.

By doing this, the cycle came out even with the solar calendar year, and the first day of the month of Nisanu – New Year's Day in the calendar – was never far off from the Vernal Equinox (the first day of Spring), resulting in the civil calendar and the seasons never being out of step.

The Levitical priesthood in Jerusalem and Judea rejected Babylon's fixed intercalation and maintained the system of intercalation by observation of the ripening barley harvest at Jerusalem, but many Jews in Babylon began to consider adopting this fixed system of the Persians because of the distance from Judea.

In the fifth century B.C., the Greek astronomer Meton of Athens (Greek: Μέτων ὁ Ἀθηναῖος; *gen.*: Μέτωνος wiki) discovered that a period of very close to 19 years was nearly a common multiple of the 365 day solar year and the synodic (present 29.5 day lunar) month. He observed that a period of 19 years is almost exactly equal to 235 synodic months and, rounded to full days, counts 6,940 days. The difference between the two periods (of 19 years and 235 synodic months) is only two hours.

Considering a year to be $\frac{1}{19}$ of this 6,940-day cycle gives a year length of $365 + \frac{1}{4} + \frac{1}{76}$ days (the unrounded cycle is much more accurate), which is slightly more than 12 synodic months.

After it was discovered by the Greek mathematician, astronomer, and engineer Meton of Athens in **432 B.C.E.** who worked closely with another Greek astronomer, Euctemon, that 235 lunar months are almost identical to 19 solar years (the difference is only 2 hours); a lunisolar calendrical system of adding months to a lunar calendar to align it with the solar calendar based on this discovery was created by the Greeks and called the "Metonic Cycle".

Alexander became king of Macedon in 336 BC and proceeded to conquer Egypt, Palestine and Babylon; bringing with him Greek culture and spreading the Greek Metonic Cycle calendar throughout the conquered lands including Judea, while adopting and maintaining the Persian [Babylonian] added fixed intercalation system.

The Jews who had remained in Babylon and those in Alexandria as well as some who were in Judea became largely Hellenized, adapting much of Greek reasoning methods and slowly apostatized away from Moses; falsely claiming that they had a hidden secret law which was above the law of Moses and which gave them authority over the written Word of God to use their own reasoning's to do as they saw fit.

From that time on the Hellenized Jews struggled with the Mosaic Pharisees, Sadducees and scribes until the Mosaic Sadducees [priests] appealed to Rome in 66 B.C. asking Rome to enter the nation and support their control of Judea. The Mosaic Pharisees, Sadducees and scribes remained in control in Judea until the destruction of Jerusalem and the Temple in 70 A.D.

When the Mosaic Pharisees were destroyed in the first century rebellion and the Roman wars, the Hellenized Jews slowly began to dominate the religion and became the forefathers of the modern Rabbins.

In c 359 A.D. the Roman emperor Constantius 2 forbade the Sanhedrin calendar committee to meet regarding calendar matters and ordered the Jews to adopt a fixed calendar. In response the Hillel 2 Sanhedrin adopted the Babylonian Calendar with its fixed months and intercalated years, adding the Biblical Festivals to this non Biblical calendar.

Most Jews Rejected the Hillel II Calendar

In fact most Jews did not accept the calendar of Hillel II and there was intense disagreement among the Rabbins for hundreds of years.

Hillel 2 did not create the present Rabbinic Calendar, he only presented the then existing Babylonian Calendar with its fixed months and intercalated years to which he added the Biblical Festivals; this Calendar then went through eight hundred more years of further development.

It is impossible to apply modern Jewish calendric rules to Talmudic dates earlier than at least 500 A.D.), because the final arithmetic **rules for calculating dates in the modern Jewish calendar** were developed over time from the 7th or 8th centuries in Babylonia by the heads of the Jewish academies of learning, known as the Geonim and were not finalized until 1178 A.D.

Today's Rabbinic Calendar went largely unnoticed until it began to gradually develop in theory during the **Geonic** period [657 to 1034 A.D.].

The postponements and final details of the modern Rabbinic Calendar were added and the principles and rules of today's modern Rabbinic Calendar were fully codified by **Maimonides** in the *Mishneh Torah* in the 12th century [1178 A.D.].

Maimonides' also began setting the months based on Molads or the average time between the darkness of conjunctions in place of God's command to begin the months with the first visible light of the new moon; bringing today's Rabbinic Calendar into full apostasy from the Word of God as given to Moses and departing from Israel's historical first visible new moon light Calendar.

Today's modern Rabbinic Calendar did not exist at the time of Christ and gradually developed until finalized in 1178 A.D. Neither the Molads of darkness nor the biblically unlawful postponements existed until they were added by Maimonides and officially accepted by the Rabbins in 1178 A.D.

Deuteronomy 4:1 Now therefore **hearken, O Israel, unto the statutes and unto the judgments, which I teach you, for to do them,** that ye may live, and go in and possess the land which the Lord God of your fathers giveth you. **4:2 Ye shall not add unto the word which I command you, neither shall ye diminish ought from it, that ye may keep the commandments of the Lord your God which I command you.**

The postponements come from Hellenic reasoning and the logic of Aristotle in defiance of the scriptures.

The issue is not calculation, the issue is about the basis of the calculation; God's first visible light, or man's darkness of conjunctions.

Instead, based on the evidence, it is now widely known that the arithmetic rules for calculating dates in the modern Jewish Calendar were not developed until at least the 7th to 8th centuries A.D. in Babylonia; While the Molads of darkness and unlawful postponement rules did not exist until finalized by Moses Maimonides in 1178 A.D.

Finally, in 1178 AD, Maimonides finalized in full, all of the rules for the modern unscriptural Jewish calendar.

> It is absolutely certain and beyond question that the Rabbinic Calendar in use today, IS NOT the calendar used by the Jews during the life of Jesus Christ, nor was it finally codified until over a thousand years later; and second, the Rabbinic Calendar has nothing to do with the Calendar that the Creator gave in the Holy Scriptures.

> The Bible tells us to begin and to end a day at sunset; and to count six days and to keep the seventh day as a Sabbath of rest. These are the only calendar instructions that the modern Hellenic Rabbins keep.

They reject the Biblical beginning of months with the first LIGHT of the moon Genesis 1:14, in favor of starting a month based on the average time between conjunctions [molads]; which is that period of darkness before the light of the sun begins to brighten the moon; and they reject adding intercalary years by the ripening of the harvest for their artificial insertion of regular intercalary months.

They then start their year in the fall, when God commands us to start our year in the spring, and they postpone the days God declares holy to other days for their own convenience. They also changed the dates of Pentecost and Passover from the biblically commanded dates.

The Rabbins have rejected God's Word for their own devising's. Is that what Moses and those who sit in Moses seat would do?

Anyone who departs from the words of Moses; does not represent Moses, or sit in Moses seat!

Should those who are called into the priesthood of Jesus Christ; reject God's Word to follow the teachings of men contrary to the Word of God? If they do so, it is pure and indefensible idolatry of men!

God commanded Moses to tell us that we are NOT to depart from God's Word, yet the Rabbinic Calendar is a departure from the Word of God; as the Rabbins themselves openly admit

Deuteronomy 5:30 Go say to them, Get you into your tents again.

5:31 But as for thee, stand thou here by me, and I will speak unto thee all the commandments, and the statutes, and the judgments, which thou shalt teach them, that they may do them in the land which I give them to possess it.

5:32 Ye shall observe to do therefore as the Lord your God hath commanded you: ye shall not turn aside to the right hand or to the left. **5:33** Ye shall walk in all the ways which the Lord your God hath commanded you, that ye may live, and that it may be well with you, and that ye may prolong your days in the land which ye shall possess.

These folks have decided to do as they please in clear defiance of the Word of God, which begs the question asked of the Sanhedrin by Peter: **Acts 4:19** But Peter and John answered and said unto them, **Whether it be right in the sight of God to hearken unto you more than unto God, judge ye.**

New Moons in Ancient Israel

1 Samuel 20:5 And David said to Jonathan, Behold, the **new moon** is tomorrow. And sitting I should certainly sit with the king to eat. And you shall send me away, and I shall be hidden in the field until the third evening.

1 Samuel 20:18 And Jonathan said to him, **Tomorrow is the new moon**, and you shall be expected, for your seat will be empty.

1 Samuel 20:24 And David was hidden in the field. And it was the **new moon.** And the king sat down by the food to eat.

We see here that David and the Israelites kept the observance of the New Moons as God had commanded.

Now let's look at the book of Kings where we will see a scripture that indicates that on the "New Moons" the people went to listen and speak with the spiritual leaders of the day, much like you would do on the Sabbath.

A woman that had been kind to Elisha by feeding him and building a room for him, was in distress because of her sons recent death. Because of this tragedy she went to find and seek help from Elisha.

Notice here what her husband says to her as she leaves…

2 Kings 4:23 And he said, Why are you going to him today; it is neither **new moon** nor Sabbath? And she said, Peace.

They would get together with the prophet of God, to learn from him **on the New Moons** just as they did on the Sabbath! It is clear to see that Israel was observing the New Moons!

Amos speaks of those sitting at the new moon gathering and wishing they were not there worshipping God; folks who would rather be going about their own ways than worshiping God on Sabbath and New Moons. This is the same as people sitting at Passover and wishing it was over so that they could do their own thing instead of obeying and worshiping God. – Amos 8:5

Solomon Kept God's New Moon Commands

2 Chronicles 8:12-13 Then Solomon offered burnt offerings to YHVH on the altar of Jehovah that he had built before the porch, **8:13** even as the matter of every day required, offering according to the commandment of Moses, on the Sabbaths, and **on the new moons,** and on the appointed feasts three times in the year, in the Feast of Unleavened Bread, and in the Feast of Weeks, and in the Feast of Booths.

God commanded Moses to order worship and sacrifices on the New Moons, much like in the Sabbaths and Holy Days!

From this we can also begin to see how much emphasis God puts on the **New Moons**…they are a very important thing to be observed!

1 Chronicles 23:27-32 For by the last words of David the Levites were numbered from a son of twenty years and above, **23:28** because their office was to wait on the sons of Aaron for the service of the house of YHVH, in the courts, and in the chambers, and in the purifying of all holy things, and the work of the service of God's house, **23:29** both for the Bread of Arrangement, and for the fine flour for food offering, and for the unleavened cakes, and for the pan, and for what is soaked in oil, and for every measure and size, **23:30** and to stand every morning to thank and praise YHVH, and likewise at evening.

23:31 And they were to offer all burnt sacrifices to YHVH in the Sabbath, in the **new moons**, and on the set feasts, by number, according to the order commanded to them, continually before the face of YHVH, **23:32** and that they should keep the charge of the tabernacle of the congregation, and the charge of the Holy Place, and the charge of Aaron's sons, their brothers, in the service of the house of YHVH.

This scripture says that David set the order of the Levites to serve and offer sacrifices to God on His Holy Days and Sabbaths and **NEW MOONS**!

Even Solomon when he was about to build the Temple said that the reason or the Temple was so that people could come and worship God in the appointed times, including the New Moons!!

2 Chronicles 2:4 behold, I am building a house to the name of YHVH my God, to dedicate to Him, to burn incense of sweet spices before Him, and for the continual Bread of Arrangement, and for burnt offerings morning and evening, on the Sabbath, and on the **new moons**, and at the set feasts of YHVH our God. **This shall be upon Israel forever**.

The New Moons are a commanded observance **forever** for all the people of God!

The King Hezekiah Restoration

2 Chronicles 31:3 And the king's portion from his substance was for burnt offerings, for burnt offerings of the morning and the evening; and the burnt offerings of the Sabbaths, and of the **new moons**, and of the appointed seasons, as it was written in the Law of YHVH.

And after Israel had gone astray, King Hezekiah restored the sacrifices in a great revival on the New Moons as Moses ordered Israel to do before God!

Originally there were 12 thirty day months in a solar year, this changed later and they had to begin to intercalate ta thirteenth month every few years o keep the months in line with the solar year and the first month in line with the spring lambing and the barley harvest.

Early civilizations around the world used calendars with months of 30 days and years of 360 days until sometime in the 8th century B.C., when suddenly it became necessary to change them. Then most civilizations around the world began to modify their calendars to allow for 5 extra days for the year and 6 fewer days for a lunar year of 12 full months; a modern lunar year is 354 days (12 months x 29.5 days).

The number of days in a year change was marked by the second King of Rome, Numa Pompilius, and by his Jewish contemporary, King Hezekiah. Later other civilizations adopted the new 365 day year as well. These events are often linked with the shadow on the sundial going back 10 degrees in the days of Hezekiah around 700-750 BC.

There was a change in the number of days in a solar year and in the lunar month as well, in about the 8th century B.C.; which then necessitated the intercalation of a 13th month every so often to keep the lunar year in line with the seasons and the solar year, about the time of Hezekiah which after that would have continued to be needed in the days of Jesus Christ and is still needed today.

After that time the Sanhedrin began to set the new moons at Jerusalem and also set the new year from Jerusalem by the lambing and the state of the barley harvest.

The Ezra Restoration

Ezra, when Judah came out of Captivity, made it a point to continue to offer God His sacrifices. And to keep the appointed worship times of God!

Ezra 3:2-5 Then Jeshua the son of Jozadak stood up, and his brothers the priests, and Zerubbabel the son of Shealtiel, and his brothers, and built the altar of the God of Israel in order to offer burnt offerings on it, as it is written in the Law of Moses the man of God. **3:3** And they set the altar on its bases, for fear was on them because of the people of those lands. And he offered burnt offerings on it to Jehovah, burnt offerings morning and evening. **3:4** They also performed the Feast of Booths, as it is written, and the burnt offerings by number, days by days, according to the ordinance, the thing of days in its day. **3:5** And afterward the continual burnt offering, both of the **new moons**, and of all the set feasts of Jehovah that were set apart, and of everyone who willingly offered a freewill offering to YHVH.

The Nehemiah Restoration

Nehemiah restored the service of God on the Holy Days and the **proper keeping of the Sabbath and the New Moons**, and tithing!

Nehemiah 10:31-33 And if the people of the land should bring **goods or any food to sell on the Sabbath**, we would **not take from them on the Sabbath, or on the holy day**. And they would forgo the seventh year, and the interest of every hand. **31:32** Also, we made stand on ourselves, to charge ourselves yearly with the third part of a shekel for the service of the house of our God, **31:33** for the Bread of Arrangement, and for the continual food offering, and for the continual burnt offering, of the Sabbaths, of the **new moons**, for the set feasts, and for the holy things, and for the sin offerings to make atonement for Israel, and all the work of the house of God.

These godly people were deeply concerned about keeping of the Law and restoring it back to what would please God... and this **included the keeping of the New Moons;**

Whenever there was a spiritual revival in Israel the observance of God's commanded new moon days was restored.

Without any doubt we are in need of a spiritual revival today: What is stopping us from doing the same?

When we pull away from God – God pulls away from us!

Our own worship, doing things our own way; made the people's worship a stench in God's nostrils. He considered it nothing more than mere lip service! Serving him according to the commandments of men; instead of doing what he had commanded.

Is this what is happening to us, his people today? Is the right worship of God lost today? Will He abhor our worship according to our own ways: or will he accept us as we seek to please him by doing what is right in His eyes??

Isaiah 1:12-14 At whose command do you come before me, making my house unclean with your feet? **12:13** Give me no more false offerings; the smoke of burning flesh is disgusting to me, so are **your new moons and Sabbaths and your holy meetings. 12:14** YOUR new moons and YOUR regular feasts are a grief to my soul: they are a weight in my spirit; I am crushed under them.

Hosea. 2:11 I will also cause all her **mirth to cease, her feast days, her new moons, and her Sabbaths, and all her solemn feasts**.

The people of God were worshiping God in **the** keeping of the New Moon as told to us by Paul in the New Testament, and by David, by Hezekiah, by Ezra, Nehemiah, Elisha, Ezekiel, Amos, Saul, Jonathan, and God trough Moses.

We can see that they did meet together and worshipped God learning of Him, they came to meet the religious authorities of the land, they broke bread together, they sacrificed, it seems clear that God is showing us that he expects us to keep His New Moons in acknowledgment of him as Creator and Moral Authority over man.

What are we to do??

It is very clear from scriptures that we need a great spiritual revival in the Ekklesia today; and that a part of that spiritual revival is the restoration of observing the New Moons as Appointed Times with Bible Study Worship Services!

When there is no physical Temple there can be no physical sacrifices, yet we can still acknowledge the sovereignty of Almighty God and dedicate ourselves to him, learning of God and His Word, on God's Commanded and Appointed New Moon days! And once the Eternal chose Jerusalem we are to establish the first light of the new moon from Jerusalem as well as establish the beginning of the new year from Jerusalem!

This has been made possible today with worldwide communications and as part of the preparation for the coming of Messiah the Christ, God is turning his people to once again look to Jerusalem the city of the King of kings!

The scripture is clear, God said to use the light and not the darkness of the moon to begin His months! Going by this instruction from God – we would have to conclude that the first sliver of light at Jerusalem would be the beginning of the new lunar month and that day would be the New Moon.

Another analogy to consider

Jesus Christ is the light of the world and He is represented as such, while Satan is darkness and he is represented as such. Would God use the LIGHT to determine the beginning of this special day or would he use darkness?

The scriptures do not give us the right to change the calendar of God. And God never, ever, told man to change what He has ordained!

The New Moon is not a Sabbath or a Holy Day.

If every New Moon Day is a Sabbath, why do we find God commanding labor upon the day, and labor being exacted upon the day?

And the LORD spake unto Moses, saying, On the first day of the first month shalt thou set up the tabernacle of the tent of the congregation. ... Thus did Moses: according to all that the LORD commanded him, so did he. And it came to pass in the first month in the second year, on the first day of the month, that the tabernacle was reared up. (Exodus 40:1,2,16,17 — read all of Exodus 40:1-33 to see how much labor was done this New Moon Day)

The New Moon is NOT a Sabbath unless it happens to fall on a Sabbath. The New Moon is NOT a Holy Day except for the first day of the Seventh Month.

The New Moon is merely the consecrating of the beginning of each month with Bible Studies [worship services] and during the temple period with special sacrifices by God's command.

New Moons are to be observed by family or local congregational Bible Studies, and they will be observed as days of worship [yet NOT Holy Days or Sabbaths just the consecration of the beginning of each month] in the Kingdom of God.

Observing the first visible light as seen from Jerusalem to begin ecclesiastical months is essential to a proper understanding of the Biblical Calendar; and the consecrating of months and Holy Days in the Biblical Calendar.

The importance of the New Moons lies in the fact that they are essential elements in determining ALL of the commanded Holy Days; except for the Sabbath. That is why God has set them apart for special recognition without calling them actual Holy Days.

They are the foundation of God's Calendar and they are the foundation for properly dating the actual commanded Holy Days! We should get in the habit now!

God calls His people to come to him and learn of him every seventh day on the weekly Sabbath, he also calls people to come before Him on the New Moons and on various Annual Festivals and Appointed Times.

God calls people to appear before him on the New Moons, on the head of every month; to acknowledge God as creator of all things and to sanctify the whole month and set it apart to godliness. We are to appear before God to acknowledge Him as our God, King, Head and Sovereign, and to rededicate ourselves to godliness!

The two silver trumpets were sounded in the temple over the special sacrifices offered by the high priest on behalf of the whole people; calling on God to remember His people and to accept the sacrifices offered on behalf of the whole people; as a type of calling on God the Father to accept the sacrifice of Jesus Christ the Lamb of God for all people in future.

The shofar are sounded in every city and town across the land in great rejoicing over the mercy of our mighty LORD in redeeming the people by giving his life for us.

Establishing the New Moon and New Year

1) God set the earth, sun and moon in motion and commanded that the light be used to establish days, months and years (Gen 1:14). Throughout history until the modern Rabbins decided to change God's Calendar away from the first visible light to the darkness of molads: The months for Israel ALWAYS began with the first visible light of the new moon until 1178 A.D.

2) If the light of the new moon is calculated to be visible, and it is observed; then the new month should be consecrated.

3) If the new moon's LIGHT is calculated to be visible and it is NOT seen at Jerusalem due to a lack of witnesses in that city, cloud cover or other adverse conditions; but it is seen in the land or within a short distance east of the land by at least two witnesses; it is evident that the moon could have been seen at Jerusalem based on the two local observation witnesses and calculation and the new month should be consecrated.

4) If the moon is calculated to be visible at the end of 29 days and it is NOT seen by witnesses [subject to statement #3] then it should NOT be consecrated, and should be delayed to the next day.

5) If the moon is calculated to be visible **at the end of 30 days** it should be consecrated regardless of whether it is seen or not; since the moon cycle is 29 1/2 days and no month may be longer than 30 days.

The New Year should be consecrated when enough barley in Jerusalem will be ready for the Wave Offering by the 14th day of the first month.

In rare years where there is no ripening barley do to great drought, the new moon CLOSEST to the spring equinox should begin the year, so as to prevent a year from being spread out over more than one complete proper year due to a lack of harvest.

To use the new moon BEFORE the equinox as a hard rule, could [in some years] start the month well before the harvest would be ready. To use the new moon AFTER the equinox as a hard rule could in some years result in the Festivals being delayed until they are out of season, for example putting the Fall Festivals in November.

The Weekly Sabbath begins when the sun sets locally. Persons living north or south of 55 degrees may observe the Sabbath from 18:00 hours [this is the average sunset time at Jerusalem], and all of the brethren in any such location should observe the Sabbath at the same time by common accord. When Christ comes he will decide on this matter.

Certain people have ridiculed the Biblical Calendar saying that there are numerous calendars out there.

That is true, however there is ONLY one Biblical Calendar which is true to Holy Scripture and true to the Calendar used during the history of Israel through the ministry of Jesus Christ and beyond: and the modern Rabbinic Calendar which they use is NOT it!

Today's modern apostate from Scripture Rabbinic Calendar was not finalized until 1178 A.D.

Since creation until Israel left Egypt the new year began in the autumn, Then in Egypt God commanded those called out of Egypt to begin their year in the spring.

This change of the beginning of the year was to separate Israel from the rest of the world as an allegory of a small early Spring Harvest of those called out of bondage to sin in our time, pictured by the Spring Festivals; and another main harvest of humanity in future pictured by the Fall

Festivals. Full details are provided in the Spring Festivals and Fall Festivals studies.

God set the new year in Egypt to begin with the Passover month in which Israel came out from Egypt. Since then the biblical new year begins with the same month [in the same season of the year] that God established in Egypt.

Later the command regarding the Wave Offering once they began to cultivate the promised land came into play, and gave us a firm starting point from that time on. The things necessary to establish the first month of the year are the birth of the spring lambs and the ripening of the barley harvest in the immediate vicinity of Jerusalem.

Originally there were 12 thirty day months in a solar year, this changed later and they had to begin to intercalate ta thirteenth month every few years o keep the months in line with the solar year and the first month in line with the spring lambing and the barley harvest.

Early civilizations around the world used calendars with months of 30 days and years of 360 days until sometime in the 8th century B.C., when suddenly it became necessary to change them. Then most civilizations around the world began to modify their calendars to allow for 5 extra days for the year and 6 fewer days for a lunar year of 12 full months; a modern lunar year is 354 days (12 months x 29.5 days).

The number of days in a year change was marked by the second King of Rome, Numa Pompilius, and by his Jewish contemporary, King Hezekiah. Later other civilizations adopted the new 365 day year as well. These events are often linked with the shadow on the sundial going back 10 degrees in the days of Hezekiah around 700-750 BC.

There was a change in the number of days in a solar year and in the lunar month as well, in about the 8th century B.C.; which then necessitated the intercalation of a 13th month every so often to keep the lunar year in line with the seasons and the solar year, about the time of Hezekiah which after that would have continued to be needed in the days of Jesus Christ and is still needed today.

After that time the Sanhedrin began to set the new moons at Jerusalem and also set the new year from Jerusalem by the lambing and the state of the barley harvest.

They did not go searching across the nation looking for maturing barley but set the new year by the barley in the immediate vicinity of Jerusalem, where it would be cut when the nation was already gathered at Jerusalem for the Passover and the Feast of Unleavened Bread.

Deuteronomy 16:16 Three times in a year **shall all thy males appear before the Lord thy God in the place which he shall choose**; in the feast of unleavened bread, and in the feast of weeks, and in the feast of tabernacles:

God commanded that when Israel entered the land and began to cultivate the land, that they should cut and bring the first sheaf of the spring barley harvest to present to God BEFORE they began the general harvest.

This was to be a sheaf of THEIR harvest, because of the meaning of this spring harvest; to be studied in the Spring Festivals study. It is for this reason that this first sheaf was required to be from the harvest cultivated by Israel, and not from the harvests of the Canaanites [which were symbolic of people not being faithful and submissive to God].

Today many search for "wild barley." This is a somewhat confusing misnomer as today's so called "wild barley" is descended from the ancient cultivated barley without the modern artificial genetic changes. It is quite right to seek out this ancient barley for biblical purposes today.

God commanded:

Leviticus 23:10 Speak unto the children of Israel, and say unto them, **When ye be come into the land which I give unto you,** and shall **reap the harvest thereof, then ye** [the nation] **shall bring a** [one] **sheaf of the firstfruits of your** [the collective national harvest] **harvest** unto the priest: **23:11** And he shall wave the sheaf before the LORD, to be accepted for you: **on the morrow after the sabbath** the priest shall wave it.

The term "ye shall" here does not mean that every individual should cut a sheaf to bring to the priest, but that ONE sheaf should be cut from the collective nation of Israel and brought to the priest; otherwise the priest would have to lift up thousands of sheaves and the symbology of one first sheaf beginning the whole harvest would be lost. This was always understood by the priests and in no case was there ever more than ONE sheaf lifted up to God.

The first sheaf represented the acceptance of the resurrected Lamb of God, by God the Father, as the first of the harvest of the early harvest of first fruits.

This was because there would be NO spiritual harvest and resurrection of men to spirit unless the First Sheaf, the Lamb of God was sacrificed for sin and was resurrected after a perfect sinless life - which took place at Jerusalem - and that Lamb of God was accepted by God the Father as the ONLY Mediator, Intercessor and spiritual High Priest forever; to effect reconciliation between sinners and God the Father in heaven.

Leviticus 23;11 And he shall wave the sheaf before the LORD, to be accepted for you: on the **morrow after the sabbath** the priest shall wave it.

History tells us that Joshua took seven years to conquer the land and it took another seven years to divide the land to all the families of Israel by lot and after that, when Israel began to cultivate the land, a First Sheaf of the harvest was cut on the day after the Sabbath on a Sunday and was then waved before the LORD on that same Sunday.

Israel did fall away many times, but when they kept the Word of God they always cut the Wave Sheaf at the very beginning of Sunday immediately after sunset ending the Sabbath and beginning Sunday, and then processed the grain overnight, lifting it up to the LOIRD after the morning Daily Sacrifice.

In the wilderness God commanded that when they entered the land they were to cut the first sheaf of the spring harvest and the Rabbins interpreted this in the Mishnah to mean that the Sheaf could be cut anywhere in Palestine: However once the Temple was built at Jerusalem this command for cutting the Wave Sheaf was qualified by God's command to appear before him at Jerusalem for the Festivals.

All able bodied persons were commanded to present themselves before God and to observe the Feasts in the place that God should choose and all being present at the place that God chose; the Wave Sheaf - which was cut during the Spring Feast - would be cut at that same place as well.

All Israel was to appear wherever the Tabernacle was, because God dwelt in the Tabernacle and the Tabernacle was movable.

Then in latter times the Ark was moved to Jerusalem by David when God revealed that God had chosen Jerusalem as the place of God's name or presence, and finally when Solomon completed the Temple and God placed His name in that Temple (2 Chron 12:16), the people were to come to that Temple to seek God during the Feasts of the LORD.

Once the Temple was built, God commanded every able bodied person to appear before him at the Temple for the Feast, and if the people obeyed God's command, they would all be at the Temple at Jerusalem during the Feast; and it is self-evident that the Wave Sheaf would have to be cut there, because all the people were already gathered there.

The point is that the Wave Sheaf was not cut many miles away but was cut in the immediate vicinity of the tabernacle and waved on the same day that it was cut. Later when the Ark was moved to the temple mount the ceremony and the cutting was also moved to Jerusalem, where God had chosen to dwell and to place his name. God has commanded that all Israel assemble before him at Jerusalem for Passover and the Unleavened Bread Feast. That is the LAW and it means that the sheaf must be cut at Jerusalem where all the people were gathered; and anyone not gathered at Jerusalem was not keeping the commandments, therefore it was unlawful to cut the Wave Sheaf anywhere else after God chose the Temple at Jerusalem.

Deuteronomy 16:16 Three times in a year **shall all thy males appear before the Lord thy God in the place which he shall choose; in the feast of unleavened bread,** and in the feast of weeks, and in the feast of tabernacles: and they shall not appear before the Lord empty:

Today God is again working to focus the whole world on Jerusalem from which Christ will rule all nations in the near future.

The Wave Sheaf must be cut at Jerusalem and therefore must be ripening at Jerusalem to begin the new year.

Since Jerusalem at 2,500 feet in elevation is the highest inhabited place in Judea, it is the last place for the barley to ripen, meaning that the whole barley harvest would be ripe and ready to be harvested when the barley is ripe at Jerusalem.

The whole nation is commanded to gather at Jerusalem from Passover through the following seven day Feast of Unleavened Bread and the Sheaf would have to be cut at Jerusalem, because that was where the people were already gathered before God.

Repeated for emphasis; The whole nation was to be present at Jerusalem for this seven Day Feast [plus an eighth day of Passover] and so the first sheaf would of necessity have to be cut at Jerusalem; and there was no need to give a specific command to cut the sheaf at Jerusalem because the people would all be gathered in that place already.

Deuteronomy 16:16 Three times in a year **shall all thy males appear before the Lord thy God in the place which he shall choose; in the feast of unleavened bread**, and in the feast of weeks, and in the feast of tabernacles: and they shall not appear before the Lord empty:

Deuteronomy 16:5 Thou mayest not sacrifice the passover within any of thy gates, which the Lord thy God giveth thee: 16:6 But at the place which the Lord thy God shall choose to place his name in,

When the barley was ripe at Jerusalem it would also be ripening across the whole land.

Various people and groups have been carrying out Aviv [ripening] barley searches for years. Overall they have all done an excellent job and are now well experienced in judging the maturing barley.

It is now time to take the Aviv search to the next level and stop searching for the minimum amount necessary to produce one sheaf for the Wave Offering while neglecting the state of the actual harvest.

We need to realize that the Wave Sheaf is meant to be the first sheaf of a much larger harvest, and finding enough anomalous barley for one sheaf in some area of Judea while the main harvest is still a month away is not acceptable.

We can waste much time, money and effort, traveling across the land to get a general impression of the readiness of the whole harvest, or we can simply follow the only correct way and accept God's command that we are to go up to Jerusalem to keep Passover and the Feast of Unleavened Bread; and assess the ripening barley in the immediate vicinity of Jerusalem where it would have to be cut since all the people would be at that location [and where it was invariably cut during the Temple period].

We also need to keep God's commandment regarding the Wave Offering concerning the barley, without any extraneous matters like bird migrations or ripening figs [NOTE: The incident of Jesus and the fig tree was where? It was in Jerusalem! Not Beer Sheva etc!] and where did God command that we use this incident to set the new year?

We know that from at least the days of Ezra, the priests were given a plot of land just outside the temple walls a few hundred yards away across the brook Kedron in the Ashes valley. It was in the sheltered Ashes Valley that the priests cultivated a plot of land for the purpose of cutting a Wave Sheaf for the First Sheaf Offering on the first Sunday during the Feast of Unleavened Bread.

From God's revival leader Ezra to the destruction of the temple in c 70 A.D. and throughout the physical life of Jesus Christ; the New Year was always set by the ripening barley in the Ashes valley just across the Kidron from the temple walls! and Jesus Christ never questioned this or taught anything contrary, indeed he confirmed this method of setting the New Year by accepting it and observing the Festivals by this method throughout his physical life!

Brethren, what was good for Jesus Christ is good for us! He set an example that we should follow!

We are to begin the New Year when the lambs are born and the barley is ready to ripen in the immediate vicinity of the Temple in Jerusalem, regardless of the condition of the harvest in Beer Sheva or Sderot or anywhere else; just like Jesus Christ did!

We are not to set the New Year by the state of the barley in Sderot or Nazareth or anywhere other than Jerusalem; for God has placed his name [temple, headquarters] at Jerusalem!

To emphasize this I want to show how the Wave Offering was actually conducted and demonstrate its meaning, which is lost when one uses a harvest from any area except Jerusalem.

Each Passover the priests would go to the Ashes Valley plot a few hundred yards from the temple and bind out a sheaf with cords, and in 31 A.D. they bound a sheaf just as Messiah was dying on the stake. Then late on the Sabbath after Passover they would go to the Ashes valley plot and prepare to cut the sheaf.

In 31 A.D. the First Sheaf was cut from the earth at the beginning of Sunday just after the Sabbath had ended and at the same time that Jesus Christ was resurrected and changed from flesh back to spirit.

Then Jesus WAITED through until the Wave Offering was lifted up to be accepted by God the Father, before he also ascended up to be accepted by God the Father. This symbolism was perfect being designed by the

Creator himself! but the symbolism would be broken if the sheaf were cut at some distant location and sent to the temple.

The Wave Sheaf MUST be cut very close to the location where it is to be offered, for the symbolism to be properly fulfilled! and since the New Year is set when the barley will be ripe enough to be cut; the New Year is to be set from Jerusalem.

Micah 4:2 And many nations shall come, and say, **Come, and let us go up to the mountain of the Lord, and to the house of the God of Jacob; and he will teach us of his ways, and we will walk in his paths: for the law shall go forth of Zion, and the word of the** Lord **from Jerusalem**.

The Ashes Valley is at the highest elevation of cultivated land in Israel, and due to that circumstance the barley there is the last to ripen. This means that when the barley is cut in the Ashes Valley by the priests, the barley harvest in all other areas will also be ripe and ready for harvest and that the national barley harvest can begin.

On the other hand if one finds a few fields of ripening barley and cuts the First Sheaf from an isolated ripening field the national barley will not be at the ready for harvest after the Wave Sheaf is cut.

There was a restriction that the sheaf be cut and offered at the place where God's tabernacle and later Temple was, simply because all the people were commanded to be there. During the tabernacle period there was no restriction on where the tabernacle was set up, the ark could be moved to any place in the land and in fact was set up at Shiloh and later at Jerusalem.

Once the Temple was built, since it was not movable and God had placed his presence there; Jerusalem became a permanent place for the cutting and offering of the Wave Offering as well as making all other offerings.

2 Chronicles 7:12 And the Lord appeared to Solomon by night, and said unto him, **I have heard thy prayer, and have chosen this place to myself for an house of sacrifice.**

The Wave Offering is included in the sacrifices as a commanded offering during the Feast of Unleavened Bread which Feast was to be observed for seven days in the presence of God which in the temple period was AT JERUSALEM.

Deuteronomy 16:16 Three times in a year **shall all thy males appear before the Lord thy God in the place which he shall choose; in the**

feast of unleavened bread, and in the feast of weeks, and in the feast of tabernacles: and they shall not appear before the Lord empty:

All Israel was gathered at Jerusalem for the seven day Feast of Unleavened Bread [and the additional Passover day] during the temple period! Why? Because God's House was there and they were appearing before God!

Therefore the Sheaf was cut at Jerusalem, [Where else could the sheaf be cut with all Israel gathered at the tabernacle or later at the Temple at Jerusalem?] just as Jesus died and was resurrected at Jerusalem!

Deuteronomy 16:1 Observe the month of Abib, and keep the passover unto the Lord thy God: for in the month of Abib the Lord thy God brought thee forth out of Egypt by night.

16:2 Thou shalt therefore sacrifice the passover unto the Lord thy God, of the flock and the herd, **in the place which the Lord shall choose to place his name there.**

16:3 Thou shalt eat no leavened bread with it; seven days shalt thou eat unleavened bread therewith, even the bread of affliction; for thou camest forth out of the land of Egypt in haste: that thou mayest remember the day when thou camest forth out of the land of Egypt all the days of thy life.

16:4 And there shall be no leavened bread seen with thee in all thy coast seven days; neither shall there any thing of the flesh, which thou sacrificedst the first day at even, remain all night until the morning.

16:5 Thou mayest not sacrifice the passover within any of thy gates, which the Lord thy God giveth thee:

16:6 But at the place which the Lord thy God shall choose to place his name in, there thou shalt sacrifice the passover at even, at the going down of the sun, at the season that thou camest forth out of Egypt.

The Feast of Unleavened Bread at the tabernacle and later at Jerusalem

16:8 Six days thou shalt eat unleavened bread: and on the seventh day shall be a solemn assembly to the Lord thy God: thou shalt do no work therein.

It is extremely obvious that the Sheaf was to be cut the same day that it was offered as was clearly done in the temple period [and approved of by Christ] and was commanded to be offered at the House of God at Jerusalem, when the whole nation was gathered there before God; and it was an offering being presented to God to be accepted by God.

Incidental signs

Of course the harvest ripens in direct relationship to the hours of sunlight and warming of the soil, meaning that the spring barley harvest will always be ripening near the spring equinox except in times of very severe conditions.

Once the ewes have lambed we must look for the ripening barley in the immediate area of Jerusalem, and that timing will be in close proximity to the spring equinox.

There are those who say that the equinox is a time of pagan celebrations and should be ignored.

I point out that I am not advocating celebrating the equinox; I am simply saying that God created the equinox as an indicator of the warming sun and the spring when the fields would begin to ripen. Remember that it was God who commanded that the sun [and moon] be used to set the seasons in Genesis 1:14.

The only God commanded signs to set the first month of the year is the lambing and the barley ripening at Jerusalem for the Wave Sheaf Offering after Passover.

Remember that the ripening fig tree cursed by Christ was at JERUSALEM not in some other location, showing that the ripening trees and harvest were to be observed at JERUSALEM - after God placed His name there - and not some other place.

The biblical new year begins with the first light of the new moon at Jerusalem when the barley is ripening enough at Jerusalem for the Wave Sheaf to be cut during the Feast of Unleavened Bread at Jerusalem.

The Biblical Calendar Summation:
1. Each day ends and a new day begins at sunset local time.
2. The Sabbath is the seventh day, Friday evening to Saturday evening; and being a complete day, begins and ends at sunset.
3. God's seventh day Sabbath is a Holy Convocation, meaning that on that day we are to meet with God. Whenever possible we are to meet with like-minded persons who seek to live by every Word of God; we are not to meet with just anyone to have a social gathering. The emphasis being on meeting and focusing on Almighty God, to learn

and internalize the Word of God; not on a social feel good experience.

4. Months begin with the first visible light of the New Moon as seen from Jerusalem.

5. Today the new moons are to be kept by holding congregational Bible Studies and sounding the Shofar at some point before the following sunset ends the new moon day.

6. The new year begins when the barley is ripening in close proximity to the Temple site in Jerusalem.

7. This Biblical Calendar is the calendar by which God's Appointed Times and High Holy Days are established during the year. All Holy Days being on specified days of specified months [except the countdown to Pentecost]

Special Situations:

1. Because of the extreme hours of sunset in the High Arctic and High Antarctic, it is appropriate to observe the Sabbath at the same time as Jerusalem time in the local time zone, above 55 degrees north or south of 55 degrees south. All members of each congregation should be in agreement and should be keeping the Sabbath at the same time

2. The new year begins when the barley harvest is ripening at Jerusalem and the first sheaf will be ready to be cut on the first Sunday after Passover.

3. During years of extreme famine when there is no barley harvest; to prevent any one year from lasting for a two year sun cycle, the new year should begin on the new moon CLOSEST to the spring equinox.

4. If the equinox is exactly midway between two new moons then the later new moon is to begin the new year, because the barley would not normally be ripening at Jerusalem two weeks before the equinox.

When Christ comes he may very well reset the orbits of the earth and moon to restore the original created calendric system.

Calendar References and Sources

"The history of the Jewish calendar may be divided into three periods--the Scriptural, the Talmudic, and the post-Talmudic. The first [Scriptural] rested purely on the observation of the sun and the moon, the second [Talmudic] on observation and reckoning, and the third [post-Talmudic--still used today] entirely on reckoning.[1]" (THE JEWISH ENCYCLOPEDIA article: "Calendar, History of" pp.498)

"The beginning of the months were determined by direct observation of the new moon. Then those beginning of months (Rosh Hodesh) were sanctified and announced by the Sanhedrin, the Supreme Court in Jerusalem, after witnesses testified that they had seen the new crescent and after their testimony had been thoroughly examined, confirmed by calculation and duly accepted." (Arthur Spier, THE COMPREHENSIVE HEBREW CALENDAR, p.1, section: HISTORICAL REMARKS ON THE JEWISH CALENDAR)

In recent years, a number of individuals and groups have begun to observe the Moon each month to practice for the commandment of observing the Moon and for determining criteria for the limits of visibility." (Above quote taken from the website of the Israeli New Moon Society [**http://www.geocities.com/royh_il/**], which was founded by Rabbi Dr. Nachum Rabinovitch, head of Yeshivat Birkat Moshe, Maale Adumim. The society works with the Institute for Kiddush Hachodesh Studies and includes scientists and rabbis from Universities, Yeshivot and elsewhere.

They are adherents of Rabbinical Orthodox Judaism and its calculated rabbinical calendar).

"The Jewish calendar as now observed is the product of a long historical development." (THE UNIVERSAL JEWISH ENCYCLOPEDIA, Vol. 2, p.631)

"There is...unimpeachable evidence from the works of writers with expert knowledge of the calendar that the present ORDO INTERCALATIONIS [sequence of intercalations--the 19 year cycle] and epochal MOLAD were not intrinsic parts of the calendar of Hillel II, these being seen still side by side with other styles of the ORDO INTERCALATIONIS and the MOLAD as late as the 11th century. Also the four DEHIYYOT [postponement rules] developed gradually. ...By the tenth century the Jewish calendar was exactly the same as today." (Cecil Roth, editor, ENCYCLOPAEDIA JUDAICA, Vol. 5, p.50, article: Calendar)

"The Talmudic Rabbis [ca. first half of the third century C.E. (i.e., prior to 250 C.E.) to the end of the fifth century C.E.] recognised the variation in length of the synodic month...and hence they determined the beginning of every month separately by observation of the new moon as well as by calculation." (W.M. Feldman, RABBINICAL MATHEMATICS AND ASTRONOMY, Hermon Press, 1965, p.123)

"Further, Gans points out, that it is hardly likely that R. Gamaliel would speak of a mean [i.e. average] synodic month, as in his time the 'fixed' calendar was not yet in use." (W.M. Feldman, Ibid, p.124)

"For as the beginning of a month was fixed on the accredited evidence of witnesses who reported having seen the new moon soon after sunset on a certain day, it was the duty of the Calendar Council not only to test their evidence by stringent cross-examination...but also to ascertain, by mathematical calculation, whether the moon could, in fact, be seen at that particular moment at the particular place from which the witnesses came." (W. M. Feldman, Ibid., p.160)

"In mishnaic times [the Mishnah was completed c 200 C.E.], though the authorities were familiar with astronomical calculations, the new moon was fixed on the basis of observation, which meant that, as a rule, the bet din formally proclaimed the New Month only after it had heard evidence of witnesses who had actually seen the new moon." (ENCYCLOPEDIA JUDAICA, Volume 14, article: Rosh Ha-Shanah, p.311)

"The Mishnaic tractate ROSH HASHANAH describes the way in which the calendar was determined in the days before there was a set, calculated calendar which we have today. Witnesses would appear before the Sanhedrin each month to testify that they had seen the 'new moon.' They were carefully cross-examined and, if the judges were satisfied, the Sanhedrin proclaimed the beginning of a new month." (BEHOLD, A MOON IS BORN! HOW THE JEWISH CALENDAR WORKS, Arnold A. Lasker and Daniel J. Lasker, Conservative Judaism, 41:4, Summer, 1989, p.8)

"But unless all indications are deceitful, they did not in the time of Jesus Christ possess as yet any fixed calendar, but on the basis of a purely empirical observation, on each occasion they began a new month with the appearing of the new moon..." [5] (Emil Schurer, THE HISTORY OF THE JEWISH PEOPLE IN THE AGE OF JESUS CHRIST, p.366)

"Now there are ten festivals in number, as the law sets them down....The third [festival] is that which comes after the conjunction, which [festival] happens on the day of the new moon in each month. ...(140) Following the order which we have adopted, we proceed to speak of the third festival, that of the new moon. First of all, because it is the beginning of the month, and the beginning, whether of number or of time, is honourable. Secondly, because at this time there is nothing in the whole of heaven destitute of light. (141) Thirdly, because at that period the more powerful and important body gives a portion of necessary assistance to the less important and weaker body; for, at the time of the new moon, the sun begins to illuminate the moon with a light which is visible to the outward senses, and then she displays her own beauty to the beholders." [6][first century Jew, Philo Judaeus, THE SPECIAL LAWS, II, XI. (41), XXVI. (140) & (141), as translated by C.D. Yonge in THE WORKS OF PHILO: New Updated Edition, Complete and Unabridged in One Volume, Hendickson Publishers, 1993, pp.572, 581]

"Jews calculated the month according to the phase of the moon, each month consisting of either twenty nine or thirty days, and beginning with the appearance of the new moon. But this opened a fresh field of uncertainty. It is quite true that every one might observe for himself the appearance of a new moon. But this would again partly depend on the state of the weather. Besides, it left an authoritative declaration of the commencement of a month unsupplied. And yet not only was the first of every month to be observed as 'New Moon's Day,' but the feasts took place on the 10th, 15th, or other day of the month, which could not be accurately determined without a certain knowledge of its beginning. To supply this want the Sanhedrin sat in the 'Hall of Polished Stones' to receive the testimony of credible witnesses that they had seen the new moon. To encourage as many as possible to come forward on so important a testimony, these witnesses were handsomely entertained at the public expense.

If the new moon had appeared at the commencement of the 30th day -- which would correspond to our evening of the 29th, as the Jews reckoned the day from evening to evening -- the Sanhedrin declared the previous month to have been one of twenty-nine days, or 'imperfect.' Immediately thereon men were sent to a signal-station on the Mount of Olives, where beacon-fires were lit and torches waved, till a kindling flame on a hill in the distance indicated that the signal had been perceived. Thus the tidings, that this was the new moon, would be carried from hill to hill, far beyond the boundaries of Palestine, to those of the dispersion, 'beyond the river.' Again, if credible witnesses had not appeared to testify to the appearance of the new moon on the evening of the 29th, the next evening, or that of the 30th, according to our reckoning, was taken as the commencement of the new month, in which case the previous month was declared to have been one of thirty days, or 'full.' It was ruled [much later in history, and by the so-called "rabbis," not God] that a year should neither have less than four nor more than eight such full months of thirty days" (Alfred Edersheim, THE TEMPLE: ITS MINISTRY AND SERVICES, pp.156-157)

"It is generally accepted that the Jewish festivals were, in Biblical times, fixed by observation of both the sun and the moon. Gradually, certain astronomical rules were also brought into requisition, primarily as a test, corroborating or refuting the testimony of observation....It has been authoritatively proved that in spite of a more advanced knowledge of astronomy the practice of fixing the new moon and the festivals by observation was in force as late as the latter part of the fifth century [C.E.]....It was only after the close of the Babylonian Talmud, in the sixth or perhaps later, in the seventh century, that the observation of the moon was entirely given up, and a complete and final system of calendation introduced [in the tenth century]." (Henry Malter, SAADIA GAON: HIS LIFE AND WORKS, Chapter IV, Saadia's Controversy with Ben Meir, pp.70-88, Philadelphia: The Jewish Publication Society of America, 1921)

"...Rejecting the fixed calendar as a heretic innovation, the Karaites held that by law of Scripture the beginning of the months must be determined by the appearance of the new crescent and no other means, and that this had been the practice of ancient Israel at all times. Rabbanite refutation of this extreme assertion found its most outspoken exponent in Saadia Gaon, who went to the opposite extreme in 'demonstrating' that the fixed calendar, computation of MOLAD and TEKUFAH, has the force of a Mosaic-Sinaitic law that had been followed at all ages of the past, while observation of the new crescent was merely a passing episode in the history of the Jews, introduced at the time of the Sadducees to show that it confirmed the correctness of the prescribed calendaric regulation by calculation. Although this contention could easily be refuted by the Karaites as fanciful to the point of ridicule, Saadia's prestige was so great that his theory was accepted even by leading scholars.....Maimonides [12th century A.D] is one of the few medieval Rabbanite authorities known to have taken issue with Saadia's and his followers' contention, and his refutation amounts to unmitigated reproach, indeed to expression of intellectual as well as religious indignation. [**Maimonides commented:**] '**I am truly astonished over a personage who rejects clear evidence, asserting that the religion of Israel was based, not on observation of the new moon, but on calculation alone**--and yet he [Saadia] affirms the authority of all these (just mentioned) Talmudic passages! I think indeed that he did not believe his own assertions, but he merely wished to repel his [Karaite] adversary by any notion that just occurred to him, be it true or false, when he had found himself unable to escape the force of (his adversary's) argument.'" (THE CODE OF MAIMONIDES, book II, treatise 8, translated by Solomon Gandz, Yale Judaica Series, Volume XI, pp.lii-liii)

"In 432 B.C.E. the Athenian astronomer Meton had reformed the Athenian calendar on the basis of a cycle of nineteen years, consisting of 235 lunar months adding one month seven times in the cycle to take care of the excess (235 is 7 more than 19 times 12). This calendar was widely adopted, and was eventually [in post-Talmudic times] followed by the Jewish teachers..." **[7]** (THE UNIVERSAL JEWISH ENCYCLOPEDIA, Vol. 2, p.632)

"The intervals of intercalation were at first irregular [i.e., they were not set in a fixed calculated pattern such as the current CRC's 19 year cycle of intercalating the 3rd, 6th, 8th, 11th, 14th, 17th, & 19th years of its cycle], intercalation being in part due to the prevailing state of the various agricultural products....R. Akiva (died 135 [A.D.]) once intercalated three successive years..." (Cecil Roth, editor, ENCYCLOPAEDIA JUDAICA, Vol. 5, p.50, article: Calendar)

"...intercalation [i.e., including a 13 month in a year] was carried out as the need arose, on the basis of an empirical observation made on each occasion without any advance calculation. The following two passages demonstrate that this was still the case in the time of the Mishnah: (1) MMEG. 1:4...(2) MEDUY. 7:7...The two passages are so clear that they require no further commentary...there was absolutely no calculation [of intercalary months] in advance." (Emil Schurer, THE HISTORY OF THE JEWISH PEOPLE IN THE AGE OF JESUS CHRIST, p.593)

"This method of observation [i.e., the first visible moon light] and intercalation [i.e., adding a thirteenth month based on the season and status of the barley crop] was in use throughout the period of the second temple (516 B.C.E. - 70 C.E.), and about three centuries after its destruction, as long as there was an independent Sanhedrin. In the fourth century, however, when oppression and persecution threatened the continued existence of the Sanhedrin, the patriarch Hillel II took an extraordinary step to preserve the unity of Israel. In order to prevent the Jews scattered all over the surface of the earth from celebrating their New Moons, festivals and holidays at different times, he made public the system of calendar calculation which up to then had been a closely guarded secret. It had been used in the past only to check the observations and testimonies of witnesses, and to determine the beginnings of the spring season." (Arthur Spier, THE COMPREHENSIVE HEBREW CALENDAR, p.2)

"The day begins and ends at sunset, or more precisely, after dusk when the first three stars of medium size appear.[8] This rule applies to the theoretical beginning and ending of Sabbaths, festivals, fast days and the hours for the daily prayers. However for calendar calculations, especially for the computation of the MOLADOTH (the times of the new moon) and the TEKUFOTH (beginnings of the seasons), the day begins and ends at 6 o-clock in the evening, Jerusalem time. -- The beginning and duration of the months depend on the MOLADOTH and the time which elapses from one MOLAD to the next one (lunation). The average figure given by tradition for this interval is 29 days and 12 hrs and 793 parts" (Arthur Spier, THE COMPREHENSIVE HEBREW CALENDAR, p.13)

"Nowadays the day, hour and parts of each Molad are announced before the Proclamation of the New Moon in the Sabbath morning service preceding the week of the New Moon. This custom keeps alive the memory of the time when the Sanhedrin sanctified the months on the basis of observation [of the new crescent]. It calls our attention to the fact that today we determine our new moons and holidays according to the decision of Hillel's Beth Din. [9]" (Arthur Spier, THE COMPREHENSIVE HEBREW CALENDAR, p.13)

"It is uncertain what the calendar of Hillel originally contained, and when it was generally adopted. In the Talmud there is no trace of it." (THE JEWISH ENCYCLOPEDIA, "Calendar, History of", pp. 502-503, Funk and Wagnalls, 1903)

"The name Rosh Ha-Shanah as it is used in the Bible (Ezek. 40:1) simply means the beginning of the year, and does not designate the festival. The months of the year were counted from the spring month (Ex. 12:2), later called by the Babylonian name Nisan. The month known by the Babylonian name Tishri is, therefore, called the "seventh month" in the Pentateuch. When the festival on the first of this month is recorded, it is referred to as the festival of the seventh month and a day of "memorial proclaimed with the blast of horns," or "a day of blowing the horn" (Lev. 23:23-25; Num. 29:1-6). In the Bible, the festival lasts one day only; the two-day festival arose out of the difficulty of determining when the new moon actually appeared." (ENCYCLOPEDIA JUDAICA, volume 14, article: Rosh Ha-Shanah, pp.305,306)

"MÔLÊD is a Hebrew word meaning renewal, rejuvenescence. It would be properly applied to the phase of the moon at the instant of time when her Conjunction with the Sun takes place. It is, however, commonly used not for the actual time of New Moon, but for the computed time, which governs the commencement of each year and of each Cycle...The length of a Lunation, as adopted by the founders of the present permanent calendar, is a constant quantity, whereas the Lunations of the true Moon are variable in their duration. The Moon of the Jewish Calendar is a mean or average Moon moving uniformly, in the same way as the artificial Moon of Hilarius [i.e., the "moon" (MOLAD) of the CRC is likewise artificial], which is used in the Julian and Gregorian Calendars." (S.B. Burnaby, "ELEMENTS OF THE JEWISH AND MUHAMMADAN CALENDARS", London: George Bell & Sons, 1901, p.40)

"The moment that the moon passes between the Earth and the sun is called the MOLAD - the birth of the moon. It is the **theoretical** beginning of the new month" **[10]** (UNDERSTANDING THE JEWISH CALENDAR, Rabbi Nathan Bushwick, pp.39-40 --emphasis mine)

"Every month of God's Calendar begins about the time of the new moon when the moon's first faint crescent is visible at sunset in Jerusalem. According to the Roman calendar a new moon may occur at any time during the month. Most people today probably don't even know when a new moon appears." (Herman Hoeh, THE CRUCIFIXION WAS NOT ON FRIDAY, p.34)

"God's months begin with the new moon....The observation of the new moon is to be made from Jerusalem, not from the North American continent. The seven to ten hours difference in time between Jerusalem and the part of the country (i.e. United States) you live in will make actual observation of the new moon from America misleading...The appearance of the new moon in the western sky just after sunset is used to determine the beginning of a new month." (Kenneth Herrmann, THE GOOD NEWS magazine, March 1953, article: "God's Sacred Calendar," p.8, col.1&2)

"The first day of the new year always begins with the day nearest the Spring equinox [11] when the new moon is first visible to the naked eye AT JERUSALEM (not in the United States)." (Herbert W. Armstrong, "WHEN, and How OFTEN, Should We Observe THE LORD'S SUPPER?," second to last paragraph--emphasis HWA's)

"This law further decreed that at the sighting of the new crescent, the first day of the seventh month would be sanctified as a solemn assembly by the blowing of trumpets" (Dwight Blevins and Carl D. Franklin, THE FEAST OF TRUMPETS 2000 A.D., p.25)

"new moon in Scripture, the visible crescent as seen from Jerusalem. Not the same as the astronomical new moon, which is not visible." (Dwight Blevins and Carl D. Franklin, THE FEAST OF TRUMPETS 2000 A.D., p.38, section: Glossary of Terms)

"One thing is for certain, the fixation of the month in Temple times was determined on the basis of BOTH calculation and observation, a fact you can be sure Jesus was aware of." (The Hebrew Calendar: Is It Reliable?, Church of God, The Eternal 1994)

Citing the JEWISH ENCYCLOPEDIA as a source, the International Standard Bible Encyclopedia likewise states: "The Hebrew or Jewish calendar had three stages of development: the preexilic, or Biblical; the postexilic or Talmudic; and the post Talmudic. The first rested on observation merely, the second on observation coupled with calculation, and the third on calculation only." (James Orr, editor, INTERNATIONAL STANDARD BIBLE ENCYCLOPEDIA, Vol.1, article: Calendar, H. Porter, pp.541).

This admission that the current Calculated Rabbinical Calendar (CRC) has only been in use for just over a thousand years is met with agreement from other Jewish sources (such as the previous quote from THE JEWISH ENCYCLOPEDIA and footnote #1, and the quote following this of the Israeli New Moon Society--that from ENCYCLOPEDIA JUDAICA, which states that the CRC was finalized in the tenth century).

Other religious sources also concur: "Such a continuous calendar, according to tradition that goes back to Hai Gaon (1038), was constructed by Patriarch Hillel II in A.D. 359 (or, according to another version, 500, though by this time the day of Patriarchs was past). But the tradition [that the CRC was fully constructed by Hillel II], which stands quite alone, is confronted with grave objections. Of these the following two are of special weight: (1) The supposed calendar is never referred to in the Talmud, which received its final redaction at the end of the fifth century. Nothing whatever is said there about the length of the month, or the nineteen-year cycle, or anything else of the kind. (2)...Moreover, from the earliest post-Talmudic age we have dates which cannot be reconciled with the regular calendar in use today. [article footnote: "One such date is the year 506, and another the year 776"]

"In point of fact, everything goes to indicate that the calendar, like all other productions of the kind, passed through a developing series of forms, and that it assumed its final shape in the schools of the official representatives of Judaism (called Geonim) in Babylonia. To the period of the Geonim, say the 7th and 8th cents., likewise belong two tractates relevant to the subject. One of these is entitled "Pirke de Rabbi Eliezer", and contains almost all the elements of the modern calendar (caps. 6-8), but it shows so many instances of self-contradiction that we must assume the presence of various interpolations..." [ENCYLOPAEDIA OF RELIGION AND ETHICS, 1908, Vol.3, article: CALENDAR (Jewish), p.118]

"After centuries of controversies between conservatives relying on observation (of moon and seasons) and innovators recommending calculation, and between religious authorities in Palestine and Babylonia, the system was settled in the 10th century A.D. (in favor of calculation and Babylon)." [Guy Ottewell, THE ASTRONOMICAL COMPANION, 1994 ed., p.30, under "Calendars (Jewish)"]

3. "Owing to inequalities in the rate of both the solar and the lunar motion in longitude, the mean conjunction [i.e., MOLAD] may precede or be preceded by the true conjunction." (Cecil Roth, editor, ENCYCLOPAEDIA JUDAICA, Vol. 5, p.46, article: Calendar). The MOLAD does not consistently match any phase of the moon. One month, the MOLAD may occur on the conjunction, while another month, the MOLAD may be on the day of the crescent, while yet another month, it may be a day or two either side of new crescent.

The Jews readily admit that the current calculated calendar in use is indeed in error and needs reform. Note the following from ENCYCLOPEDIA JUDAICA: "the present [calendar] system was expected to be replaced again by a system based on true values more akin to the earlier Jewish calendar in which New Moon (days of the phasis) and intercalations were proclaimed on the basis of both observation and calculation." (Cecil Roth, editor, ENCYCLOPAEDIA JUDAICA, Vol. 5, p.47, article: Calendar). "The rebirth of the state of Israel rekindles in us the hope that a new Sanhedrin, recognized by the whole people of Israel, will be established again in our time. It will be the task of the Sanhedrin to make a decision as to when and how the sanctified calendar of Hillel II is to be modified in accordance with the requirements of astronomy and the Torah." (Arthur Spier, THE COMPREHENSIVE HEBREW CALENDAR, p.227). While God's Word does state that we are to walk within the bounds of the laws of the land (i.e., Romans 13:1-7; Titus 3:1; I Pet 2:11-20), this by no means suggests that we need wait for a new "Sanhedrin" to be formed to follow God's commands for His appointed times. When the established laws of men are at odds with the Laws of God, we are by no means bound to such- -God's Law always reigns above (see Acts 5:29 where Peter and the others plainly rejected a ruling of the Sanhedrin in order to obey God instead).

The Mishnah, spanning the time period of 200 B.C. - 200 A.D., contains evidence that the CRC was not in use in the first century, nor even at that time of the Mishnah's collection into book form (ca. 200 A.D.). It shows that, unlike the CRC with its postponements, Yom Teruah (Day of Trumpets) could be observed on a Sunday, Wednesday, and Friday; the Day of Atonement could be observed on Fridays and Sundays; the seventh day of the Feast of Tabernacles could be observed on a Sabbath; etc.

Philo a Jew who lived from about 20 B.C. to about 50 A.D., and was thus a contemporary of Jesus and His disciples. Philo here testifies of the reckoning of the new moon in their day stating that it occurs "AFTER the conjunction....at this time there is NOTHING in the whole of heaven destitute of light...because at that period the more powerful and important body gives a portion of necessary assistance to the less important and weaker body; for, at the time of the new moon, the sun begins to illuminate the moon with a light which is visible to the outward senses." (italicized emphasis mine). Plainly, Philo testifies that the new moon is the fresh visible crescent.

"The Assuan Papyri yield ample proof of the fact that at the time after the Exile no such fixed cycle was in use among the Jews, and this would appear to be true also of the Talmudic period....Explicit mention of the nineteen-year cycle is first made in post-Talmudic writings. [article footnote: "It is related in the Talmud (SANHEDRIN, 12A) that Akiba (first half of 2nd cent. A.D.) reckoned three successive years as intercalary--a fact which proves the non-existence of any intercalary cycle at that time."]." [ENCYLOPAEDIA OF RELIGION AND ETHICS, 1908, Vol.3, article: CALENDAR (Jewish), p.117]

"As already indicated, the Jewish year is a composite arrangement. Its months are lunar, but from time to time an extra month is intercalated in order to effect an adjustment with the solar year. This was done even before the establishment of a continuous calendar. It was regarded as a matter of special importance that the month of Nisan should not begin before its TEQUFA (beginning of spring), and a second Adar was intercalated as required; but at that time nothing was as yet known of a regular and periodic intercalation, recurring according to definite rules. Such an arrangement was in all probability first introduced along with the continuous calendar itself, when the Metonic cycle was adopted." [ENCYLOPAEDIA OF RELIGION AND ETHICS, 1908, Vol.3, article: CALENDAR (Jewish), p.122]

"The earliest known reference to the 'TEQUFA of R. Adda' under that designation is made by Isaac b. Baruch Albalia of Cordova (A.D. 1035-1094); cf. Abraham b. Hiya's SEFER HA-'IBBUR, iii. 4), but the period it indicates is already referred to by al-Biruni (Arab. text, p. 183 = Eng. tr. p. 163)...this TEQUFA...agrees with a date (776) mentioned in the BARAITHA of Samuel...Moreover, **the intercalary system in common use among the Jews**, of which we shall treat presently, **could never have**

been framed except on the basis of R. Adda's--not Samuel's--TEQUFA. In all probability, therefore, its duration was calculated about the 8th cent. A.D., I.E. at the period in which the Jews in the East began to study astronomy, and became acquainted with the Almagest." [ENCYPLOPAEDIA OF RELIGION AND ETHICS, 1908, Vol.3, article: CALENDAR (Jewish), p.122--boldface emphasis mine]

As Spier relates in the next sentence, the usage of the three stars of the second magnitude is a "THEORETICAL beginning and ending"--not an actual one. This is of Jewish tradition. The former demarcation (i.e., sunset) IS the precise end of a day according to Holy Scripture: "...from sunset to sunset..." (Lev 23:32, SCHOCKEN BIBLE VOL. 1, FIVE BOOKS OF MOSES, translated by Everett Fox). The CRC however, is not calculated according to the Scriptural "sunset to sunset" reckoning, or even the traditional "three stars" method, but rather is calculated using 6pm as the beginning/ending of a day. Hence, the CRC not only utilizes an erroneous reckoning of the month (i.e., MOLAD), but likewise, an erroneous reckoning of the day.

Spier claims this goes back to Hillel, but historic documents show otherwise:

"Here, therefore, we find a corroboration of our theory that the constant calendar of modern Judaism is of relatively late date. The calculation of conjunctions, for instance, cannot have been finally established even as late as A.D. 776, for, according to the BARAITHA of Samuel, the conjunction of Tishri in that year took place as 4 d. 0 h. 363 p.; while, according to the modern reckoning, it did not occur till 4 d. 3 h. 363 p. This fact is of great importance in the history of the Jewish calendar." [ENCYPLOPAEDIA OF RELIGION AND ETHICS, 1908, Vol.3, article: CALENDAR (Jewish), p.122, col.1, footnote 3]

As stated above, the MOLAD does not consistently match the actual conjunction, or any phase of the moon. The actual conjunction of the sun, earth, and moon occurs in the midst of what is generally three days of the moon being concealed. Given that MOLAD means "birth," would this concealed moon constitute a birth (i.e., MOLAD)? Is a baby "birthed" at 4 and 1/2 months from conception, in the midst of the nine month gestation period, or rather is it birthed at the conclusion of its concealment in the womb? It is born when we see it (i.e., just as the crescent moon), and not before.

For in depth studies on these subjects visit our website
theshininglight.info

www.ingramcontent.com/pod-product-compliance
Lightning Source LLC
Chambersburg PA
CBHW081147230426
43664CB00018B/2836